IP Telephony Using CallManager Express

Lab Portfolio

Cheryl A. Schmidt

Ernie Friend

Cisco Press

800 East 96th Street

Indianapolis, Indiana 46240 USA

P9-DUY-948

IP Telephony Using CallManager Express Lab Portfolio

Cheryl Schmidt, Ernie Friend

Copyright® 2007 Cisco Systems, Inc.

Published by:
Cisco Press
800 East 96th Street
Indianapolis, IN 46240 USA

Printed in the United States of America 1 2 3 4 5 6 7 8 9 0

First Printing: December 2006

Library of Congress Cataloging-in-Publication data is on file.

ISBN: 1-58713-176-5

Warning and Disclaimer

This book is designed to provide information about configuring and understanding voice over IP (VoIP) in a CallManager Express (CME) environment. Every effort has been made to make this book as complete and accurate as possible, but no warranty or fitness is implied.

The information is provided on an "as is" basis. The authors, Cisco Press, and Cisco Systems, Inc. shall have neither liability nor responsibility to any person or entity with respect to any loss or damages arising from the information contained in this book or from the use of the discs or programs that may accompany it.

The opinions expressed in this book belong to the authors and are not necessarily those of Cisco Systems, Inc.

Feedback Information

At Cisco Press, our goal is to create in-depth technical books of the highest quality and value. Each book is crafted with care and precision, undergoing rigorous development that involves the unique expertise of members of the professional technical community.

Reader feedback is a natural continuation of this process. If you have any comments about how we could improve the quality of this book or otherwise alter it to better suit your needs, you can contact us through e-mail at feedback@ciscopress.com. Please be sure to include the book title and ISBN in your message.

We greatly appreciate your assistance.

Trademark Acknowledgments

All terms mentioned in this book that are known to be trademarks or service marks have been appropriately capitalized. Cisco Press or Cisco Systems, Inc. cannot attest to the accuracy of this information. Use of a term in this book should not be regarded as affecting the validity of any trademark or service mark.

Publisher
Paul Boger

Cisco Representative
Anthony Wolfenden

Cisco Press Program Manager
Jeff Brady

Executive Editor
Mary Beth Ray

Managing Editor
Patrick Kanouse

Senior Development Editor
Christopher Cleveland

Senior Project Editor
San Dee Phillips

Copy Editor
Gayle Johnson

Technical Editors
Tomoo Esaka, Katalin Filzen, David Harris, Artem Tokarev, Joel Wilkinson

Team Coordinator
Vanessa Evans

Book and Cover Designer
Louisa Adair

Proofreader
Karen A. Gill

Americas Headquarters	Asia Pacific Headquarters	Europe Headquarters
Cisco Systems, Inc.	Cisco Systems, Inc.	Cisco Systems International BV
170 West Tasman Drive	168 Robinson Road	Haarlerbergpark
San Jose, CA 95134-1706	#28-01 Capital Tower	Haarlerbergweg 13-19
USA	Singapore 068912	1101 CH Amsterdam
www.cisco.com	www.cisco.com	The Netherlands
Tel: 408 526-4000	Tel: +65 6317 7777	www-europe.cisco.com
800 553-NETS (6387)	Fax: +65 6317 7799	Tel: +31 0 800 020 0791
Fax: 408 527-0883		Fax: +31 0 20 357 1100

Cisco has more than 200 offices worldwide. Addresses, phone numbers, and fax numbers are listed on the Cisco Website at www.cisco.com/go/offices.

©2006 Cisco Systems, Inc. All rights reserved. CCVP, the Cisco logo, and the Cisco Square Bridge logo are trademarks of Cisco Systems, Inc.; Changing the Way We Work, Live, Play, and Learn is a service mark of Cisco Systems, Inc.; and Access Registrar, Aironet, BPX, Catalyst, CCDA, CCDP, CCIE, CCIP, CCNA, CCNP, CCSP, Cisco, the Cisco Certified Internetwork Expert logo, Cisco IOS, Cisco Press, Cisco Systems, Cisco Systems Capital, the Cisco Systems logo, Cisco Unity, Enterprise/Solver, EtherChannel, EtherFast, EtherSwitch, Fast Step, Follow Me Browsing, FormShare, GigaDrive, GigaStack, HomeLink, Internet Quotient, IOS, IP/TV, iQ Expertise, the iQ logo, iQ Net Readiness Scorecard, iQuick Study, LightStream, Linksys, MeetingPlace, MGX, Networking Academy, Network Registrar, Packet, PIX, ProConnect, RateMUX, ScriptShare, SlideCast, SMARTnet, StackWise, The Fastest Way to Increase Your Internet Quotient, and TransPath are registered trademarks of Cisco Systems, Inc. and/or its affiliates in the United States and certain other countries.

All other trademarks mentioned in this document or Website are the property of their respective owners. The use of the word partner does not imply a partnership relationship between Cisco and any other company. (0609R)

About the Authors

Cheryl A. Schmidt is a full-time faculty member in the network engineering technology department at Florida Community College at Jacksonville (FCCJ). She has a master's degree in computer and information resource management. Schmidt started her career in computers while in the Navy. She has been working on computers and networks ever since. For the past ten years, she has taught courses such as computer repair, CCNA, CCNP, VoIP, QoS, and wireless. FCCJ is one of the few Cisco Academy Advanced Training Centers for CCNP, wireless, and security. Schmidt lives with her husband and children in Jacksonville, Florida.

Ernie Friend is the director of academic systems at Florida Community College at Jacksonville (FCCJ). FCCJ is one of the largest community colleges in the United States, with more than 60,000 students. Friend manages the Network Engineering Technology Department at FCCJ. He previously managed the college's network and computer infrastructure. Friend has a bachelor's degree in electronics management. He spent more than ten years in the Navy, managing several computer-based aviation repair facilities. He has managed computer and networking departments for more than 14 years at the college. He continues to explore and teach the latest networking technologies.

About the Technical Reviewer

Tomoo Esaka has been a systems engineer for Cisco for more than six years. In his current capacity as a technical marketing engineer, he has helped develop technical solutions and concepts for Call Unified CallManager Express (CUCME). He has communicated complex technical solutions to both internal sales and partner channels to help drive CUCME sales. He also has developed technical marketing collateral including technical papers, hands-on training, presentations, and troubleshooting guides.

Dedications

Cheryl Schmidt: This book is dedicated to educators who change people's lives. May we all continue to remember why we like sharing knowledge with others. This book is also dedicated to those who are always striving to learn new technologies. As always, I would like to thank my family for their support. I could not be who I am without them to complement me.

Ernie Friend: I would like to thank my wife, Timara, and children, Cayla and Coral, for allowing me to take time away from their lives to write this book. Each of them showed tremendous patience over the many nights and weekends spent writing this book. I am not sure they understood my excitement when the labs worked and the phones finally rang, but they rarely complained when the fans on the equipment drowned out the television.

Acknowledgments

We both would like to thank our Cisco Press team, especially Mary Beth Ray and Christopher Cleveland, who make our writing so much better. Chris is a true wordsmith.

We want to say a really big thank-you to Tomoo Esaka, our technical editor. We really appreciated the technical input and depth of knowledge that he brought to our book.

Some very special technical editors helped us test this book. They include students at Florida Community College and instructors from Costa Rica, Virginia, and Georgia. Very valuable contributions came from the following individuals, who tested the labs multiple times:

- Joel Wilkinson

- Katalin Filzen

- Artem Tokarev

- David Harris

Their recommendations for new labs, modifications, and corrections were invaluable to us, and we thank them very much.

Cheryl Schmidt: I would like to thank my coauthor, Ernie Friend. We both knew how much time this would take out of our lives. Ernie realizes how hard it is to be in the classroom without at least some labs to get you started on a specific subject. Ernie had a passion for Voice over IP even when he was over LANs and WANs for Florida Community College. His passion is contagious, and he recruited me into this wonderful technology.

Ernie Friend: I would like to thank Cheryl for sharing the vision of writing a hands-on lab book that anybody with a basic knowledge of networking can use to learn VoIP. Cheryl is an accomplished author who has crafted many computer-related books, and her experience made this effort that much more rewarding. It isn't always easy to coauthor a book, but this project was an enjoyable and satisfying experience for me.

Contents at a Glance

Contents

Icons Used in This Book

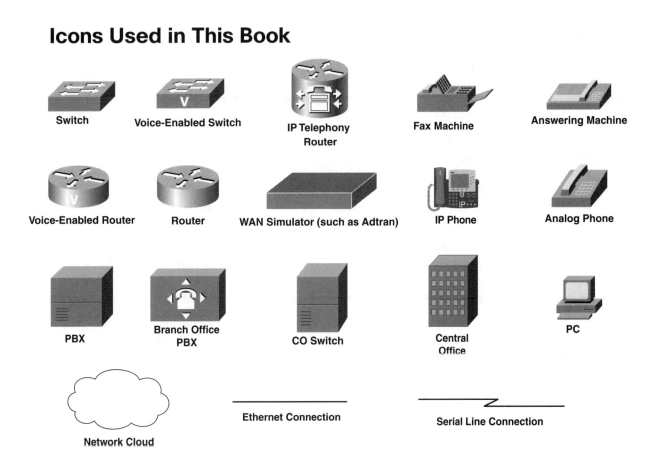

Command Syntax Conventions

The conventions used to present command syntax in this book are the same conventions used in the IOS Command Reference. The Command Reference describes these conventions as follows:

- **Bold** indicates commands and keywords that are entered literally as shown. In actual configuration examples and output (not general command syntax), bold indicates commands that are manually input by the user (such as a **show** command).

- *Italic* indicates an argument for which you supply an actual value.

- Vertical bars (|) separate alternative, mutually exclusive elements.

- Square brackets ([ ]) indicate an optional element.

- Braces ({ }) indicate a required choice.

- Braces within brackets ([{ }]) indicate a required choice within an optional element.

Introduction

When you're first learning any new technology, it is most difficult in the beginning stages—that place where you do not know where to begin and how to avoid pitfalls that will cost you many hours and even days. This book was written to help anyone who wants to know how VoIP works and how to configure it in a small deployment using Cisco CallManager Express (CME).

Goals and Methods

The most important and somewhat obvious goal of this book is to help you learn about VoIP using CME. After doing these labs, you should be able to deploy a basic phone system. CallManager Express is run on a router that has a voice IOS installed. You can install, configure, and customize IP Phones as well as traditional analog telephony devices.

One key methodology used in this book is the paper exercises in topics such as dial plans, IP addressing, and dial peers. These are areas that many people find difficult to understand when just reading a book. Even though this is a lab book, it also contains exercises to help you succeed in a VoIP deployment.

Another methodology used is case studies that allow you to combine the methods learned in this book so that you can see if you can apply those methods to a different scenario. This is analogous to a customer giving you criteria for how they want their telephone system to work.

Who Should Read This Book?

This book is intended to introduce and familiarize you with VoIP topics using CME. Although other objectives can be achieved from using this book, it was written with one goal in mind: to help you deploy VoIP. Even if you will eventually be using CallManager, the concepts presented and configured in this book will help you succeed in any VoIP deployment.

VoIP is becoming so popular in industry that even PC repair technicians are expected to understand the basic concepts of how VoIP works. If you can perform basic router and switch configurations, you can learn about VoIP using this book.

This book was written to provide a hands-on approach to learning Cisco voice technologies using CME. It can also be used to supplement the books *Cisco IP Communications Express: CallManager Express with Cisco Unity Express* and *Cisco Voice over IP (CVOICE)*. Although this book was not specifically designed to adhere to a specific Cisco certification, the labs can reinforce the content in the Cisco IP Communications Express Specialist (IPTX) certification. Understanding voice technologies is also a part of the new CCNP Optimizing Converged Cisco Networks (ONT) certification. In addition, this book can be used in conjunction with CCNA, CCNP, and Cisco Academy courses. Voice technologies will continue to penetrate corporate networks; this book can provide the basic knowledge and skills you need to implement voice on a CME platform.

What You Need to Perform the Labs

You can configure these labs on several Cisco router platforms, including the 2600XM, 2800, 3700, and 3800 series. This lab book focuses on using the 2800 series, but you can easily substitute other CME-capable platforms. Several hardware options might be available for each platform of router. If you are unsure whether your Cisco lab equipment can handle Cisco CallManager Express or which parts to purchase, you can contact your local Cisco technical representative or authorized Cisco reseller. You do not need all the equipment listed here to complete every lab. Some labs require a minimum amount of equipment and some require a more complex configuration. Each lab within the book gives a specific list of the equipment needed to complete that lab. The following comprehensive list highlights the basic equipment needed if you plan to complete all labs contained in this book:

- **CallManager Express-related equipment:**

  - Cisco CallManager Express (CME) capable router.

  - Cisco router IOS version that supports CallManager Express.

  - A version of Cisco IOS Software for a router that supports gatekeeper and CallManger. Any IOS image that includes *ivs* in its filename supports gatekeeper. One valid IOS version is *c2800nm-ipvoice_ivs-mz.124-2.T5*.

  - Two CME capable routers with a serial interface and the appropriate serial cables.

  - Cisco CME-capable router with switch module.

  - Two Cisco CME-capable routers with specific files for IP Phone (basic CME .tar file).

  - Cisco CME-capable router (with DSPs to support voice channels) and an FXS port.

  - Cisco CME-capable router with an FXO port.

  - Two Cisco CME-capable routers with T1 PRI ports installed.

  - Cisco CME-capable router with Unity Express module installed.

- **Network Devices/Phones:**

  - Cisco external 3550 (or higher) switch.

  - Two switches/switch modules.

  - Inline power capable switch/switch module or noninline power switch/switch module with power injectors.

  - Four Cisco IP Phones.

  - Cisco IP Phone 7940/60 series.

  - Cisco IP Phone 7970 series (powered using any method.)

  - Four analog phones.

  - One analog phone with RJ-11 cable.

  - One analog phone connected to an FXS port.

  - Adtran unit or a similar device that simulates WAN connectivity.

  - Adtran (or other WAN simulation device) with T1 capability.

  - Adtran (or other WAN simulation device) with two T1-capable ports.

  - Adtran Atlas 550 with octal FXS, single T1 module, and a Quad T1/PRI module configured as per Table D-1.

- Unity Express Advanced Integration Module (AIM).

- 2811 series router.

- **PC Capabilities/Software:**

  - Two workstations with an Ethernet 10/100 NIC installed.

  - Workstation with FastEthernet 10/100 NIC installed.

  - Windows XP computer with administrator rights to load a software application and Internet Explorer 5.5 or higher.

  - Appropriate licensed copy of Cisco IP Communicator application.

  - Application that can extract zipped files.

  - Trivial File Transfer Protocol (TFTP) software.

  - Access to Cisco.com with a CCO account and rights to download software.

  - PC access to the CME GUI Administrator.

- **Connections/Cables:**

  - Adtran 9-pin to RJ-45 connector.

  - Two T1 cables.

  - Router serial cables.

  - RJ-11 cable.

How This Book Is Organized

Although this book could be read cover-to-cover, it is designed to be flexible. You can easily move between chapters and sections of chapters to cover just the material you need more work with. If you intend to read all the chapters, the order in the book is an excellent sequence to use.

The chapters and appendixes cover the following topics:

Chapter 1, "Traditional Phone and IP Telephony," provides basic information on traditional phone concepts and IP telephony. It discusses basic terms and configuring basic voice router interfaces. It offers examples of what the topology will look like when migrating a traditional company phone network to IP telephony. Labs include the process to install Cisco CallManager Express IOS.

Chapter 2, "Router, Integrated Switch, and IP Phone Basic Configuration," provides the steps to configure a router and switch. Labs in this chapter provide step-by-step commands to configure routers with an internal switch module and a router that uses an external switch.

Chapter 3, "Managing and Configuring Cisco VoIP Devices," examines how to configure Cisco CallManager Express using a variety of methods: VoIP telephony setup dialog, manual configuration of the router for CME, a partially automated process, Quick Configuration Tool (QCT), and Cisco Network Assistant. Each of these methods is discussed in detailed labs. You can explore each one so that you can determine the most appropriate method to deploy Cisco CallManager Express.

Chapter 4, "Dial Plans and Dial Peers," examines the use of dial peers in a VoIP network. Dial peers are used to configure dial plans and to identify call source and destination endpoints. They also define each call leg in the call connection. Dial peers are a critical component of VoIP. This chapter includes detailed simple and complex dial peer labs.

Chapter 5, "Configuring VoIP Ports," focuses on configuring Foreign Exchange Station (FXS), Foreign Exchange Office (FXO), and T1 ports for transporting voice traffic. Labs in this chapter include configuring FXS interfaces, configuring analog phones, configuring FXO interfaces, and configuring T1/PRI interfaces.

Chapter 6, "Digit Manipulation," covers digit manipulation. Digits (phone numbers) can be manipulated at different points throughout the voice network. Digits can be added, removed, or changed, depending on the dial plan. Several digit manipulation options are available, depending on the situation. This chapter discusses some of the common digit-manipulation strategies, including digit stripping and prefixes, forward digits, number expansion, and translation rules for VoIP.

Chapter 7, "Configuring Inter-Pod Connectivity," focuses on connecting two pods via a T1 connection as well as a serial port connection. The T1 connectivity simulates connectivity between two different companies. The serial connection is more indicative of connectivity between two sites of the same company. The last lab introduces the idea of class of restriction (COR). Labs include configuring T1/PRI between two pods, configuring COR, and configuring serial connectivity between two pods.

Chapter 8, "GUI and IOS Intermediate Administration," focuses on using the graphical user interface (GUI) and command-line interface (CLI) to manage the CME router and Cisco IP Phones. Labs include configuring GUI for system administrator, customer administrator, phone users, call transfer and call forward, call park, intercom, and paging groups.

Chapter 9, "H.323," focuses on H.323, gateways, and gatekeepers. H.323 is a commonly used protocol suite that connects multiple CME sites. H.323 is also commonly used for multimedia conferencing. Other options are available, but the concepts are similar, and it is important to understand how this protocol works as it relates to voice. Labs include simple H.323 between two pods, H.323 with a gatekeeper and analog phones, and H.323 with analog and IP Phones.

Chapter 10, "VoIP Quality of Service and Security," covers the fundamentals of VoIP quality of service (QoS) and security. Typically, networks operate on a best-effort delivery basis. This means that all traffic has equal priority and an equal chance of being delivered in a timely manner. Similarly, when congestion occurs, all traffic has an equal chance of being dropped. QoS can be implemented on each network device. It provides an end-to-end solution to ensure that the important traffic gets through but that it does not use so much bandwidth that it prevents other traffic from reaching its destination. Labs include configuring AutoQoS on a router with an integrated switch module, configuring AutoQoS on a router with an external switch, using NBAR, and VoIP security measures.

Chapter 11, "Unity Express," covers the fundamentals and configuration of Cisco Unity Express. Cisco Unity Express provides voice mail and automated attendant services in a small office environment. The automated attendant allows callers to reach any phone extension without the assistance of an operator 24 hours a day, seven days a week. Unity Express can be used in conjunction with CallManager Express. Labs include accessing Unity Express for the first time, configuring Unity Express from a GUI interface, and configuring business hours with night service bell features.

Chapter 12, "Case Studies," provides three case studies designed to give you practice with configuration concepts from Chapters 1 through 11. You can work through these case studies individually or in a group setting.

Appendix A, "Reference Tables," provides three tables—IP addressing, dial plan, and dial peers. These are a combination of addresses and numbers given throughout the labs.

Appendix B, "Command Reference," provides IOS commands and descriptions used in the labs.

Appendix C, "Installing a Unity Express AIM in a 2811 Router," provides instructions for installing the Cisco Unity Express AIM module in a 2800 series router.

Appendix D, "Configuring the Adtran Dial Plan," provides a lab to verify and configure the dial plans using the Adtran 550. The correct dial plan is critical to ensuring that the labs work as written.

Appendix E, "Resetting 7970 Cisco IP Phones," provides instructions to reset a Cisco 7970 IP Phone. The 7970 Cisco IP Phone cannot be reset with the same procedures as the 7940 or 7960 IP Phone. Instead, a similar process is used. This appendix is provided for anyone who might use 7970 Cisco IP Phones as part of their lab equipment.

Appendix F, "Configuring Cisco IP Communicator," provides a lab to configure the Cisco IP Communicator software. The Cisco IP Communicator software can be installed on a desktop or laptop computer to emulate a 7960 IP Phone.

CHAPTER 1

Traditional Phone and IP Telephony

Before doing any voice configuration on a router, you should have basic knowledge of traditional telephone operation and the goals of implementing IP telephony. This chapter helps you understand how telephony fits into the big picture of phone technology. It also helps with some of the basic terms, explains basic router interfaces, and gives examples of what the topology looks like when you migrate a traditional company phone network to IP telephony.

The first two labs help with the basic terminology and router interfaces. The last lab helps when you install a router IOS that supports voice. These labs, together with the information provided, will help you when you configure the other chapters' labs.

Overview of Traditional Phone Networks

Traditionally in the United States, an analog phone connects via the *local loop* to a *central office (CO) switch*. From there it can cross an *interoffice trunk* to another CO switch. The CO switch is located in the *local exchange (LEX)*. Figure 1-1 illustrates this concept.

Figure 1-1   Analog Phone to CO Switch

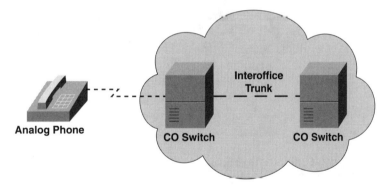

All the local phones in one area connect to a central office, also known as a telephone exchange or local exchange. The central office can connect to another central office, to a long-distance switch or point of presence (POP) if a long-distance call is made in the same country, or to an international exchange if a long-distance call is made to another country. Figure 1-2 shows another way of looking at this.

Figure 1-2   Multiple Central Offices Connection

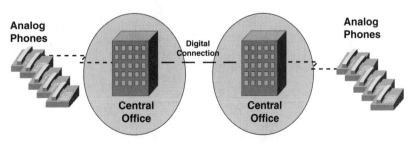

In Figure 1-2, you can see that a digital connection is used between the COs. If you make a call from the analog phone on the right and it is outside the calling area of the CO to which the phone connects, the call is routed through a trunk (a digital connection) to another CO to the remote phone.

Understanding Basic Analog Technologies

There's a difference between a conventional two-wire telephone interface such as Foreign Exchange Station (FXS) or Foreign Exchange Office (FXO) and an Ear and Mouth (E&M) or Earth and Ground, depending on the source (E&M) interface. The E&M interface has wires that pass the audio signals, plus additional wires to act as an input (to sense an incoming call) or an output (to indicate an outgoing call). These control leads are normally called the E lead (input) and the M lead (output). Depending on the type of E&M interface, the signaling leads could be controlled by connecting them to the ground, switching a –48-volt DC (VDC) source, or completing a current loop between the two devices.

More Connectivity

Phones in a business frequently connect to a Private Branch Exchange (PBX). The PBX uses one or more trunks to connect to the central office, as shown in Figure 1-3.

Figure 1-3   PBX Connections to the Central Office

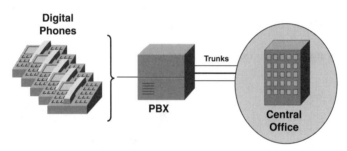

A company that has multiple sites uses trunks to connect to the public switched telephone network (PSTN).

Figure 1-4   Multiple Branch Office Connections

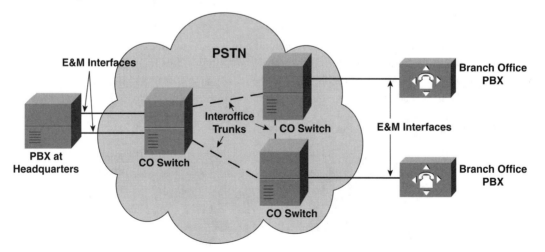

Notice in Figure 1-4 how E&M interfaces are used to connect the PBXs to the central office switches.

A company that is switching to voice over IP (VoIP) normally migrates departments to IP Phones over time. Figure 1-5 shows how routers connect to the IP WAN and can be used to interface with the company's existing PBXs.

Figure 1-5   VoIP and Traditional Phones During Migration

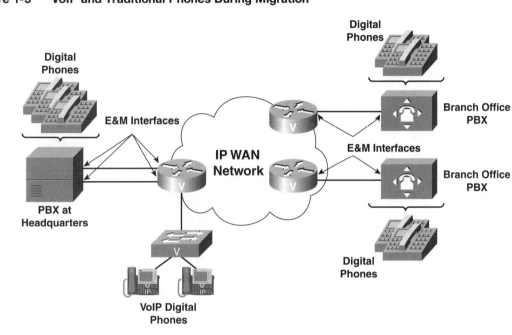

The router can contain FXS ports to connect traditional analog devices, such as a fax machine or answering machine, to the network. Figure 1-6 illustrates FXS connectivity.

Figure 1-6   FXS Connectivity

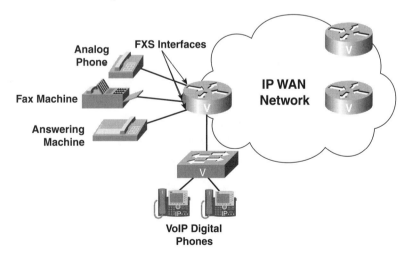

Another type of router interface for telephone is FXO. The FXO port connects the router to the phone company switch or a PBX. You could connect a router's FXO port directly to the RJ-11 phone jack in your house or to a traditional RJ-11 phone jack found in a small business. FXO ports can also be used to connect from the service provider to a PBX or key system. Only one call can be sent over an FXO connection at a time. Figure 1-7 shows an FXO connection.

Figure 1-7   FXO Connectivity

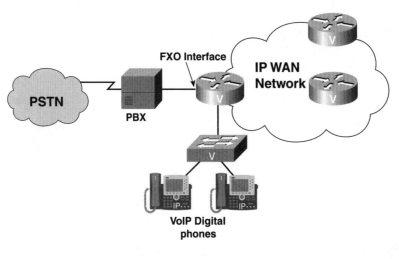

The labs in this chapter familiarize you with VoIP terms and VoIP ports used on a Cisco router. They also guide you through installing IOS on a Cisco router so that it has VoIP capabilities.

Lab 1-1: VoIP Ports

This lab emphasizes the various VoIP ports that can be installed on a router. This information is useful during a VoIP implementation. It is important for a technical support person to know how these ports might be used.

The objective of this lab is to identify the purpose of common VoIP ports. No equipment is required to complete this lab.

In Table 1-1, match the interface on the left to its description on the right.

Table 1-1   VoIP Ports

Interface	Description
__ FXO	A. Analog trunk that connects PBXs and switches
__ FXS	B. Lets you connect the IP Phone via a switch to the router
__ E&M	
__ T1	C. Analog interface that connects analog edge devices, such as telephone or fax
__ FastEthernet	D. Carries data at a rate of ~2 Mbps and carries 32 channels of 64 kbps each
__ E1	E. Lets you make 24 connections to the router over a single interface
	F. Lets you connect office equipment such as a PBX or a central office switch to the router

Lab 1-2: IP Telephony Terms

This lab covers some of the numerous IP telephony terms that are used in the industry.

The objective of this lab is to familiarize you with IP telephony terminology.

No equipment is required to complete this lab.

In Table 1-2, match the term on the left to its definition on the right.

Table 1-2   IP Telephony Terms

Term	Definition
__ Codec	A. A way to separate networks on a switch
__ Bandwidth	B. A way to classify traffic and determine the order in which packets are transmitted
__ Trunk	C. An acronym for the telephone network
__ CME	D. A phone switch that might be owned by a medium or large company
__ CallManager	E. A device such as a router that tracks bandwidth and permits or denies voice calls based on the amount of available bandwidth
__ PSTN	
__ Inline power	F. The protocol that carries voice after it has been digitized
__ VLAN	G. The protocol that the IP Phone uses to communicate with the CME router or CallManager server
__ Skinny	
__ RSVP	H. Special software on a server that lets you control and manipulate IP Phones
__ RTP	I. The amount of data that can be carried from one point to another, measured in bits per second
__ Voice gateway	
__ PBX	J. A communications channel that can handle numerous simultaneous voice and data signals between two telephone exchange switching systems
__ QoS	
__ Gatekeeper	K. A router that converts data from a VoIP network and another type of network, such as a PBX or PSTN
	L. A chip or software routine that converts sound into digital code and vice versa and compresses/decompresses the data
	M. The protocol used to signal a router to reserve bandwidth for voice or video traffic
	N. A method of providing –48VDC to an IP Phone using a data cable
	O. Special software on a router that lets you control and manipulate IP Phones

Lab 1-3: Installing Cisco CallManager Express (CME)

In this lab, the company OCSIC.org has configured the router with a basic configuration, but the version of IOS on the router does not support CallManager Express features. The version of IOS needs to be updated. The router should already be configured.

The objective of this lab is to install Cisco CallManager Express (CME) software on the router.

To perform this lab, you need the following equipment:

- CME-capable router

- Cisco router IOS version that supports CME

- Workstation with Ethernet network interface card (NIC) installed

- Trivial File Transfer Protocol (TFTP) software

- Access to www.cisco.com, with a valid user ID and rights to download software

Note: This lab might not be necessary if the VoIP IOS and CME are already installed. Use the **show flash:** command on the router and reference the Cisco website to see if the version of IOS is correct. For CME 3.2, used in this lab, Cisco IOS Software Release 12.3(11)T IP Voice or later is required.

The procedure for this lab consists of these tasks, as described in the following sections:

- **Task 1**—Configure the TFTP server.

- **Task 2**—Update and install the Cisco CME IOS.

Task 1: Configure the TFTP Server

Note: If the router has multiple FastEthernet interfaces, use the lowest-numbered interface. For example, if it has two FastEthernet interfaces numbered Fa0/0 and Fa0/1, use the Fa0/0 interface.

Step 1.   Ensure that the computer being used (the one that holds the TFTP server application) is connected to the FastEthernet port of the router (either using a crossover cable or going through a switch using a straight-through cable). Be sure that the computer has an IP address assigned in the same subnet as the router interface.

Step 2.   Download the appropriate IOS from www.cisco.com. You are required to have a CCO account login and rights to download IOS files.

Step 3.   Ensure that the appropriate router IOS file that supports CallManager Express is placed in the default folder for the TFTP server application.

Step 4.   Open the TFTP server application.

Step 5.   Console to the router. From the router, test connectivity with the PC that holds the TFTP server application. Do not proceed unless the ping is successful.

Task 2: Update and Install the Cisco CME IOS

Step 1.   From enable mode, copy the IOS image from the TFTP server to the router using the **copy tftp: flash:** command. The prompts may vary from what is shown here because of a difference in router model and/or IOS. When and if you are prompted to overwrite the existing files, enter **y** for yes. *Source filename* is the filename of the Voice IOS located on the TFTP server. *Address or name of remote host* is the TFTP server's IP address. *Destination filename* is the same name as the Source filename.

```
RouterVoIPX# copy tftp: flash:
Address or name of remote host? [Enter the address assigned to the TFTP
    server.]
Source filename? [Enter the IOS filename. It is best to copy and paste the
    filename into this section.]
Destination filename? [The filename should be the same as what was placed in
    the source filename.]
```

Note: Here's an example of the process:
```
RouterVoIP1# copy tftp flash:
Address or name of remote host? 10.10.0.12
Source filename? c2800nm-ipvoice-mz.123-11.T3.bin
Destination filename? c2800nm-ipvoice-mz.123-11.T3.bin
Accessing tftp://10.10.0.12/ c2800nm-ipvoice-mz.123-11.T3.bin...
```

Step 2.   Ensure that the TFTP transfer was successful by using the **show flash** command to verify that the IOS file is present in flash memory. Do not proceed until the IOS has been transferred.

```
RouterVoIPX# show flash
```

Note: Here's an example of the process:
```
-#- --length-- -----date/time------ path
1      24119024 Mar 24 2005 22:17:00 +00:00 c2800nm-ipvoice-mz.123-11.T3.bin
32143304 bytes available (24119024 bytes used)
```

Step 3.   The following commands allow you to load and use the new system IOS image:

```
RouterVoIPX(config)# boot system flash new system_image_filename
RouterVoIPX(config)# exit
RouterVoIPX# copy running-config startup-config
RouterVoIPX# reload
```

Step 4.   When prompted to save the system configuration, enter **no**.

Step 5.   When prompted to confirm the reload, enter **y**.

Step 6.   Verify that the system image file (IOS image) is the correct one by using the **show flash:** or **show version** command:

```
RouterVoIPX# show flash:
RouterVoIPX# show version
```

Note: For example:

```
Cisco IOS Software, 2800 Software (C2800NM-IPVOICE-M), Version 12.3(11)T3, RELEASE
 SOFTWARE (fc4)

Technical Support: http://www.cisco.com/techsupport

Copyright (c) 1986-2005 by Cisco Systems, Inc.

Compiled Wed 26-Jan-05 02:49 by pwade

ROM: System Bootstrap, Version 12.3(8r)T7, RELEASE SOFTWARE (fc1)

RouterVoIP1 uptime is 11 minutes

System returned to ROM by power-on

System image file is "flash:c2800nm-ipvoice-mz.123-11.T3.bin"

Cisco 2821 (revision 53.51) with 249856K/12288K bytes of memory.

Processor board ID FHK0847F0QH

4 FastEthernet interfaces

2 Gigabit Ethernet interfaces

2 Serial(sync/async) interfaces

DRAM configuration is 64 bits wide with parity enabled.

239K bytes of non-volatile configuration memory.

62720K bytes of ATA CompactFlash (Read/Write)

Configuration register is 0x2102
```

CHAPTER 2

Router, Integrated Switch, and IP Phone Basic Configuration

The most basic IP telephony configuration is to make two IP Phones ring. Before making two phones ring and entering the telephony commands, you must configure the router and switch and connect the Cisco IP Phones. Labs 2-4 and 2-5 in this chapter provide configuration basics and deal with routers and either an external switch or an internal switch module. The type of configuration needed depends on what hardware is being used.

Overview of VoIP Basic Configuration

Voice over IP (VoIP) is an exciting technology being implemented by businesses today. It allows a company to attach a special IP Phone to an RJ-45 data outlet just like a PC connects to a network. The phone uses the same network connectivity as traditional network devices such as PCs, servers, and network printers.

VoIP can be implemented using special Cisco software installed on specific models of routers or software installed on a traditional network server. Servers use Cisco CallManager, and routers use CallManager Express (CME).

CME is typically used in small business installations (fewer than 240 phones). CME is supported on specific router models such as the 1700, 2600XM, 2691, 2800, 3700, and 3800 series. CallManager typically is used in larger corporate installations with more than 240 phones. CME is used to demonstrate the basics of IP telephony in this book.

Basic Requirements for VoIP Implementation

Implementing VoIP means buying special IP Phones and using the CallManager software (on the router or on the server) to control the phones. When planning for a VoIP installation, you must consider several things, all of which are discussed throughout this chapter. Two important considerations are the VoIP Phone's power and data outlets. Power can be applied to the phone in one of three ways:

- External 48VDC power brick

- Power over Ethernet (PoE) connectivity from a PoE switch

- Connectivity to a PoE patch panel

Most companies use one of the PoE solutions.

Some routers can have an optional 4-, 9-, 16-, or 36-port Ethernet switch module. You can also upgrade a router so that the switch module can be made into a PoE switch and provide power to IP Phones. The labs of this chapter demonstrate this switch module as well as an external switch providing power to the IP Phones.

It is important to have the proper Cisco IOS Software version to run CME in the labs. You must have a CCO account to download Cisco IOS. To obtain the correct version, do not use the Voice Software download option; instead, use the Cisco IOS Software download option on the Cisco website. To locate Cisco IOS, go to www.cisco.com and log in. Point to the Technical Support and Documentation option, select the Software Downloads option, and use either the Cisco IOS Upgrade Planner link or the Cisco

IOS Software link. Cisco IOS Software Release 12.3T was used to create the labs. At the time of writing, the CME files required to provision phones and configure CME from a web interface were located at the following URL:

www.cisco.com/cgi-bin/tablebuild.pl/ip-key

VLAN Review

Virtual LANs (VLANs) allow you to create different networks on a Layer 2 switch. VLANs break up broadcast domains because they allow different networks to be created. A broadcast is sent only over the same network. The VLAN assigned to every port on a switch by default is VLAN 1.

VLAN 1 gets confusing because it has many names—default VLAN, management VLAN, native VLAN. Each of these names is correct for a switch that has not had its configuration changed to anything else. The following list clarifies these terms and a related term for the purposes of this chapter:

- **Default VLAN**—The VLAN that is assigned to a switch port without changes being made. All switch ports belong to VLAN 1 (and that probably will never change). So, calling VLAN 1 the default VLAN is a good name and a good practice.

- **Management VLAN**—The VLAN that is used to connect to the switch from a remote location. All switches by default have a management VLAN of 1. Changing the management VLAN to another VLAN besides VLAN 1 is a good idea. This way, broadcasts that are sent over the management VLAN cannot be captured easily by a workstation that is on VLAN 1.

- **Tagging the frame**—When frames are sent across a trunk (a line that carries more than one VLAN), they have a special section to designate the VLAN to which the frame belongs. This is called *tagging the frame*. A frame coming from a host on VLAN 2 that crosses a trunk would have its frame tagged with the VLAN identifier (VLANID) of 2.

- **Native VLAN**—Traffic from the native VLAN is not tagged as it crosses the trunk. If the trunk fails, but connectivity still exists, traffic from the native VLAN is still allowed across the link.

IP Phone Connectivity Options

One common connectivity option used by companies is connecting the existing networked office PC to an RJ-45 jack on the IP Phone and using the existing PC-to-wall outlet cable to connect to the IP Phone. Figure 2-1 illustrates this type of connectivity.

Figure 2-1   PC Connecting to an IP Phone Using an Existing Connection

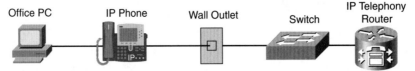

The connectivity method shown in Figure 2-1 saves the company from having to install another cable run from the patch panel to the office and allows for the use of existing wiring. The existing wiring can also provide power to the phone if a PoE power panel or switch is being used.

The PC and the Cisco IP Phone need to be on different networks even though they both use a single connection to the switch. This is done using VLANs. The connection from the phone to the switch is a trunk that carries both the data VLAN (the information from the PC) and the voice VLAN (the data from the IP Phone). Figure 2-2 illustrates the concept of different networks for the two VLANs.

Figure 2-2   PC on a Different VLAN Than the IP Phone

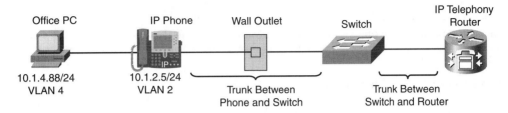

Notice in Figure 2-2 how the PC and the phone are on two different networks and have IP addresses assigned accordingly. The trunk between the IP Phone and the switch carries the two VLANs. Configuring the trunk is an important concept and configuration step.

Special Commands for the Labs

Whether the switch ports are on a specialized module in a router or a separate network device, the **switchport trunk native vlan** *x* command is used on the port that has an IP Phone attached (with a PC attached to the phone).

The **native** keyword defines this VLAN as the one that is not tagged with VLAN information when a frame (from the native VLAN) crosses the trunk between the IP Phone and the switch. In an IP telephony configuration, this native VLAN is the data VLAN—the VLAN to which the PC attaches. This allows the PC that connects to the IP Phone to be on a different subnet than the IP Phone and still receive an IP address from a DHCP server. The command also allows data traffic to still traverse the link between the phone and the switch even if the trunk fails. The **show interfaces trunk** or **show interfaces** *interface-id* **switchport** commands can be used to verify trunk operations.

For the ports that connect to the IP Phones, you must configure the switch so that 802.1Q knows which VLAN contains voice traffic. You can accomplish this configuration with the **switchport voice vlan** command.

On switches such as the 3560, the **switchport trunk** command is not required. Only the voice VLAN (**switchport voice vlan**) and the data VLAN (**switchport access vlan**) commands are required to define which VLAN is used for voice and which VLAN is used for data. The **switchport trunk** command is still required on the switch modules installed in routers and older switches.

When you configure the router, it is important to program the correct interface; this can get quite confusing. For example, some routers have the first FastEthernet interface shown as Fa0, whereas other routers show the same first interface as Fa0/0. This is not an issue with routers that support CME. All onboard interfaces are in 0/0 format. This becomes even more confusing with the switch module that inserts into a router. The specific *slot/port-adapter/port* parameter used with the **interface** command depends on the physical router slot that contains the switch module. A sample command is **interface fastethernet 0/1/0**. Use the **show diag** and **show ip interface brief** commands to verify the naming of the installed interfaces.

Lab 2-1: Connecting the IP Phone to a Switch

In this lab, the company OCSIC.org has decided to deploy CallManager Express in the enterprise. You have decided to connect the phones to a switch and test basic phone power.

The objectives of this lab are as follows:

■ Cable two Cisco IP Phones to a switch.

■ Provide power to the phones using any method.

To perform this lab, you need the following equipment:

■ Inline power-capable switch/switch module or noninline power switch/switch module with power injectors

■ Two Cisco IP Phones

Figure 2-3 illustrates the topology that is used for this lab.

Figure 2-3   Lab Topology: Cisco IP Phone Connectivity

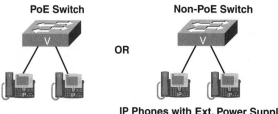

Notice in Figure 2-3 how the IP Phone can be powered with an inline PoE switch/switch module or through an external power supply.

The procedure for this lab consists of the following tasks. The following sections describe each task in detail:

■ **Task 1**—Understand the power capability of switches.

■ **Task 2**—Cable the IP Phone to an inline power switch/switch module.

■ **Task 3**—Cable the IP Phone to a noninline power switch/switch module.

Task 1: Understand the Power Capability of Switches

Two types of switches can be used with Cisco IP Phones:

■ An inline power switch/switch module

■ A noninline power switch/switch module

An inline power external switch has the words INLINE POWER or PoE (Power over Ethernet) stenciled on it, as shown in Figure 2-4. Determine what type of switch model is being used. Task 2 describes the process of cabling using an inline power switch. Task 3 describes the process of cabling using a noninline power switch. Also, a router can contain an inline power or noninline power switch module. To provide inline power through a switch module, the router has a special router power supply.

If you use a switch module, be sure to go to the router privileged mode prompt. It might take a moment for the phone to be sensed.

Figure 2-4 illustrates a typical inline power switch.

Figure 2-4   Inline Power (Power Over Ethernet) Switches

Notice in Figure 2-4 the way Cisco labels the power capability of the external switch. Ensure that you know the type of switch being used for the lab before you start a voice lab.

Task 2: Cable the IP Phone to an Inline Power Switch/Switch Module

Note: If an inline power switch/switch module is not available, skip to Task 3.

Step 1.   Locate the two RJ-45 ports on the back of the IP Phone. Figure 2-5 illustrates the ports on the back of a Cisco IP Phone.

Figure 2-5   Cisco IP Phone Ports

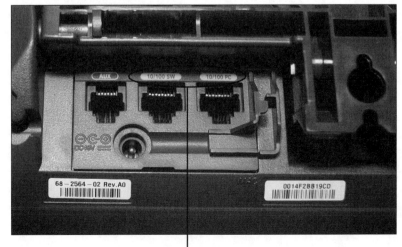

Port Labels

Figure 2-5 points out the port labeling. When performing this lab, ensure that you are using the proper port.

What are the names of the two RJ-45 ports located on the back of a Cisco IP Phone?

_____

Step 2.   If necessary, connect a power cord to the switch that is to provide the inline power. The switch should power on.

Step 3.   Connect a straight-through Ethernet cable from the 10/100 SW port on the IP Phone to any 100-MB port on the inline power switch/switch module. Observe the phone to answer the following question. Figure 2-6 illustrates the cabling of a Cisco IP Phone to a switch.

Figure 2-6   Cisco IP Phone Cabling

How do you know that the phone is receiving power?

_____

_____

Task 3: Cable the IP Phone to a Noninline Power Switch/Switch Module

Step 1.   Connect power to the noninline power switch.

Step 2.   To connect a Cisco IP Phone to a noninline power switch/switch module, you need a power injector, or you can directly connect the phone to a power brick. Look at the power injector illustrated in Figure 2-7; notice the two RJ-45 jacks on one end of the power injector. The port on the left, labeled 10/100BaseTX To Device, is used to connect to the IP Phone (via a straight-through cable). The port on the right, labeled 10/100BaseTX To Network, is used to connect to a noninline power switch such as a 2950 switch (via a straight-through cable).

Figure 2-7   Cisco IP Phone Power Injector

Step 3.   Connect a straight-through cable from the left power injector port, labeled 10/100BaseTX To Device, to the IP Phone port labeled 10/100 SW.

Step 4.   Connect a second straight-through cable from the right power injector port, labeled 10/100BaseTX To Network, to any noninline power switch port.

Step 5.   At the opposite end of the power injector module (away from the RJ-45 connectors) is a cable that goes to the power supply adapter (see Figure 2-8). Attach the power supply adapter connector to the power injector module (48VDC hole). The opposite end of the power supply adapter requires an AC power cord. Attach one end of the AC power cord to the power injector module and the other end to a power outlet.

Figure 2-8   Cisco IP Phone Cabling When Using a Power Injector Module

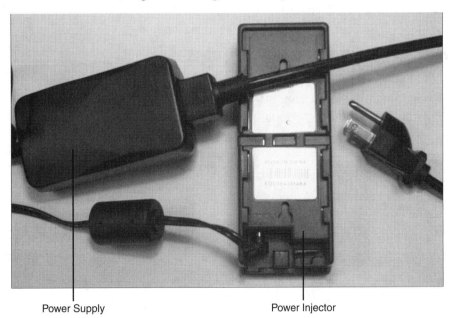

Power Supply   Power Injector

How do you know that power has been applied on the phone?

Lab 2-2: Resetting a Cisco IP Phone

In this lab, OCSIC.org has decided to deploy CallManager Express in the enterprise. IP Phones must be reset if they have been used before. In this company, the network staff used IP Phones in a test lab, and they currently have various configurations. This process should be used when you configure any IP Phone that might have been previously configured.

The objectives of this lab are as follows:

- Erase the current configuration from an IP Phone.

- Reset the phone to factory defaults.

To perform this lab, you need the following equipment:

- Cisco IP Phone 7940/60 series

- Inline power-capable switch or noninline power switch with power injectors

Figure 2-9 illustrates the topology used for this lab.

Figure 2-9   Lab Topology: Cisco IP Phone

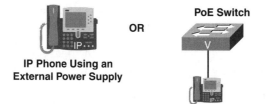

The procedure for this lab consists of the following tasks. The following sections describe each task in detail:

- **Task 1**—Provide power to the switch.

- **Task 2**—Reset the Cisco IP Phone.

Task 1: Provide Power to the Switch

Connect a Cisco IP Phone to an inline power switch using a straight-through cable, cable the phone (with a straight-through cable) to a power module that connects to a noninline power switch, or connect an external power brick to the IP Phone. Power on the switch if necessary.

What is an advantage of using an inline power switch?

_____

_____

_____

_____

_____

_____

Task 2: Reset the Cisco IP Phone

Note: In the following steps, a symbol of either a closed lock or an open lock is shown. The only way that the phone can be reset is if the symbol is of an open lock. If the symbol appears as a closed lock, press the **#** keys on the keypad.

Step 1.   On the IP Phone, press the **settings** button (the one with a check mark) followed by the **#** keys on the keypad to unlock the Network Configuration menu. Note that no feedback appears on the screen. A menu appears.

Step 2.   Press the number **3** on the keypad to select the **Network Configuration** option.

Step 3.   Using the up and down arrow keys on the IP Phone, scroll in both directions to view the various network configuration options.

Step 4.   Either scroll to the number **33** option or press the number **33** on the keypad to go directly to option 33. Verify that an open lock symbol appears beside the words **Network Configuration**. If it does not, press the **#** keys again. The **Erase Configuration** option should appear on the IP Phone.

Step 5.   Press the **softkey** button located under the **Yes** option at the bottom of the phone display.

Step 6.   Press the button under the **Save** option.

What message appears very quickly on the IP Phone screen?

_____

Step 7.   Press the button that corresponds to **Cancel**.

Step 8.   Press the **Save** option.

What message quickly appears on the IP Phone screen?

_____

_____

Lab 2-3: IP Addressing with IP Telephony

IP Phones and PCs need to be on different networks, but they commonly connect to the same switch. This is a perfect place for VLANs. IP Phones need to be on a separate VLAN for the following reasons:

- The voice traffic can be tagged and prioritized over other traffic using quality of service.

- No other traffic in the same broadcast domain interferes with the voice traffic.

Voice traffic cannot tolerate any delay, because the packets cannot be resent.

This lab exercise helps you practice voice network design concepts related to IP addressing and VLANs in different scenarios.

The objective of this lab is to be able to address a small network that has both voice and data networks. You do not need equipment to perform this lab.

Using the information and IP addressing pattern given for a specific scenario, complete the IP addressing and VLAN numbering.

Figure 2-10 shows the first scenario to apply the IP addressing and VLAN numbering.

Figure 2-10   Scenario 1

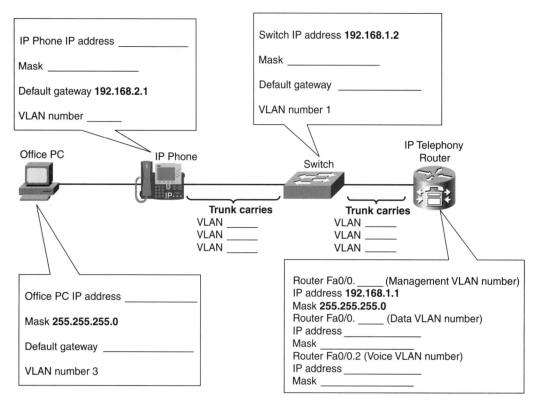

Figure 2-11 shows the second scenario to apply the IP addressing and VLAN numbering.

Figure 2-11   Scenario 2

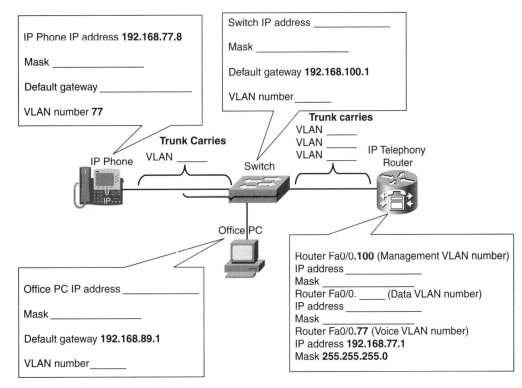

Figure 2-12 shows the third scenario to apply the IP addressing and VLAN numbering.

Figure 2-12   Scenario 3

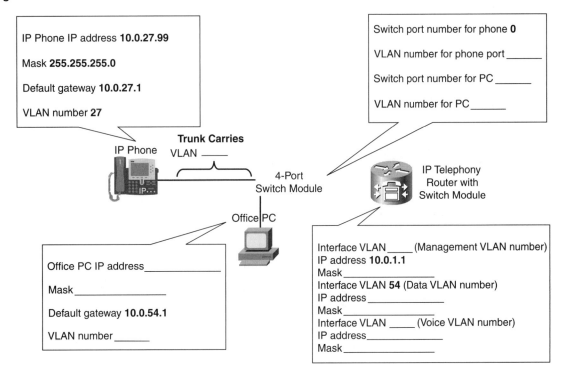

Figure 2-13 shows the last scenario to apply the IP addressing and VLAN numbering. The last valid IP address in a subnet is used as the default gateway for each VLAN.

Figure 2-13   Scenario 4

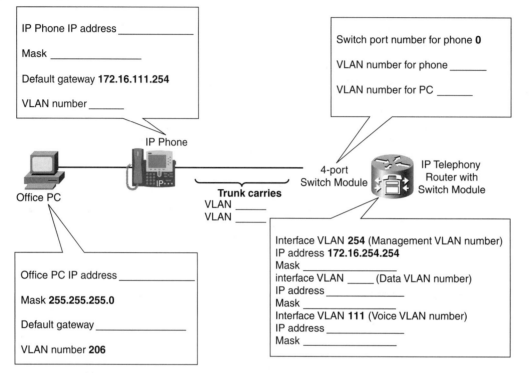

Lab 2-4: Configuring a Cisco CallManager Express-Capable Router and an Integrated Switch

In this lab, OCSIC.org has decided to deploy CallManager Express in the enterprise. Before configuring CallManager, you must configure the router portion and the integrated switch module using the information found in Table 2-1.

Table 2-1   IP Addressing Scheme with an Internal Switch

Pod	Hostname of Router or Switch	Ethernet IP Addresses	VLAN Type
Pod 1	RouterVoIP1	10.10.0.1/24	Data
		10.15.0.1/24	Voice
		10.1.0.1/24	Management
Pod 2	RouterVoIP2	10.20.0.1/24	Data
		10.25.0.1/24	Voice
		10.2.0.1/24	Management
Pod 3	RouterVoIP3	10.30.0.1/24	Data
		10.35.0.1/24	Voice
		10.3.0.1/24	Management
Pod 4	RouterVoIP4	10.40.0.1/24	Data
		10.45.0.1/24	Voice
		10.4.0.1/24	Management

Table 2-1 lists four different pods. Later labs have a phone from one pod calling a phone from another pod.

The objectives of this lab are as follows:

- Configure a Cisco router in preparation for CallManager Express.

- Configure a switch module in preparation for CME.

To perform this lab, you need the following equipment:

- Cisco CallManager Express-capable router with a switch module

- Workstation with an Ethernet 10/100 NIC installed

- Two Cisco IP Phones

Figure 2-14 shows the topology used with this lab.

Figure 2-14   Lab Topology: A Router with an Integrated Switch Module

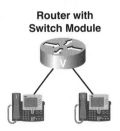

The procedure for this lab consists of the following tasks. The following sections describe each task in detail:

- **Task 1**—Select a pod number.

- **Task 2**—Erase the configuration from the router and switch module.

- **Task 3**—Perform basic router configuration.

- **Task 4**—Configure the router switch module ports.

- **Task 5**—Verify the VLAN configuration.

- **Task 6**—Save the router configuration.

Task 1: Select a Pod Number

From Table 2-1, select a pod number. The commands given on the router reference this pod number. Make a note of which pod you choose.

Task 2: Erase the Configuration from the Router and Switch Module

From privileged mode, erase the VLAN database and startup-configuration file by using the **delete flash:vlan.dat**, **erase startup-config**, and **reload** commands. If you see an error message saying that the vlan.dat file was not found, this is normal if the router does not have VLANs in the VLAN database.

```
Router# delete flash:vlan.dat
Router# erase startup-config
Router# reload
```

If you're prompted to enter the configuration dialog, enter **no** and press **Enter**. If you're prompted to terminate autoinstall, enter **yes**.

Task 3: Perform Basic Router Configuration

Step 1. From configuration mode, change the router's hostname. Use the following command:

```
Router(config)# hostname RouterVoIPx
```

where *x* is the pod number you chose. Throughout the rest of this lab, use the parameters from Table 2-1 based on the pod number you chose.

Step 2. From privileged mode, use the following commands to go into the VLAN database and manually create two VLANs—the voice VLAN and the data VLAN:

```
RouterVoIPX# vlan database
RouterVoIPX(vlan)# vlan x name Management state active
RouterVoIPX(vlan)# vlan x0 name Data state active
RouterVoIPX(vlan)# vlan x5 name Voice state active
RouterVoIPX(vlan)# exit
```

This command sequence also names the VLAN and places it in an active state. Note that the *x* shown in the commands is the pod number.

Step 3. From global configuration mode, access the management VLAN. The *x* in the command is the pod number chosen from Table 2-1.

```
RouterVoIPX(config)# interface vlan x
```

Step 4. Configure the management VLAN interface with an IP address appropriate for the management VLAN taken from Table 2-1. The *x* in the command is the pod number:

```
RouterVoIPX(config-if)# ip address 10.x.0.1 255.255.255.0
```

Step 5. From global configuration mode, access the data VLAN:

```
RouterVoIPX(config)# interface vlan x0
```

The *x* used in the command is the pod number. For example, if the group was assigned to Pod 1, the command would be **interface vlan 10**.

Step 6. From interface configuration mode, configure the data VLAN IP address based on the information found in Table 2-1. The *x* in the command is the pod number:

```
RouterVoIPX(config-if)# ip address 10.x0.0.1 255.255.255.0
```

If a host was configured on the same data VLAN, what would be the default gateway IP address on the host?

Step 7. From global configuration mode, access the voice VLAN using the **interface vlan *x*5** command (where *x* is the pod number):

```
RouterVoIPX(config)# interface vlan x5
```

Step 8. Configure the voice VLAN with the appropriate IP address based on the information found in Table 2-1. The *x* used in the command example is the pod number:

```
RouterVoIPX(config-if)# ip address 10.x5.0.1 255.255.255.0
```

Step 9. Bring *each* of the created VLAN interfaces to a useable condition. Remember to do this for the management VLAN, the voice VLAN, and the data VLAN:

```
RouterVoIPX(config)# interface vlan x
RouterVoIPX(config-if)# no shutdown
RouterVoIPX(config)# interface vlan x0
RouterVoIPX(config-if)# no shutdown
RouterVoIPX(config)# interface vlan x5
RouterVoIPX(config-if)# no shutdown
```

Step 10. Configure the EIGRP routing protocol by using the **router eigrp 100** global configuration command. Then enable and advertise EIGRP updates on all 10.0.0.0-configured interfaces and turn off automatic summarization.

```
RouterVoIPX(config)# router eigrp 100
RouterVoIPX (config-router)# network 10.0.0.0
RouterVoIPX (config-router)# no auto-summary
```

Task 4: Configure the Router Switch Module Ports

Step 1. Verify the slot into which you will insert the router switch four-port module by viewing the router and using the **show diag** command. Look for the words **4 Port FE Switch**. Use the **show ip interface brief** command to verify the slot and the format used for the interface. For example, in a 2811 Integrated Services Router (ISR), the four ports (0 through 3) are listed as FastEthernet 0/1/0, 0/1/1, 0/1/2, and 0/1/3. Make a note of the interface format, because it will be needed with these commands:

```
RouterVoIPX# show diag
RouterVoIPX# show ip interface brief
```

Note: Ports 0 and 1 of the switch module will be used to connect the IP Phones. These ports require four configuration tasks. Each port must

- Be configured in trunking mode
- Have the IEEE 802.1Q trunking protocol configured
- Identify the native VLAN
- Identify the voice VLAN

The **interface fastethernet** *slot/port-adapter/port* command is required on both port 0 and port 1.

Step 2.   From global configuration mode, prepare ports 0 and 1 for trunk mode using the IEEE 802.1Q protocol, and identify both the native VLAN and the voice VLAN. The *x* in the command is the pod number:

```
RouterVoIPX(config)# interface fastethernet slot/port-adapter/0
RouterVoIPX(config-if)# switchport trunk encapsulation dot1q
RouterVoIPX(config-if)# switchport trunk native vlan x0
RouterVoIPX(config-if)# switchport mode trunk
RouterVoIPX(config-if)# switchport voice vlan x5
RouterVoIPX(config-if)# no shutdown
RouterVoIPX(config)# interface fastethernet slot/port-adapter/1
RouterVoIPX(config-if)# switchport trunk encapsulation dot1q
RouterVoIPX(config-if)# switchport trunk native vlan x0
RouterVoIPX(config-if)# switchport mode trunk
RouterVoIPX(config-if)# switchport voice vlan x5
RouterVoIPX(config-if)# no shutdown
```

Task 5: Verify VLAN Configuration

Step 1.   Connect a Cisco IP Phone using a straight-through cable to switch module port 0. Visually verify the port number on the switch module. It is labeled 0*x*. The port on the bottom of the IP Phone is labeled 10/100 SW. The IP Phone gets power but does not connect to another phone until CallManager Express has been configured later, in a different lab.

Step 2.   Using a second straight-through cable, connect the second Cisco IP Phone to switch module port 1 on the router.

Step 3.   From privileged mode, verify that the port is properly configured as a trunk port by using the following command:

```
RouterVoIPX# show interfaces fastethernet slot/port-adapter/port switchport
```

Step 4.   Verify trunking operations on ports 0 and 1 of the switch module using the following command. Do not proceed unless trunking is enabled:

```
RouterVoIPX# show interfaces trunk
```

Step 5.   From privileged mode on the router, issue the following command to verify that VLAN1, *x*0, and *x*5 (where *x* is the pod number) have IP addresses and that their status is up and up:

```
RouterVoIPX# show ip interface brief
```

If the interfaces are not displayed, if they do not have an IP address or the correct IP address, or if their status is not up and up, troubleshoot as necessary.

Task 6: Save the Router Configuration

Step 1.   Save the router configuration by entering the following command:

```
RouterVoIPX# copy running-config startup-config
```

Step 2.   Save the router configuration to a text file as well. This basic configuration will be required in future labs.

Lab 2-5: Configuring a Cisco CallManager Express-Capable Router with an External Switch

In this lab, OCSIC.org has decided to deploy CallManager Express in the enterprise. Before you configure CallManager, the router and the external switch using the information shown in Table 2-2.

Table 2-2   IP Addressing Scheme with an External Switch

Pod	Hostname of Router or Switch	Ethernet IP Address	VLAN Type
Pod 1	RouterVoIP1	10.10.0.1/24	Data
		10.15.0.1/24	Voice
		10.1.0.1/24	Management
	SwitchVoIP1	10.1.0.4/24	Management
Pod 2	RouterVoIP2	10.20.0.1/24	Data
		10.25.0.1/24	Voice
		10.2.0.1/24	Management
	SwitchVoIP2	10.2.0.4/24	Management
Pod 3	RouterVoIP3	10.30.0.1/24	Data
		10.35.0.1/24	Voice
		10.3.0.1/24	Management
	SwitchVoIP3	10.3.0.4/24	Management
Pod 4	RouterVoIP4	10.40.0.1/24	Data
		10.45.0.1/24	Voice
		10.4.0.1/24	Management
	SwitchVoIP4	10.4.0.4/24	Management

Table 2-2 lists four different pods. Later labs have a phone from one pod calling a phone from another pod.

The objectives of this lab are as follows:

- Configure a Cisco router in preparation for CallManager Express.

- Configure a switch in preparation for CME.

To perform this lab, you need the following equipment:

- Cisco CallManager Express-capable router

- Inline power-capable switch or noninline power switch with power injectors

- Workstation with an Ethernet 10/100 NIC installed

- Two Cisco IP Phones

Figure 2-15 illustrates the topology used in this lab.

Figure 2-15   Lab Topology: A Router with an External Switch

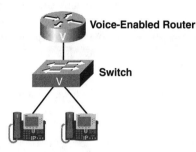

The procedure for this lab consists of the following tasks. The following sections describe each task in detail:

- **Task 1**—Select a pod number.
- **Task 2**—Erase the router configuration.
- **Task 3**—Assign a router name and cable.
- **Task 4**—Configure Layer 3 trunking.
- **Task 5**—Configure the routing protocol.
- **Task 6**—Erase the switch.
- **Task 7**—Assign a switch name.
- **Task 8**—Configure Layer 3 access to the switch.
- **Task 9**—Enable the management VLAN.
- **Task 10**—Configure a switch port as a trunk port.
- **Task 11**—Create VLANs on the switch.
- **Task 12**—Test connectivity across the trunk.
- **Task 13**—Configure switch ports for IP Phones.

Task 1: Select a Pod Number

From Table 2-2, select a pod number. The commands given on the router reference this pod number. Make a note of which pod you chose.

Task 2: Erase the Router Configuration

Erase the startup-configuration file on the router by using the following commands. If you're prompted to enter the configuration dialog, enter **no** and press **Enter**. If you're prompted to terminate autoinstall, enter **yes**.

```
Router# erase startup-config
Router# reload
```

Task 3: Assign a Router Name and Cable

Step 1.   Configure the router's hostname using the following command, where *x* is the pod number assigned to the group:

```
Router(config)# hostname RouterVoIPx
```

Throughout the rest of the lab, use the parameters in Table 2-2 based on the pod number chosen.

> **Note:** Depending on the router model and physical configuration, the router interface used to connect to the switch could be a FastEthernet port or a Gigabit Ethernet port. Also, the router may have a different physical interface number (that is, FastEthernet 0 or GigabitEthernet 2/0). If you're unsure of which interface is installed, verify the name of the router Ethernet ports by using the **show running-config** or **show ip interface brief** command. Make a note of how the interface is numbered. This information is used in commands that follow.

Step 2. Attach a straight-through cable between the lowest-numbered router FastEthernet port and port 1 on the switch.

Task 4: Configure Layer 3 Trunking

Step 1. On the router Ethernet interface used to connect to the switch, create a subinterface for the management VLAN by entering global configuration mode. The *x* in the following command is the pod number:

```
RouterVoIPX(config)# interface fastethernet 0/0.x
```

Note that the **fastethernet 0/0** portion of the command might change based on the router model being used.

Step 2. Configure the same subinterface for trunking by entering the following command, where the *x* is the pod number:

```
RouterVoIPX(config-subif)# encapsulation dot1q x
```

If a warning message appears, ignore it. If this command does not work, the proper router is not being used.

Step 3. Configure the management VLAN subinterface with an IP address appropriate for the management VLAN based on the information found in Table 2-2. The *x* used in the command is the pod number:

```
RouterVoIPX(config-subif)# ip address 10.x.0.1 255.255.255.0
```

If a switch was configured with an IP address on the same management VLAN, what would be the default gateway IP address configured on the switch?

_____

Step 4. Create a subinterface for the data VLAN by entering global configuration mode and entering the following command (where *x* is the pod number):

```
RouterVoIPX(config)# interface fastethernet 0/0.x0
```

For example, if Pod 1 were being used, you would use the **interface fastethernet 0/0.10** command.

Step 5. Configure the data VLAN subinterface for trunking by entering the following command (where *x* is the pod number):

```
RouterVoIPX(config-subif)# encapsulation dot1q x0 native
```

The **native** keyword defines this VLAN as the one that is not tagged with VLAN information when a frame (from VLAN *x*0) crosses the trunk between the router and the switch. This allows the PC that connects to the IP Phone to be on a different subnet than the IP Phone and still receive an IP address from a DHCP server.

Step 6. Configure the data VLAN subinterface with an IP address appropriate for the data VLAN based on the information found in Table 2-2. Use the following command (where *x* is the pod number):

```
RouterVoIPX(config-subif)# ip address 10.x0.0.1 255.255.255.0
```

If a host were configured on the same data VLAN, what would be the host default gateway IP address?

Step 7. From global configuration mode, create a subinterface for the voice VLAN using the following command (where *x* is the pod number):

```
RouterVoIPX(config-subif)# interface fastethernet 0/0.x5
```

Step 8. Configure the voice VLAN subinterface for trunking using the following command (where *x* is the pod number):

For example, if Pod 2 were being used, you would enter the **interface fastethernet 0/0.25** command.

```
RouterVoIPX(config-subif)# encapsulation dot1q x5
```

Step 9. Configure the voice VLAN subinterface with an IP address appropriate for the voice VLAN based on the information found in Table 2-2. Use the following command (where *x* is the pod number):

```
RouterVoIPX(config-subif)# ip address 10.x5.0.1 255.255.255.0
```

Step 10. Bring the Ethernet interface to a useable condition:

```
RouterVoIPX(config)# interface fastethernet x
RouterVoIPX(config-if)# no shutdown
```

Task 5: Configure the Routing Protocol

Step 1. Configure the EIGRP routing protocol by using the **router eigrp 100** command to start an EIGRP process with an autonomous system number of 100. Then enable and advertise EIGRP updates on all 10.0.0.0-configured interfaces and turn off automatic summarization.

```
RouterVoIPX(config)# router eigrp 100
RouterVoIPX (config-router)# network 10.0.0.0
RouterVoIPX (config-router)# no auto-summary
```

Step 2. Verify connectivity by viewing the Ethernet interface on the router using the following command:

```
RouterVoIPX# show ip interface brief
```

If the Ethernet interface is not functional, troubleshoot and resolve the problem. Do not proceed until the interface is up and up.

Step 3. Save the router configuration to NVRAM by entering the following command:

```
RouterVoIPX# copy running-config startup-config
```

Step 4. Save the router configuration to a text file as well. This basic configuration will be required in future labs.

Task 6: Erase the Switch

Erase the switch VLAN database and startup-configuration file and reload the switch by using the following commands. If you're prompted to enter the configuration dialog, enter **no** and press **Enter**. If you're prompted to terminate autoinstall, enter **yes**. If a message appears that states **%Error deleting flash:Vlan.dat (File not found)**, no action is necessary. This simply means there were no preexisting VLANs.

```
Switch# delete flash:vlan.dat
Delete filename [vlan.dat]? [Enter]
Delete flash:vlan.dat? [confirm] [Enter]
Switch# erase startup-config
Switch(config)# reload
```

Note: The configuration output used in this lab is produced from a 2950 switch. Any other switch or IOS version might produce different output. You should execute the following steps on each model of switch unless specifically instructed otherwise.

Task 7: Assign a Switch Name

From global configuration mode, assign to the switch the hostname of SwitchVoIPx (where x is the pod number chosen), as follows:

```
Switch(config)# hostname SwitchVoIPx
```

Task 8: Configure Layer 3 Access to the Switch

Step 1.   On the management VLAN, set the switch IP address to **10.x.0.4/24** (where x is the pod number):

```
SwitchVoIPX(config)# interface vlan x
SwitchVoIPX(config-if)# ip address 10.x.0.4 255.255.255.0
SwitchVoIPX(config-if)# description Management VLAN
```

Step 2.   From global configuration mode, set the switch default gateway to **10.x.0.1** (where x is the pod number):

```
SwitchVoIPX(config)# ip default-gateway 10.x.0.1
```

Task 9: Enable the Management VLAN

Enable the virtual interface using the **no shutdown** command:

```
SwitchVoIPX(config)# interface vlan x
SwitchVoIPX(config-if)# no shutdown
```

Task 10: Configure a Switch Port as a Trunk Port

Step 1.   From global configuration mode, access switch port 1, which connects to the router:

```
SwitchVoIPX(config)# interface fastethernet 0/1
```

Step 2. From interface configuration mode, set the port to use the IEEE 802.1Q trunking protocol. The **switchport trunk encapsulation dot1q** command does not have to be programmed on switches that do not support another trunking protocol. (It is IEEE 802.1Q by default.)

```
SwitchVoIPX(config-if)# switchport trunk encapsulation dot1q
```

Note: If this command does not work on the switch, the switch supports only the 802.1Q trunking protocol and therefore does not have to be programmed with the **switchport trunk encapsulation dot1q** command.

Step 3. From interface configuration mode, set the port to trunking mode:

```
SwitchVoIPX(config-if)# switchport mode trunk
```

Step 4. From interface configuration mode, specify which VLAN is the native VLAN (where *x* is the pod number):

```
SwitchVoIPX(config-if)# switchport trunk native vlan x0
```

Step 5. From enable mode, verify that the port is properly configured as a trunk port by using the **show interfaces** *interface-id* **switchport** command (where *interface-id* is the switch port used to connect to the router). Some switches have another command that can be used to verify trunking operations—**show interfaces trunk:**

```
SwitchVoIPX# show interfaces fastethernet 0/1 switchport
SwitchVoIPX# show interfaces trunk
```

Task 11: Create VLANs on the Switch

From privileged mode, use the following commands to go into the VLAN database and manually create two VLANs—the voice VLAN and the data VLAN:

```
SwitchVoIPX# vlan database
SwitchVoIPX(vlan)# vlan x name Management state active
SwitchVoIPX(vlan)# vlan x0 name Data state active
SwitchVoIPX(vlan)# vlan x5 name Voice state active
SwitchVoIPX(vlan)# exit
```

These commands also name the VLAN and place it in an active state. These commands might not be necessary on the latest switch models (but they can still be added). Note that the *x* shown in the command is the pod number.

Task 12: Test Connectivity Across the Trunk

Step 1. After the management VLAN has come up (use the **show ip interface brief** command), go to enable mode on the switch and ping the router IP address for the management VLAN. Refer to Table 2-2 for this address (*x* refers to the pod number):

```
SwitchVoIPX# ping 10.x.0.1
```

Ensure that the ping was successful. If the ping was unsuccessful, do not proceed until you have performed appropriate troubleshooting and the ping is successful. Note that on some models of routers and switches, you must manually configure the speed and duplex on both ports.

Step 2. Ping the router IP address for the voice VLAN and the data VLAN. Refer to Table 2-2 for the IP addresses. All pings should be successful when the trunk is working correctly. Troubleshoot as necessary until all pings succeed.

Task 13: Configure Switch Ports for IP Phones

Step 1.   Cable the two IP Phones to switch ports 2 and 3 using straight-through cables.

Step 2.   From interface configuration mode, configure the two IP Phone ports to use the IEEE 802.1Q trunking protocol using the following commands.

Note: The **switchport trunk encapsulation dot1q** command does not have to be programmed on switches that do not support another trunking protocol. (It is IEEE 802.1Q by default.)

```
SwitchVoIPX(config)# interface fastethernet 0/2
SwitchVoIPX(config-if)# switchport trunk encapsulation dot1q
SwitchVoIPX(config)# interface fastethernet 0/3
SwitchVoIPX(config-if)# switchport trunk encapsulation dot1q
```

Step 3.   Configure the two IP Phone ports to be trunk ports with the **switchport mode trunk** command. You execute this command from interface configuration mode:

```
SwitchVoIPX(config)# interface fastethernet 0/2
SwitchVoIPX(config-if)# switchport mode trunk
SwitchVoIPX(config)# interface fastethernet 0/3
SwitchVoIPX(config-if)# switchport mode trunk
```

Step 4.   Configure both switch ports that are used to connect IP Phones to identify the voice VLAN traffic with the **switchport voice vlan** command. The x in the command is the pod number:

```
SwitchVoIPX(config)# interface fastethernet 0/2
SwitchVoIPX(config-if)# switchport voice vlan x5
SwitchVoIPX(config)# interface fastethernet 0/3
SwitchVoIPX(config-if)# switchport voice vlan x5
```

Step 5.   For the IP Phone to operate on a different VLAN from the PC, you must use the **switchport trunk native vlan x0** command (where x is the pod number) from interface configuration mode. The native VLAN must be the same as the data VLAN for this to work:

```
SwitchVoIPX(config)# interface fastethernet 0/2 (and 3)
SwitchVoIPX(config-if)# switchport trunk native vlan x0
```

Note: The IP Phones do not register at this point, because CallManager Express has not yet been configured on the router.

Step 6.   Save the switch configuration by using the following command:

```
SwitchVoIPX# copy running-config startup-config
```

Step 7.   Save the switch configuration to a text file as well. This basic configuration will be required in future labs.

CHAPTER 3

Managing and Configuring Cisco VoIP Devices

This chapter examines how to configure VoIP using a variety of methods: VoIP telephony setup dialog, manual configuration of the router for Cisco CallManager Express (CME), a partially automated process, Quick Configuration Tool (QCT), and Cisco Network Assistant. Each of these methods is addressed in a lab that allows you to explore each one so that you can determine the most appropriate method or tool to use.

IP Telephony IP Addresses

No matter what method of configuration is used, a Cisco IP Phone needs an IP address and a configuration file to operate. An IP address is normally assigned using DHCP. A DHCP pool of addresses can be created on the router or on a separate server. In these labs, the DHCP pool is created on the router. When either method is used, the CME router has to be able to let the phone know the IP address of the router or server that can provide the IP address. This is true even if the IP address is the same router that is providing CME.

DHCP Option 150

The Cisco IP Phone uses DHCP option 150 to identify the location of the device that contains the IP Phone's configuration file. The Cisco IP Phone receives its configuration file from a TFTP server. DHCP (specifically, the 150 option) can be used to let the IP Phone know the IP address of the device that contains the phone configuration file. This IP address is a TFTP server, and it can be located on the router providing CME.

In the DHCP pool configuration process on the router, this **option 150** parameter must be configured, or the Cisco IP Phone will not function.

PC IP Addressing

Additionally, if a PC is to be used, it, too, needs an IP address. If the PC is using DHCP, the DHCP pool needs to be a different one from the pool used for the IP Phones. Lab 3-2 details how to create a separate DHCP pool for PC addresses on the router. This information is useful and can be used in later labs when a PC is required.

ephone-dn

When dealing with CME, an IP Phone is configured using the **ephone** option. The term *ephone* is short for Ethernet phone. The telephone line associated with the ephone is known as an *ephone-dn*, which stands for Ethernet phone directory number. The ephone-dn represents a line that connects a voice channel to a phone so that calls can be made. When you enable the VoIP telephony service, ephones and ephone-dns can be created and seen in the running configuration output.

An ephone-dn has one or more extensions or phone numbers associated with it that allow calls to be made. An ephone-dn is similar to a phone line. Each ephone has a number to identify it during the configuration process.

The **ephone-dn** command creates one virtual voice port and one or more dial peers (covered in the next chapter). The number of ephone-dns that are created corresponds to the number of simultaneous calls that can be made, because each ephone-dn represents one virtual voice port in the router. This means that if you want more than one call to the same number to be answered simultaneously, multiple ephone-dns (virtual voice ports) are needed.

There are two types of ephone-dns:

- **Single-line**—The single-line option should be used when phone buttons have a one-to-one correspondence to the regular phone lines that come into a CME system. The dual-line option lets you make two call connections at the same time using one phone line button.

- **Dual-line**—Dual-line IP Phones have one voice port with two channels to handle two independent calls. This capability enables call waiting, call transfer, and conference functions on a phone-line button. In dual-line mode, each IP Phone and its associated line button can support one or two calls. You select one of two calls on the same line using the **Navigation** button located below the phone display.

Cisco Network Assistant

To access Network Assistant, you need a registered www.cisco.com CCO account but no special access privileges. Network Assistant is a Cisco application that manages standalone devices and device groups—communities and clusters from a computer on your intranet. Network Assistant was free at the time of writing. A community can manage up to 20 devices such as routers, access points, and switches. A cluster can manage up to 16 switches. With a community, CDP does not have to be enabled, because you can manually add a device. Clusters require that CDP be enabled. Lab 3-5 demonstrates a community.

Cisco Network Assistant uses a GUI interface to interact with a network device that has an IP address assigned and HTTP enabled. The interface allows you to apply actions to multiple devices and ports at the same time for VLAN and quality of service (QoS) settings, inventory and statistics reports, link and device monitoring, and software upgrades.

Lab 3-1: Configuring VoIP Using the telephony-service setup Program

The company OCSIC.org has decided to experiment with using the **telephony-service setup** program to determine what commands are deployed as a result.

You must use the information in Tables 3-1 and 3-2 to perform some of the steps in the setup process.

Table 3-1   IP Telephony Addressing Scheme

Pod	Hostname of Router or Switch	IP Address on Ethernet Interface	DHCP Pool Exclusion	DHCP Pool Network	Default Router	DHCP Option 150
1	RouterVoIP1	10.10.0.1/24	10.10.0.1 – 10.10.0.10	10.10.0.0/24	10.10.0.1	
		10.15.0.1/24	10.15.0.1 – 10.15.0.10	10.15.0.0/24	10.15.0.1	10.10.0.1
		10.1.0.1/24				
	SwitchVoIP1	10.1.0.4/24			10.1.0.1	
2	RouterVoIP2	10.20.0.1/24	10.20.0.1 – 10.20.0.10	10.20.0.0/24	10.20.0.1	
		10.25.0.1/24	10.25.0.1 to 10.25.0.10	10.25.0.0/24	10.25.0.1	10.20.0.1
		10.2.0.1/24				
	SwitchVoIP2	10.2.0.4/24			10.2.0.1	
3	RouterVoIP3	10.30.0.1/24	10.30.0.1 – 0.30.0.10	10.30.0.0/24	10.30.0.1	
		10.35.0.1/24	10.35.0.1 – 10.35.0.10	10.35.0.0/24	10.35.0.1	10.30.0.1
		10.3.0.1/24				
	SwitchVoIP3	10.3.0.4/24			10.3.0.1	
4	RouterVoIP4	10.40.0.1/24	10.40.0.1 – 10.40.0.10	10.40.0.0/24	10.40.0.1	
		10.45.0.1/24	10.45.0.1– 10.45.0.10	10.45.0.0/24	10.45.0.1	10.40.0.1
		10.4.0.1/24				
	SwitchVoIP4	10.4.0.4/24			10.4.0.1	

Table 3-2   IP Telephony Dial Plan

Pod	Extension Numbers	First E.164 DID Number	Voice Mail Extension Number
Pod 1	5000 to 5029	5105555000	5555028
Pod 2	5030 to 5059	5105555030	5555058
Pod 3	5060 to 5089	5105555060	5555088
Pod 4	5100 to 5129	5105555100	5555128

The objectives of this lab are as follows:

- Cable two Cisco IP Phones to a switch/switch module.

- Provide power to the phones using either method of connectivity.

- Configure Cisco CallManager Express.

- Configure two IP Phones using the **telephony-service setup** dialog routine.

- Verify IP Phone registration and connectivity.

To perform this lab, you need the following equipment:

- Cisco CallManager Express-capable router

- Switch/switch module

- Workstation with FastEthernet 10/100 NIC installed

- Two Cisco IP Phones (powered using any method)

Figure 3-1 shows the topology used for this lab. Keep in mind that an integrated switch module in the router could be used instead of the external switch.

Figure 3-1   Lab Topology: Cisco Router, Switch/Switch Module, and IP Phone Connectivity

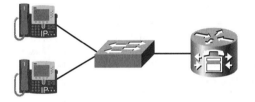

The procedure for this lab consists of the following tasks. The following sections describe each task in detail:

- **Task 1**—Configure the Cisco IP Phones using the **telephony-service setup** command.

- **Task 2**—Verify connectivity between the Cisco IP Phones.

- **Task 3**—Connect a PC to the Cisco IP Phone, and verify the configuration.

- **Task 4**—Erase and reboot the router.

Task 1: Configure the Cisco IP Phones Using the telephony-service setup Command

Step 1.   Ensure that the router has no previously configured commands except for the commands created in Lab 2-4 or Lab 2-5. Copy the configuration from Lab 2-4 or Lab 2-5 (depending on whether a switch module or external switch is being used). Reprogram the VLANs *or* reprogram the router and switch module/external switch with the commands necessary to create the voice, data, and management VLANs and route between them.

Step 2.   From global configuration mode, enter the **telephony-service setup** command to enter CME telephony setup mode:

```
RouterVoIPX(config)# telephony-service setup
```

Note: If you make a mistake while you are in the setup program, you can correct it at the end of the utility.

Step 3. When prompted with the choice to set up the DHCP service for your IP Phones, enter **y** and press **Enter**.

Step 4. The IP network for the telephony-service DHCP pool is **10.X5.0.0** (where *X* is the pod number). This is a DHCP pool to be used by the IP Phones.

Step 5. The subnet mask for the DHCP network is **255.255.255.0**.

Step 6. The TFTP server IP address for DHCP option 150 is an address on the Cisco CME router— **10.X5.0.1** (where *X* is the pod number).

Step 7. The default router for the pool also is **10.X5.0.1** (where *X* is the pod number).

Step 8. When you are asked if you want to start the telephony-service setup, answer **y** for yes.

Step 9. For the source IP address, enter **10.X5.0.1** (where *X* is the pod number).

Step 10. Accept the default port of 2000 by pressing the **Enter** key. Skinny is a protocol used by Cisco IP Phones. It uses TCP port 2000.

Step 11. When asked how many phones to configure, respond with **4**, even though only two phones are connected. You can change this value from the command prompt if necessary.

Step 12. When asked whether you want dual lines, answer **y** and press **Enter**.

Step 13. Select the language you want on the phone. (You can accept the default of English by simply pressing the **Enter** key.)

Step 14. When asked which Call Progress tone to use, select a number relating to the country for call progress tones. (If you're in the United States, you can use the default by just pressing the **Enter** key.)

Note: In-band call progress tones (such as ringback and busy tones) and announcements ("The number you have dialed is no longer in service") are required to successfully signal voice calls. Call progress tones can be generated by the originating, terminating, or intermediate devices.

Step 15. Refer to Table 3-2 to find the appropriate first extension number. The second column lists extension numbers. Find the appropriate row for the pod number being used. Select the first number in the range for the pod being used. For example, if Pod 1 is being used, the first extension number is 5000.

Step 16. When you're asked if Direct Inward Dialing (DID) is used, answer **y** and press **Enter**.

Note: DID is a local phone company service that provides a block of phone numbers used to call into a company's PBX system. With DID, individual phone numbers can be assigned to each person or PC without having a physical line into the PBX for each person's connection.

Step 17. When you're asked for the full E.164 number, enter the value from Table 3-2 for the pod being used. For example, if Pod 2 is being used, the E.164 DID number is 5105555030.

Note: A fully qualified E.164 number contains a country code (issued by the ITU), area code (sometimes called an STD code), and the local telephone number. Because the country has been selected already, it is just the area code and the phone number.

Step 18. When you're asked if you want forwarding to a voice message service (voice mail), enter **y** and press **Enter**.

Step 19. When you're asked to enter an extension or pilot number of the voice message service, refer to Table 3-2 for the voice mail extension number. For example, if pod 3 is being used, the voice mail extension number is 5555088.

Step 20. Press the **Enter** key to accept the default of 18 seconds for Call Forward timeout.

Step 21. You are asked if any of the information needs to be changed. Select **no** to use the current settings and to exit the utility, or select **yes** to change an option. If you did not make mistakes in the previous steps, enter **n**, press **Enter**, and proceed to the next step. If you made mistakes, enter **y**, press **Enter**, and go back to the first step.

Step 22. Watch the console output to see if the phones register. You should see router output similar to the following:

```
Mar 2 23:57:09.080: %IPPHONE-6-REGISTER: ephone-1 :SEP000F2470F92E
   IP:10.15.0.11
   Socket:1 DeviceType:Phone has registered.
```

Note that this may take several minutes. Another indication that the phone has registered is that the phone number appears in the upper-right corner of the phone display.

Note: Ensure that the phones are inserted into the correct switch/switch module ports that have been configured for VoIP.

The power to the phone may need to be removed and reapplied to get the phone to rerequest an IP address and register with the CME router.

Also, the phone may need to have its configuration erased and rebooted to register with the CME router.

How important is it to pick the extension numbers that will be used for IP Phone extensions? Do you think any numbers should be avoided? If so, which ones?

_____

_____

_____

_____

Task 2: Verify Connectivity Between the Cisco IP Phones

Place a call between the two IP Phones by picking up the handset on one phone and entering the number of the second IP Phone.

After a connection has been made, reverse the process. Make a call from the second IP Phone to the first one.

Note: Calls can also be placed by pressing the speaker button on the bottom right of the Cisco IP Phone and then entering the number of the other IP Phone.

If the phones do not connect to one another, perform troubleshooting as necessary. Reset the phone using steps from Lab 2-2 if necessary.

Task 3: Connect a PC to the Cisco IP Phone Port, and Verify the Configuration

Step 1. Connect a PC using a straight-through cable to the port labeled 10/100 PC on the bottom of one of the Cisco IP Phones. Ensure that the RJ-45 connector inserts fully into the connector.

Step 2. Ensure that the PC is configured to receive an IP address from a DHCP server. On a Windows-based computer, use the Network Control Panel to configure TCP/IP to "Obtain an IP address automatically."

Step 3. On the router from global configuration mode, create a DHCP pool for the data VLAN. The PC will connect to the data VLAN and receive an IP address. In the following commands, the x in the **network** and **default-router** commands represents the pod number chosen previously:

```
RouterVoIPX(config)# ip dhcp pool DATA
RouterVoIPX(dhcp-config)# network 10.x0.0.0 255.255.255.0
RouterVoIPX(dhcp-config)# default-router 10.x0.0.1
```

Step 4. From global configuration mode, reserve the first ten IP addresses of the DATA DHCP pool for networking devices. The x in the **ip dhcp excluded-address** command represents the pod number:

```
RouterVoIPX(config)# ip dhcp excluded-address 10.x0.0.1 10.x0.0.10
```

Step 5. Renew the IP address on the PC. It might be necessary to use the commands **ipconfig /release** and **ipconfig /renew** from a command prompt if the PC has already gotten an address in the excluded IP address range.

Did the PC receive an IP address? If so, what address did it receive? If the PC did not receive an IP address, troubleshoot as necessary.

_____

_____

Step 6. From the PC command prompt, ping the default gateway. The ping should succeed. Troubleshoot as necessary.

Task 4: Erase and Reboot the Router

Do *not* save the router configuration. However, it is recommended that you copy the current configuration to a text file that can be used later.

Reload the router so that a manual configuration can be completed in the next lab. Do *not* save the changes. If an integrated switch module is being used, the **del vlan.dat** command needs to be used on the router:

```
RouterVoIPX# del vlan.dat
RouterVoIPX# reload
```

Lab 3-2: Manually Configuring a CME Router for VoIP Phones

In this lab, OCSIC.org has decided to use the manual setup process to configure the Cisco CallManager Express router and phones.

The objective of this lab is to configure two Cisco IP Phones using commands entered on the router.

To perform this lab, you need the following equipment:

- Cisco CME-capable router with specific files for an IP Phone (basic CME .tar file)

- Switch/switch module

- Workstation with an Ethernet 10/100 NIC installed

- Two Cisco IP Phones (powered using any method)

Figure 3-2 shows an example of the topology used for this lab. Keep in mind that an integrated switch module in the router can be used instead of the external switch.

Figure 3-2   Sample Lab Topology

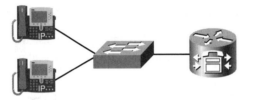

The procedure for this lab consists of the following tasks. The following sections describe each task in detail:

- **Task 1**—Configure a DHCP pool for Cisco IP Phones.

- **Task 2**—Verify and optionally load the Cisco firmware file.

- **Task 3**—Perform basic router configuration for a Cisco IP Phone.

- **Task 4**—Verify Cisco IP Phone registration.

- **Task 5**—Add configuration for a second Cisco IP Phone.

Task 1: Configure a DHCP Pool for Cisco IP Phones

Step 1.   Ensure that the router has no previously configured commands *except* for commands necessary to create the voice, data, and management VLANs and route between them. Use the **show running-config | begin tele** command to verify that the IP telephony service has not been configured or executed. The pipe symbol (|) is normally created by holding down the **Shift** key and pressing the \ key. Nothing should appear as a result of issuing this command if the IP telephony service has been deleted or has not been executed. If Lab 3-1 has just been completed, move into global configuration mode and remove the **telephony-service** commands:

```
RouterVoIPX# show running-config | begin tele

RouterVoIPX(config)# no telephony-service
```

Note: The **begin tele** parameter searches the running configuration for the first instance of "tele," which is really meant to be telephony-service. If **no telephony-service** is configured, nothing is displayed, and the RouterVoIPX prompt is seen again. If a configuration exists, use the **no telephony-service** command to erase any existing configuration.

Step 2. If you just completed Lab 3-1, from global configuration mode remove the DHCP pool for the IP Phones and any **tftp-server** commands:

```
RouterVoIPX(config)# no ip dhcp pool ITS
RouterVoIPX(config)# no tftp-server P003xxxxxxxx.bin
RouterVoIPX(config)# no tftp-server P003xxxxxxxx.sbn
RouterVoIPX(config)# no tftp-server P004xxxxxxxx.bin
```

Step 3. Create the DHCP pool for Cisco IP Phone addresses. From global configuration mode, use the command **ip dhcp pool Voice** to name the DHCP pool and begin DHCP parameter configuration:

```
RouterVoIPX(config)# ip dhcp pool Voice
```

Step 4. Use the **network 10.X5.0.0 255.255.255.0** command to set the range of IP addresses to use in the DHCP:

```
RouterVoIPX(dhcp-config)# network 10.X5.0.0 255.255.255.0
```

Step 5. Enter the command **default-router 10.X5.0.1** (where X is the pod number) to assign a default gateway to the Cisco IP Phone:

```
RouterVoIPX(dhcp-config)# default-router 10.X5.0.1
```

Note: With CallManager Express, the Cisco IP Phones receive their initial configuration information and phone firmware from the TFTP server associated with the CME router. The phones usually get the IP address of their TFTP server using the DHCP **option 150** command. When CME is used, the TFTP server address obtained by the phone should point to an IP address on the CME router, because that is where the phone image will be located.

The Cisco IP Phone downloads the image configuration file from the device that has the IP address obtained through the DHCP option 150.

Step 6. Use the command **option 150 ip 10.X5.0.1** (where X is the pod number) to assign the TFTP server address as the CME router:

```
RouterVoIPX(dhcp-config)# option 150 ip 10.X5.0.1
```

Step 7. Exit the DHCP pool configuration mode. From global configuration mode, enter **ip dhcp excluded-address 10.X5.0.1 10.X5.0.10** (where X is the pod number) to prevent this range of defined addresses from being used out of the DHCP pool:

```
RouterVoIPX(dhcp-config)# exit
RouterVoIPX(config)# ip dhcp excluded-address 10.X5.0.1 10.X5.0.10
```

Step 8. Optionally, if a DHCP pool has not already been created for PCs, you can create one using the steps demonstrated in Task 3 of the preceding lab.

Task 2: Verify and Optionally Load the Cisco Firmware File

From privileged mode, use the **show flash:** command to verify the IP Phone firmware files that are present:

```
RouterVoIPX# show flash:
```

The firmware files for 7960 and 7940 start with **P003**, such as P00303020214.bin. For other phones, research on www.cisco.com what .bin file is used. Do not continue until the IP Phone firmware file is present in flash.

Note: For a 28x1 router: If these files are not there, you must obtain them from the Cisco site. The .bin files are located in a file that has an extension of .tar. An example of the filename is cme-basic-123-11T.tar.

The .tar file must match the IOS version on the CME router.

You can find the firmware files that are needed for each model of IP Phone by performing a search for Cisco CallManager Express using any of the search engines. (At the time of writing, the URL was www.cisco.com/univercd/cc/td/doc/product/voice/its/cme32/cme322sp.htm.)

The file must be extracted and uploaded to the router flash memory from a TFTP server. Copy the .tar file into the appropriate TFTP server folder. From privileged mode, use the following command:

```
archive tar /xtract tftp://tftp_server_ip_address/.tar_filename flash:
```

An example of this command is as follows:

```
archive tar /xtract tftp://10.3.0.33/cme-basic-123-11T.tar flash:
```

For a 1760 router (on an older IOS): If these files are not there, you must download the IOS zip file; the P*xxx* files are part of the zip file. For this model of router and this IOS, upload any and all files that start with P003 from the downloaded file to the router flash memory using a TFTP server. An example of this command is **copy tftp:P00303020214.bin flash:**.

Task 3: Perform Basic Router Configuration for a Cisco IP Phone

Step 1. From privileged mode, view flash memory for the exact filenames for the files needed for the model of IP Phone being used. Either make a note of the exact filenames or copy the names into a word processing program such as Notepad. These filenames will be needed in the next step.

```
RouterVoIPX# show flash:
```

Step 2. From global configuration mode, use the **tftp-server flash:P00**xxxxx.xxx command to allow the firmware files to be accessed through the TFTP server service running on the router. Here's an example of this command for 7940 and 7960 Cisco IP Phones:

```
tftp-server flash:P00303020214.bin
```

If any other phone model is being used, substitute the correct .bin filename.

Note: The filename entered after the **flash:** parameter is case-sensitive.

Step 3. Repeat this command for all P00*x* firmware files present in flash memory. A 7960 phone requires a second file called P00305000301.sbn.

```
RouterVoIPX(config)# tftp-server flash:P00xxxxxxxxx.xxx
RouterVoIPX(config)# tftp-server flash:P00xxxxxxxxx.xxx
```

Step 4. From global configuration mode, enter telephony service mode by using the command **telephony-service**:

```
RouterVoIPX(config)# telephony-service
```

Step 5. To see the maximum allowable number of ephones (another name for IP Phones) that this system can use, enter the command **max-ephones ?**.

```
RouterVoIPX(config-telephony)# max-ephones ?
```

What is the maximum number of phones supported by the current router?

Step 6. Set the maximum number of IP Phones to 2, because this is sufficient for this lab:

```
RouterVoIPX(config-telephony)# max-ephones 2
```

The **max-dn** command specifies the maximum number of directory numbers or virtual voice ports that the router supports. The maximum number is IOS- and platform-dependent. The default number is 0.

Step 7.   To see the maximum allowable number of directory numbers that this system can use, enter the command **max-dn ?**:

```
RouterVoIPX(config-telephony)# max-dn ?
```

Step 8.   Configure the maximum number of directory numbers to 20 for this lab:

```
RouterVoIPX(config-telephony)# max-dn 20
```

Note: A separate **load** command (used in the next step) is needed for each type of phone. However, the 7940 and 7960 phones have the same firmware and share the **7960-7940** keyword.

Another keyword used with this command is the name of the firmware file. It is *very* important when using the **load** command that you *do not* specify the file extension.

Step 9.   The **load** command identifies which Cisco IP Phone firmware file is to be used by a specific IP Phone type when it registers with the CME router. Cisco IP Phones update themselves with new phone firmware whenever they are started or reloaded.

Use the command **load** *model filename*. Do not put the filename extension (.bin) in this command. An example of this command when using a 7940 or 7960 Cisco IP Phone is **load 7960-7940 P00303020214.** Use **load ?** to see the proper syntax for Cisco IP Phone models:

```
RouterVoIPX(config-telephony)# load ?
RouterVoIPX(config-telephony)# load model filename
```

Step 10.   Use the **create cnf-files** command to build XML configuration files that will be used by the phones during the boot process. The XMLdefault.cnf.xml configuration file contains the IP address that the Cisco IP Phones use to register with the CallManager.

```
RouterVoIPX(config-telephony)# create cnf-files
```

Note: The **keepalive** command sets the time interval (in seconds) between messages that are sent from the phone to the CME router. The default value is 30 seconds, which normally is adequate. If the default value is set to too large a value, it is possible that notification will be delayed when a system goes down.

Step 11.   Set the keepalive interval to 10 seconds:

```
RouterVoIPX(config-telephony)# keepalive 10
```

Step 12.   Use the **show running-config | begin tele** command to view the results of the manual configuration:

```
RouterVoIPX# show running-config | begin tele
```

Step 13.   Ensure that no Cisco IP Phones connect to the switch/switch module. Use the global configuration command **ephone-dn** to add an IP Phone for the first line appearance on the first phone in the pod. The **dual-line** parameter defines the type of ephone-dn being created (two calls per line/button).

```
RouterVoIPX(config)# ephone-dn 1 dual-line
```

Step 14.   In ephone-dn configuration mode, enter the **number** *xxxx* command. (Use Table 3-3 to locate the number that corresponds to the appropriate pod.) For example, Pod 2 would use the number 5030.

```
RouterVoIPX(config-ephone-dn)# number xxxx
```

Table 3-3   **IP Telephony Dial Plan: Beginning Extension Numbers**

Pod	Dial Plan: Beginning Extension Numbers
Pod 1	5000
Pod 2	5030
Pod 3	5060
Pod 4	5100

Step 15.   Enter a name that will be associated with this DN by entering the **name firstname lastname** command. Either make up a name or use your own:

```
RouterVoIPX(config-ephone-dn)# name firstname lastname
```

Step 16.   From global configuration mode, enter the command **ephone 1** to enter ephone configuration mode for the first phone in the pod:

```
RouterVoIPX(config)# ephone 1
```

Note: The MAC address of the IP Phone will be needed in the next step. The MAC address is on a sticker on the bottom of the phone. The sticker is normally located in the center. Upon close inspection, you can see that the letters MAC are stenciled directly to the left of the white sticker that contains the MAC address.

Step 17.   Write down the MAC address of the first IP Phone. Write your MAC address in the format of HHHH.HHHH.HHHH (where each H is a hexadecimal character).

Step 18.   Assign the MAC address to ephone 1 with the **mac-address** *HHHH.HHHH.HHHH* command (where *H* is a hexadecimal character). Note that the periods must be inserted between each set of four characters, and the letters are not case-sensitive. A sample entry is **mac-address 0013.c43b.4999**.

```
RouterVoIPX(config-ephone)# mac-address HHHH.HHHH.HHHH
```

Step 19.   The **button** command is used to define properties for the buttons located to the right of the IP Phone's LCD. The **button** command has a number after it; the number 1 represents the top button on the IP Phone. The number is followed by a separator character that specifies phone characteristics. For example, the colon separator assigns the phone a normal ring—a single pulse for internal calls and a double pulse for external calls. The last 1 is the ephone-dn with which the button is associated.

```
RouterVoIPX(config-ephone)# button 1:1
```

Step 20.   The phones use the Skinny Client Control Protocol (SCCP) to communicate with CallManager. SCCP is commonly called Skinny or the Skinny protocol.

Enter the **ip source-address** command from telephony-service configuration mode to define the address and port number where the Cisco CME router is listening for registrations (Skinny messages). This address should correspond to a valid CME router IP address. The *X* in the command is the pod number.

```
RouterVoIPX(config-telephony)# ip source-address 10.X5.0.1 port 2000
```

Task 4: Verify Cisco IP Phone Registration

Step 1. From privileged mode, enter the **debug ephone register** command:

    RouterVoIPX# debug ephone register

Step 2. Plug in the Cisco IP Phone that has the MAC address that was configured in the previous task.

Step 3. View the ephone registration debugging output. This might take a few moments. Verify that the phone registers and that the proper DN appears with the line.

Step 4. Use the **undebug all** command to turn off all debugging:

    RouterVoIPX(config)# undebug all

Task 5: Add Configuration for a Second Cisco IP Phone

Step 1. View the running configuration file to see the results of the configuration thus far.

Step 2. Using commands demonstrated in the previous task, add **ephone-dn** and **ephone** configuration commands for a second IP Phone. The name associated with the phone will be John Doe. The number assigned to the phone is one number larger than the number used for the first phone.

Step 3. Attach the second Cisco IP Phone, and view the IP Phone registration process. Verify that the phone registers with the CallManager router:

    RouterVoIPX# debug ephone register

Step 4. After the phone has successfully registered, use the **undebug all** command to turn off all debugging:

    RouterVoIPX(config)# undebug all

Note: If the second Cisco IP Phone appears with the same phone number as the original IP Phone, change the **button 1:1** command to **button 1:2** on the second IP Phone configuration.

Step 5. After the second phone registers and you can call from one phone to the other phone, delete all commands related to the second Cisco IP Phone:

    RouterVoIPX(config)# no ephone-dn 2
    RouterVoIPX(config)# no ephone 2

Step 6. Save the router configuration. It will be used to complete the next lab.

    RouterVoIPX# copy running-config startup-config

Lab 3-3: Connecting a Second IP Phone Using the auto assign Command

In this lab, OCSIC.org has decided to use the partially automated setup process to configure the Cisco CallManager Express router and phones.

The objective of this lab is to configure a Cisco IP Phone using the partially automated process.

To perform this lab, you need the following equipment:

- Cisco CME-capable router with .tar configuration files already extracted

- Switch/switch module

- Workstation with an Ethernet 10/100 NIC installed

- Two Cisco IP Phones (powered using any method)

Figure 3-3 shows a typical IP Telephony network topology used for this lab. Keep in mind that an integrated switch module in the router could be used instead of the external switch.

Figure 3-3   Lab Topology: Partially Automated Setup

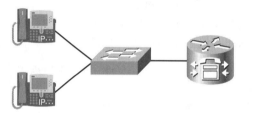

The procedure for this lab consists of the following tasks. The following sections describe each task in detail:

- **Task 1**—Add a second Cisco IP Phone using the **auto assign** command.

- **Task 2**—Connect and verify the phone configuration.

Task 1: Add a Second Cisco IP Phone by Using the auto assign Command

Step 1.   Either copy the configuration file from Lab 3-2 *or* reprogram the router and external switch (if they're being used) with the commands necessary to create the voice, data, and management VLANs and route between them. Note that Lab 3-2 requires Lab 2-4 or Lab 2-5 to be completed as well.

Step 2.   Ensure that the second Cisco IP Phone is not connected to the switch. Add a second ephone-dn by using the **ephone-dn 2** command:

```
RouterVoIPX(config)# ephone-dn 2 dual-line
```

Step 3.   Use the **number** *xxx***1** command to program the second phone number extension (refer to Table 3-4):

```
RouterVoIPX(config-ephone-dn)# number xxx1
```

Table 3-4　IP Telephony Dial Plan: Second Extension Numbers

Pod	Dial Plan: Second Extension Number
Pod 1	5001
Pod 2	5031
Pod 3	5061
Pod 4	5101

Step 4.　Enter telephony service mode:

```
RouterVoIPX(config)# telephony-service
```

Note:　The **auto assign** command is used to partially automate the IP Phone configuration process. This command specifies a range of ephone-dn numbers to assign newly discovered IP Phones. This method is used when several phones must be installed and each phone has a unique extension number.

A phone type can be specified so that all 7940 IP Phone models receive an extension in a particular range and all 7960 models receive an extension in a different range of numbers. For the purposes of this lab, the basic concept of automatic number assignment is all that is being demonstrated.

Step 5.　View the models supported by the **auto assign** command by entering the following command:

```
RouterVoIPX(config-telephony)# auto assign 2 to 2 type ?
```

Step 6.　Use the **auto assign** command without specifying a phone model:

```
RouterVoIPX(config-telephony)# auto assign 2 to 2
```

Task 2: Connect and Verify the Phone Configuration

Step 1.　From privileged mode, use the **debug ephone pak** command, which allows ephone packets to be displayed:

```
RouterVoIPX# debug ephone pak
```

Step 2.　Connect the second IP Phone to the appropriate switch/switch module port that has been configured for IP telephony. Verify the switch configuration if necessary.

Step 3.　View the debugging output. It might take a few moments to see that the Cisco IP Phone registers with the CallManager Express router.

Step 4.　Verify that both phones are registered and configured by entering the **show ephone** command:

```
RouterVoIPX# show ephone
```

What indication is shown in the output to prove that both phones are configured properly?

Step 5.　Lift the handset of the first IP Phone and dial the other IP Phone by pressing the second phone's four-digit identifier. This number is located in the second phone's upper-right display.

Step 6.　If the second IP Phone rings, the lab has been successful. If it's unsuccessful, troubleshoot as necessary. Save your configuration only if you want it as a reference.

Lab 3-4: Using the Quick Configuration Tool to Set Up Cisco CME

In this lab, OCSIC.org has decided to use the Quick Configuration Tool setup process to configure the Cisco CallManager Express router and phones.

The objective of this lab is to configure Cisco CallManager Express using the Quick Configuration Tool.

To perform this lab, you need the following equipment:

- Cisco CallManager Express-capable router with .tar configuration files already extracted
- Switch/switch module
- Workstation with an Ethernet 10/100 NIC installed
- Two Cisco IP Phones (powered using any method)
- CCO account at www.cisco.com
- Windows XP computer with administrator rights to load a software application and Internet Explorer 5.5 or higher
- Application that can extract zipped files

Figure 3-4 shows the topology used for this lab. Keep in mind that an integrated switch module in the router could be used instead of the external switch.

Figure 3-4   Lab Topology: QCT Software

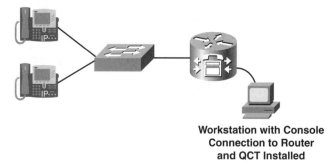

**Workstation with Console
Connection to Router
and QCT Installed**

The procedure for this lab consists of the following tasks. The following sections describe each task in detail:

- **Task 1**—Install the QCT software.
- **Task 2**—Configure the QCT software.

Task 1: Install the QCT Software

Step 1.   Ensure that the router has no previously configured commands. If an external switch or switch module is installed, ensure that no VLANs exist. After the router and switch reboot, make sure that the prompt is at privileged mode (and not in the configuration dialog) before proceeding.

```
RouterVoIPX# erase startup-config
RouterVoIPX(or SwitchVoIPX)# del vlan.dat
RouterVoIPX(and/or SwitchVoIPX)# reload
```

Step 2.   Go to www.cisco.com, log in with a valid CCO account name and password, and search for the Quick Configuration Tool Download. The page should contain a link to download the file.

Step 3. From the download page, select the latest CME QCT, and download it to a local folder on the computer. For best results, create a local folder on the drive's root. For instance, create the folder C:\QCT. Errors can occur when the folder is created at deeper levels in the subdirectory structure. At the time of this writing, the site for downloading was www.cisco.com/ cgi-bin/tablebuild.pl/cme-qct. These labs are based on QCT version 2.0.3.

Step 4. Extract all files into the folder that contains the downloaded file.

Step 5. From within the folder that contains the extracted files, open the **NetCommOCX** subfolder. Double-click the **Setup.exe** filename to start the installation process. If a security window appears, click the **Run** button.

Step 6. At the Welcome screen, click **Next**. Enter a name in the **Name** field and a company name in the **Company** field, and click **Next**.

Step 7. Browse to the appropriate folder to install the software, or accept the default by clicking **Next**.

Step 8. Accept the **NETCommOCX** program folder by clicking **Next**. Verify the settings and click **Next**. Files are copied. A prompt may appear to restart the computer; click the **Finish** button to restart the computer.

Task 2: Configure the QCT Software

Step 1. From the folder where the files were originally extracted, double-click the QCT.htm file to launch IPC Express QCT.

Step 2. If a dialog box asks if you want to allow ActiveX control, click the **Yes** button.

Step 3. Click the link to read the licensing agreement, and then click the **Accept** button if the terms are agreeable. Some browser security settings might require you to unblock pop-ups before you can proceed.

Step 4. The Cisco IPC Express Quick Configuration Tool window appears, as shown in Figure 3-5. Ensure that a console connection to the router is in place from the PC that has this tool loaded. Ensure that *no other application* (such as HyperTerminal) is active.

Figure 3-5   Cisco IPC Express Quick Configuration Tool

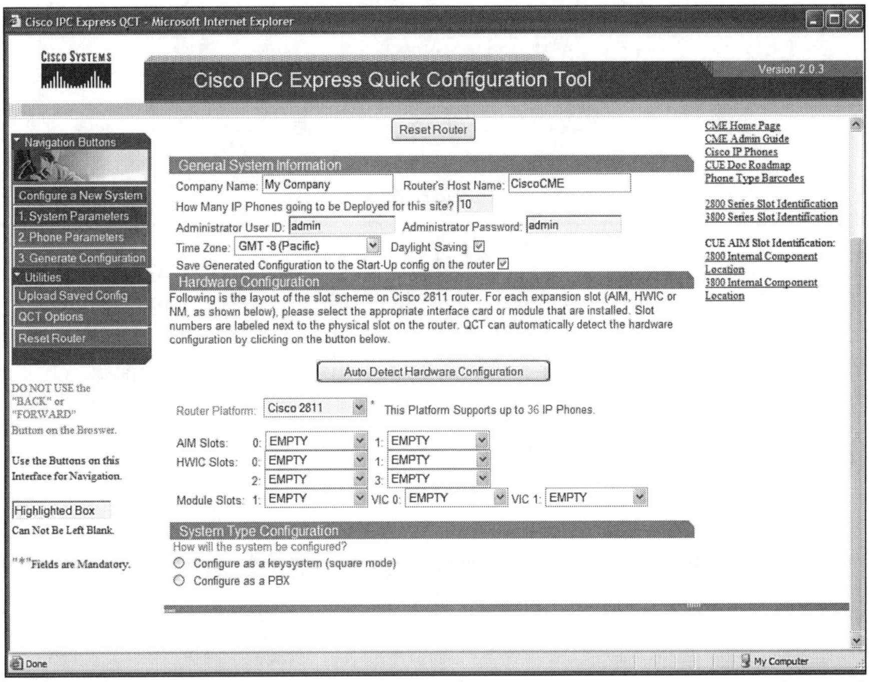

Step 5.   Select a pod number from Table 3-5. In the General System Information field, locate the Router's Host Name textbox and enter the appropriate name based on the information shown in Table 3-5.

Table 3-5   IP Addressing Scheme with Internal Switch

Pod	Hostname of Router or Switch
Pod 1	RouterVoIP1
Pod 2	RouterVoIP2
Pod 3	RouterVoIP3
Pod 4	RouterVoIP4

Step 6.   In the How Many IP Phones going to be Deployed for this site? textbox, enter **2**.

Step 7.   In the Administrator Password textbox, enter **cisco** for the router password.

Step 8.   In the Time Zone drop-down menu, select the correct time zone. Figure 3-6 shows the basic steps in configuring QCT.

Figure 3-6   Configuring QCT

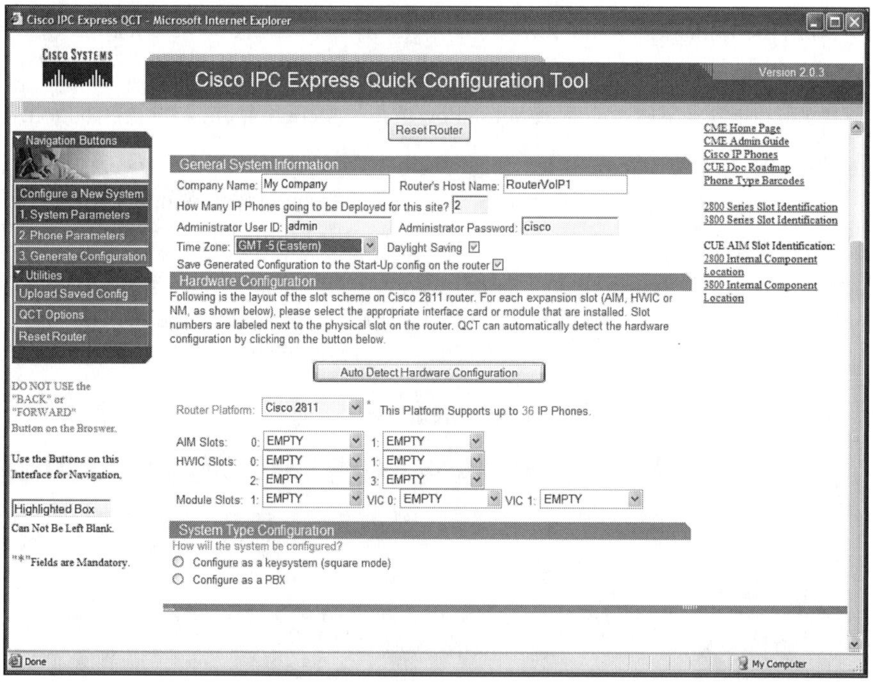

Step 9.   In the Hardware Configuration section, click the **Auto Detect Hardware Configuration** button. Ensure that the correct serial port is listed in the PC Serial Port drop-down menu, as shown in Figure 3-7. Click the **Detect** button. If an ActiveX dialog box appears, click the **Yes** button. Verify the information detected.

Figure 3-7   QCT Auto-Detect Hardware

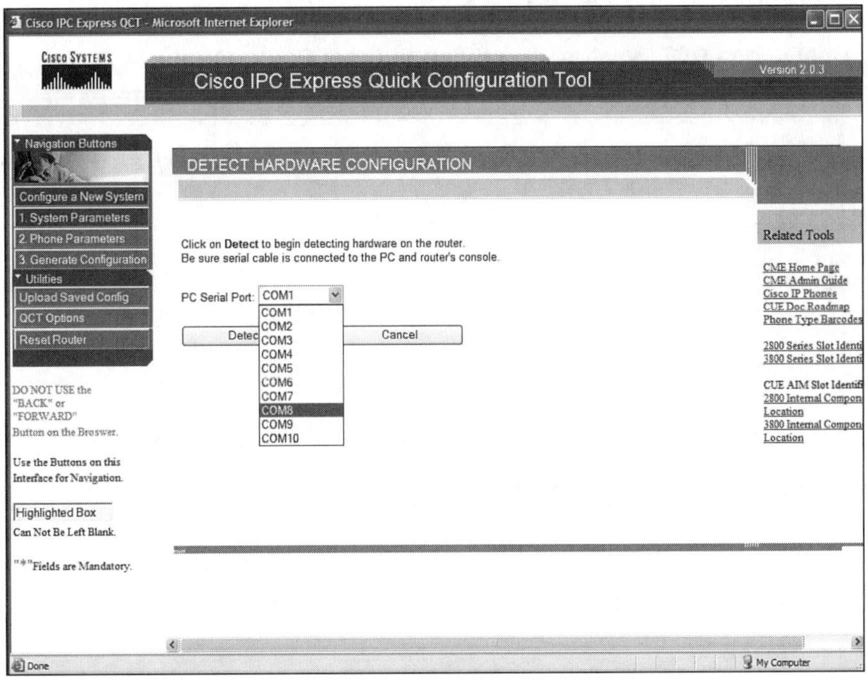

Step 10. In the System Type Configuration section, select the **Configure as a PBX** radio button. This selection allows each IP Phone to have its own separate line and extension number. Features such as intercom, call park, hunt groups, and caller-ID blocking can be supported. The Configure as a keysystem option allows each IP Phone to share the same line. This means that an incoming call rings on all phones. Figure 3-8 shows the basic steps in configuring QCT as a PBX.

Figure 3-8   Configuring QCT as a PBX

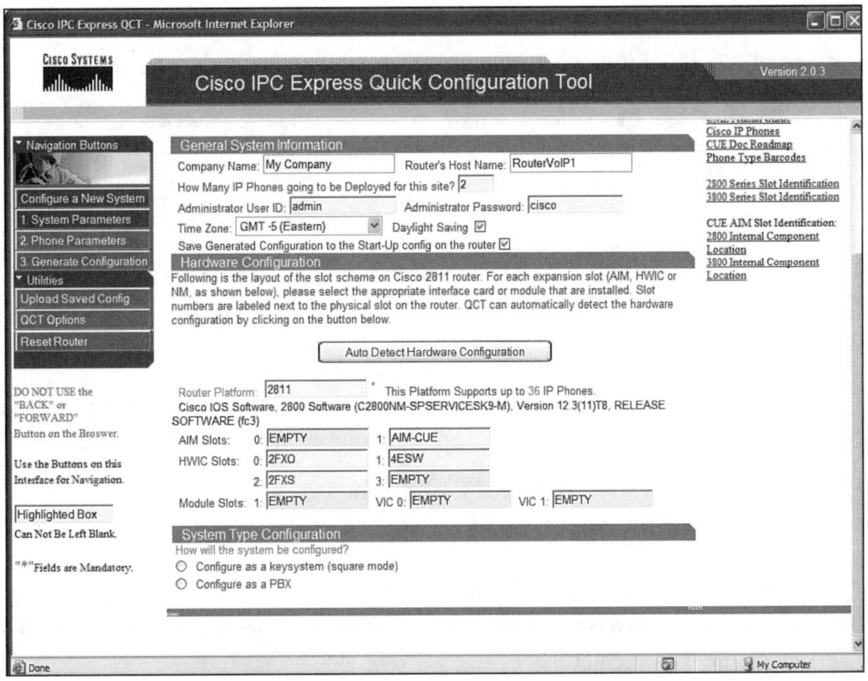

Step 11. In the Select configuration type subsection, select the **Typical Configuration (Recommended)** radio button, as shown in Figure 3-9.

Figure 3-9   Configuring QCT Type Configuration and Other Parameters

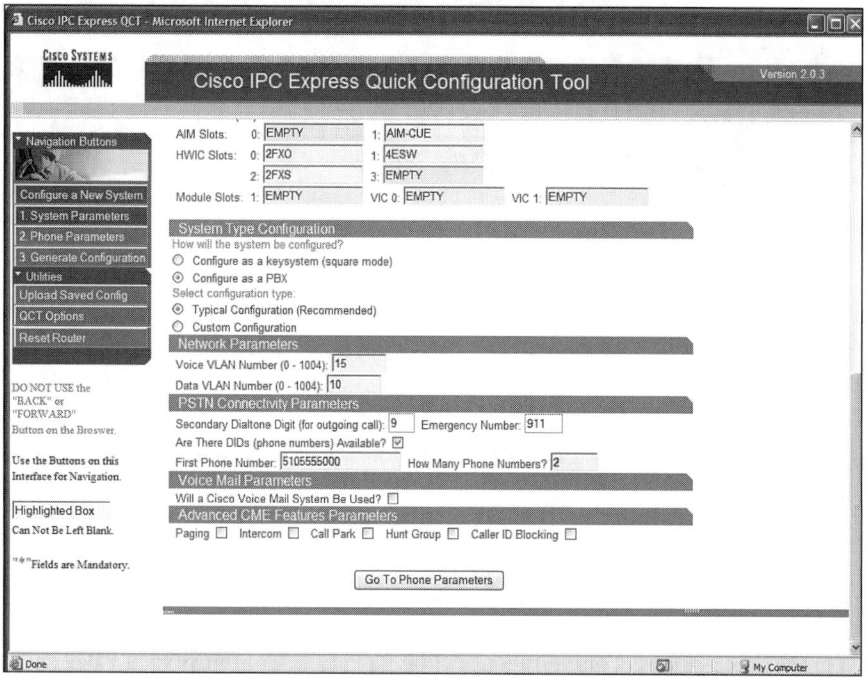

Step 12. In the Network Parameters section, in the Voice VLAN Number textbox, enter *x*5, where *x* is the pod number you selected previously. In the Data VLAN Number textbox, enter *x*0, where *x* is the pod number you selected previously.

Note: Refer to Table 3-6 to perform the next steps.

Table 3-6   IP Telephony Dial Plan

Pod	Dial Plan Extension Numbers	First E.164 DID Number
Pod 1	5000 to 5029	5105555000
Pod 2	5030 to 5059	5105555030
Pod 3	5060 to 5089	5105555060
Pod 4	5100 to 5129	5105555100

Step 13. In the first Phone Number textbox, enter the appropriate number based on the First E.164 DID number column and corresponding pod. An example for pod 3 is 5105555060.

Step 14. In the How Many Phone Numbers? textbox, enter **2**.

Step 15. Click the **Go to Phone Parameters** button at the bottom of the window.

Step 16. In the MAC Address column, shown in Figure 3-10, enter the MAC addresses of the two IP Phones connected to the router or switch. The MAC address is located on the bottom of the IP Phone on the white center label.

Figure 3-10   Configuring QCT MAC Addresses

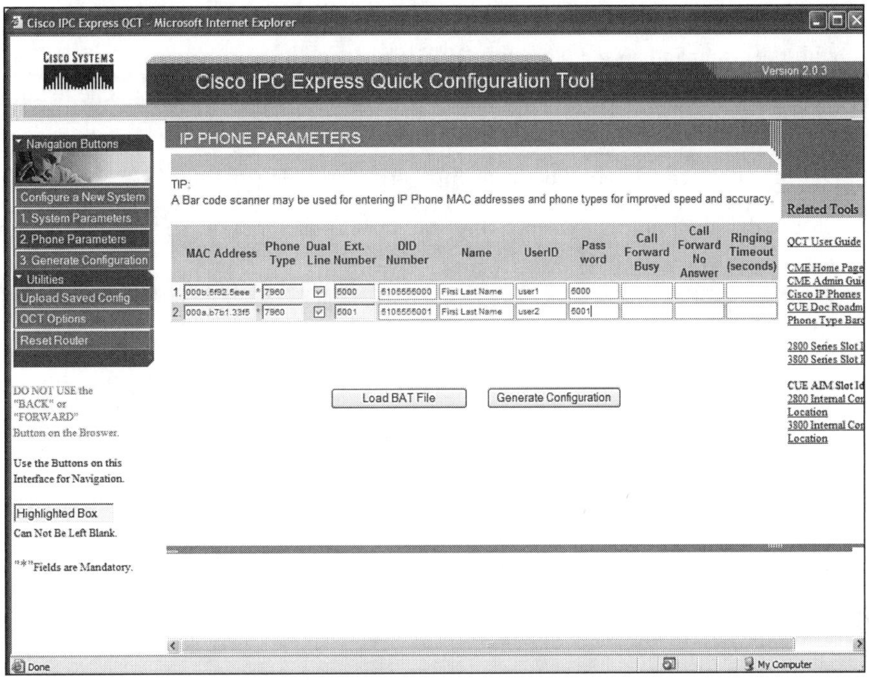

Step 17.   Click the **Generate Configuration** button.

Step 18.   When a dialog box appears, asking if the configuration is to be pushed to the router, click **OK**. If an ActiveX dialog box appears, click **Yes**. Figure 3-11 shows the QCT configuration upload process.

Figure 3-11   QCT Configuration Upload Process

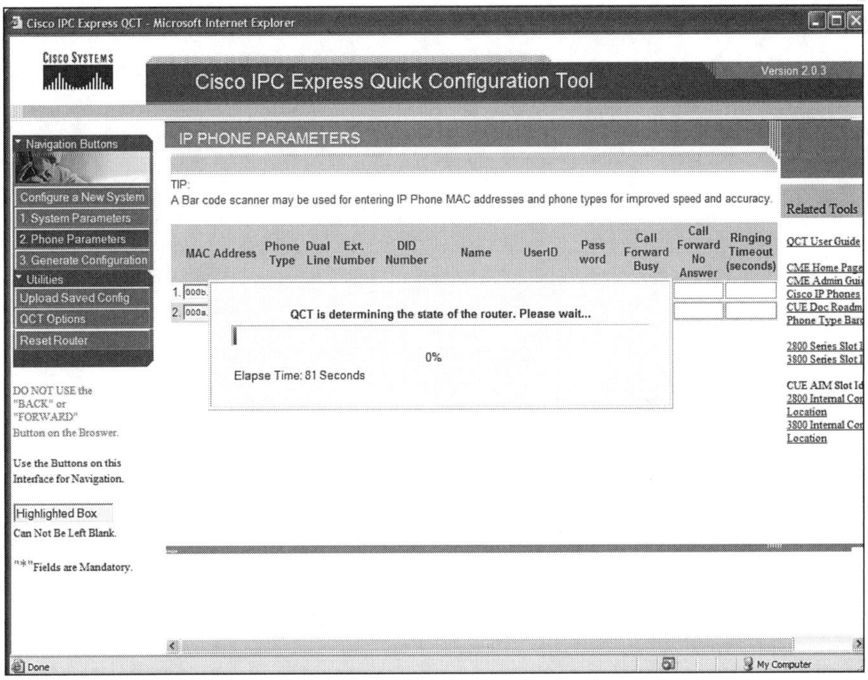

Step 19.   When a dialog box appears, stating that IPC Express is now configured, click **OK**.

Step 20.   After a couple minutes, the IP Phones should be attached to the CCME router and configured with the commands issued through QCT. The four-digit extension is shown in the upper-right corner of the phone's LCD display. From one phone, dial the other phone using the four-digit extension.

Step 21.   Did the phone ring? If not, perform appropriate troubleshooting.

Step 22.   Ensure that the router's startup configuration is deleted before you perform another lab:

```
RouterVoIPX# erase startup-config
RouterVoIPX (or SwitchVoIPX)# del vlan.dat
RouterVoIPX(and/or SwitchVoIPX)# reload
```

Lab 3-5: Using Cisco Network Assistant

In this lab, OCSIC.org has decided to use Cisco Network Assistant to manage the Cisco CallManager Express router and switch.

The objective of this lab is to install and configure Cisco Network Assistant.

To perform this lab, you need the following equipment:

- Cisco CallManager Express-capable router with .tar configuration files already extracted

- Switch/switch module

- Workstation with an Ethernet 10/100 NIC installed

- Two Cisco IP Phones (powered using any method)

- CCO account at www.cisco.com

- Windows XP computer with administrator rights to load a software application and Internet Explorer 5.5 or higher

- Application that can extract zipped files

Note: This lab is best demonstrated with an external Cisco switch (not a switch module inserted into the router).

Figure 3-12 shows the lab topology to be used. Keep in mind that an integrated switch module in the router could be used instead of the external switch.

Figure 3-12   Lab Topology: Cisco Network Assistant

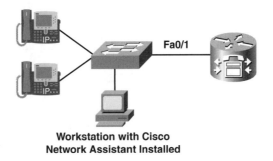

Fa0/1

**Workstation with Cisco
Network Assistant Installed**

The procedure for this lab consists of the following tasks. The following sections describe each task in detail:

- **Task 1**—Preconfigure the router and switch/switch module.

- **Task 2**—Install the Cisco Network Assistant software.

- **Task 3**—Configure the Cisco Network Assistant software.

Task 1: Preconfigure the Router and Switch/Switch Module

Step 1.   Ensure that the two Cisco IP Phones are configured so that a call can be made between them and they are attached to either a switch module that is installed in the router or an external switch.

Even though this step can be done manually using previously demonstrated methods: CLI, the **telephony-service setup** configuration dialog, or QCT.

Step 2.   Ensure that the external switch attaches to the router, has an IP address assigned to VLAN 1, has a default gateway configured (**ip default-gateway**), and has HTTP enabled (**ip http server**).

Task 2: Install the Cisco Network Assistant Software

Step 1.   Go to Cisco.com, log in with a CCO account name and password, and search for the Cisco Network Assistant download. On the search results page, the first result normally has a link to the site to download this tool. At the time of this writing, the site was www.cisco.com/ pcgi-bin/tablebuild.pl/NetworkAssistant. (Note that this URL is case-sensitive.) Click the latest Cisco Network Assistant version filename, and follow the prompts to download the file.

Step 2.   After the file is downloaded, double-click the Network Assistant installer executable. Follow the instructions to install the software.

Step 3.   To join a community, a device must have an IP address assigned and HTTP enabled. The PC that has Cisco Network Assistant installed must be able to ping the device that is to be added to Cisco Network Assistant.

Step 4.   Before you start this lab, it is best to have an idea of IP addresses assigned to the router, PC, IP Phones, and the external switch. Use the following table to document IP addresses assigned. If IP addresses are not assigned to any of the devices, preconfigure the device with an IP address before beginning this lab. Switches are assigned IP addresses through VLAN 1. Do not forget to apply a default gateway to both the PC and the switch.

Device	Interface or VLAN Number	IP Address

Note: Note that a router will be logged more than once because multiple interfaces are used. Ensure that all active interfaces and IP addresses are documented.

Step 5.   From the PC, ping the default gateway IP address. Do not proceed until the ping is successful.

Step 6.   On the router, create a username and encrypted password:

```
RouterVoIPX(config)# username MrBig8 privilege 15 secret cisco
```

Note: Whenever the Authentication Device window appears, use the username of **MrBig8** and a password of **cisco**.

Task 3: Configure the Cisco Network Assistant Software

Step 1.   To begin using Cisco Network Assistant, click the **Start** button, point to **All Programs**, point to **Cisco Network Assistant**, and click the **Cisco Network Assistant** option.

Step 2.   As shown in Figure 3-13, ensure that the **Connect to a new community** radio button is enabled, and then click the **Connect** button.

Figure 3-13   CNA Community Configuration

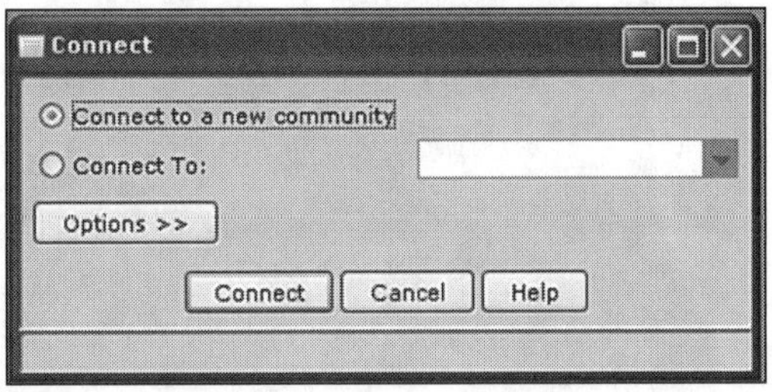

Step 3.   In the Create Community window, shown in Figure 3-14, enter **VoIP**x (where x is the pod number chosen in previous labs) in the Name textbox.

Figure 3-14   Creating the CNA Community

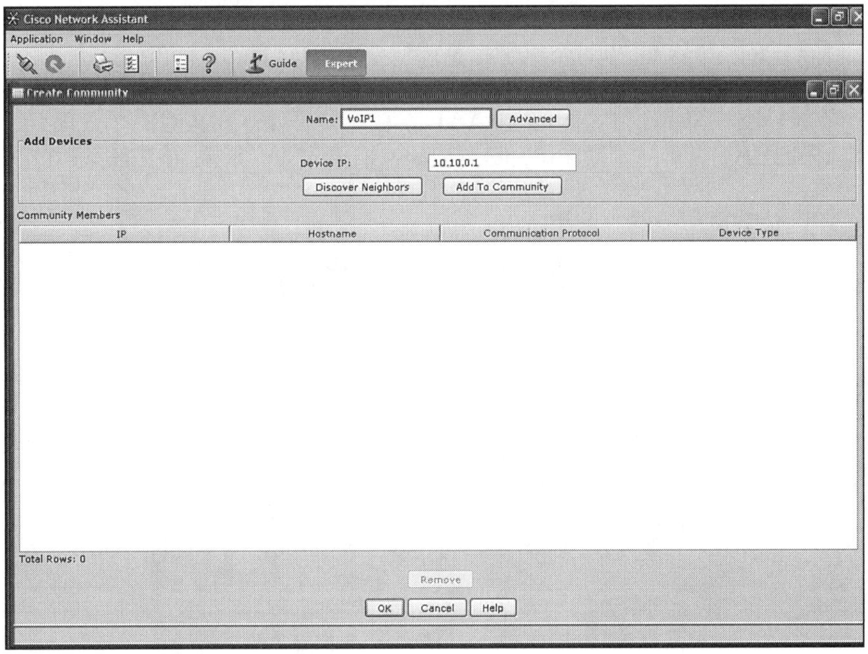

Step 4.   In the **Add Devices** section, in the Device IP textbox, enter the router IP address. The default gateway for the PC is an appropriate IP address to use.

Step 5.   Click the **Add To Community** button. In the Create Community window, click **OK**. The Topology View window appears, as shown in Figure 3-15.

Figure 3-15   Sample Cisco Network Assistant Topology View

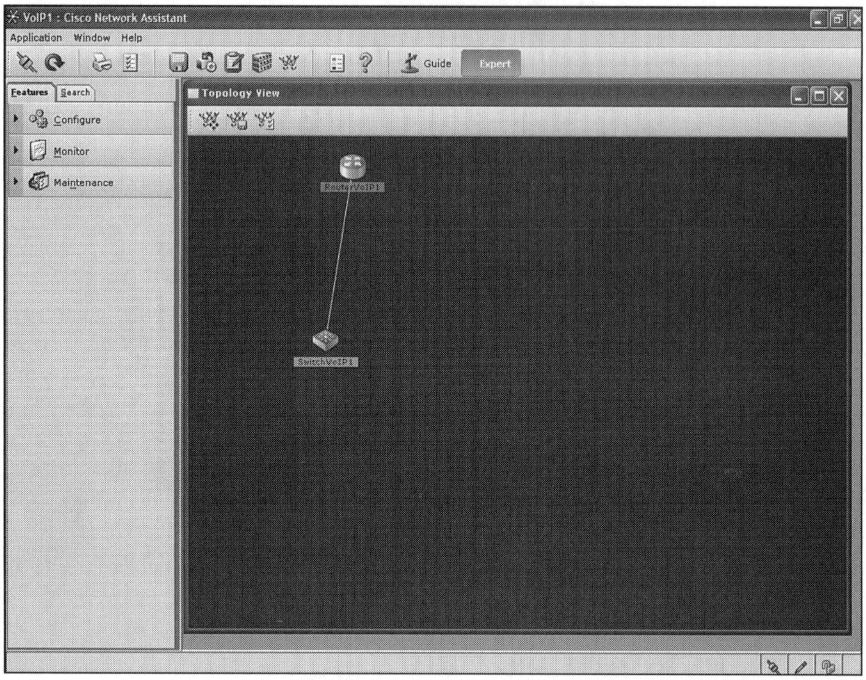

Step 6.   In the top left of the Topology View window, click the third icon from the left; it is the icon that looks like a tree with a checklist. The Topology Options window appears, as shown in Figure 3-16. Click the **Node** tab. Select the **IP Address** checkbox and click **OK**. The IP addresses assigned to the devices appear in the Topology View window, as shown in Figure 3-17.

Figure 3-16   Configuring CNA Node Options

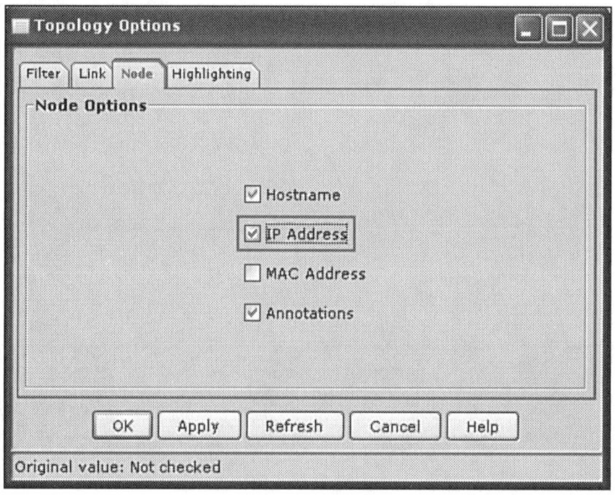

Figure 3-17   CNA Topology View with IP Address

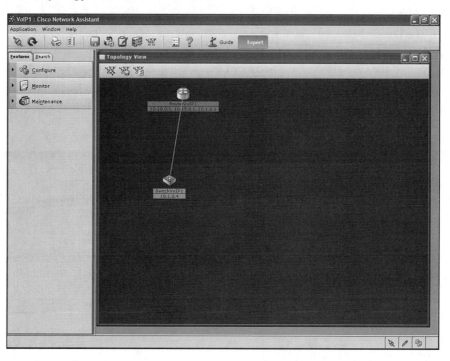

Step 7.   Right-click the router icon. A menu appears, as shown in Figure 3-18.

Figure 3-18   CNA Router Options in the Topology View

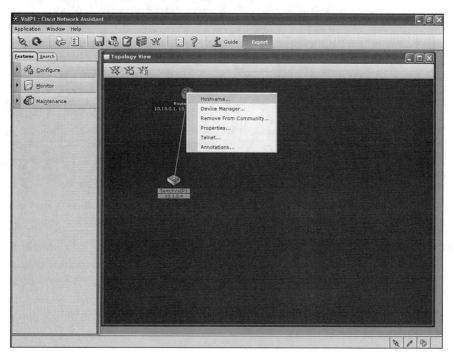

The Hostname option is used to change the router name. It is the same as using the **hostname** command. It changes the router configuration to reflect this, not just the Topology View window.

The Device Manager option is used to configure the device. If the Cisco Router and Security Device Manager software is installed on the device, it can be used through this particular selection. If the Cisco Router and Security Device Manager software is not installed on a device, the HTML web configuration window is accessible through the Device Manager option.

The Remove From Community option is used to remove a device from the Cisco Network Assistant community.

Step 8.   Click the **Properties** option. The Device Properties window appears, with the model, IP address, IOS version, and MAC address information displayed. Click **OK** to close the window.

Step 9.   Right-click the switch icon and select the **Add To Community** option, as shown in Figure 3-19. This adds the external switch to the VoIPx community. After the topology view updates, right-click the switch icon. A switch has a Bandwidth Graphs option that the router did not. This option shows bandwidth utilization over a period of time.

Figure 3-19   CNA Topology View with IP Address

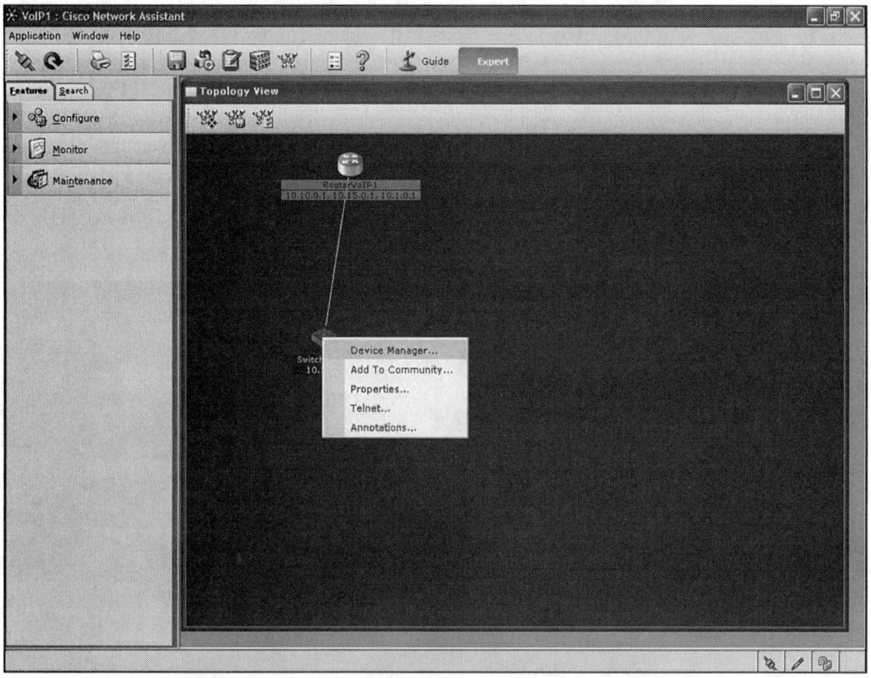

Step 10.   To the left of the Topology View window on the Features tab, click the **Configure** option to expand it, as shown in Figure 3-20. The Configure option is used to make configuration changes to the switch. For example, if switch port 2 will have an IP Phone attached, Cisco Network Assistant allows you to configure those ports.

Figure 3-20   CNA Configure Features Options

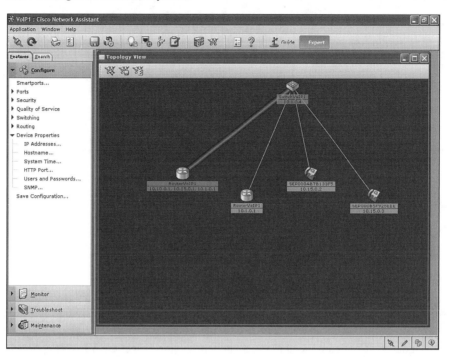

Step 11.   Expand the Switching section by clicking the arrow icon beside the word Switching or by clicking the word **Switching**. Click the **Voice VLAN** option. Figure 3-21 shows CNA Switch VLAN options.

Figure 3-21   CNA Switch VLAN Options

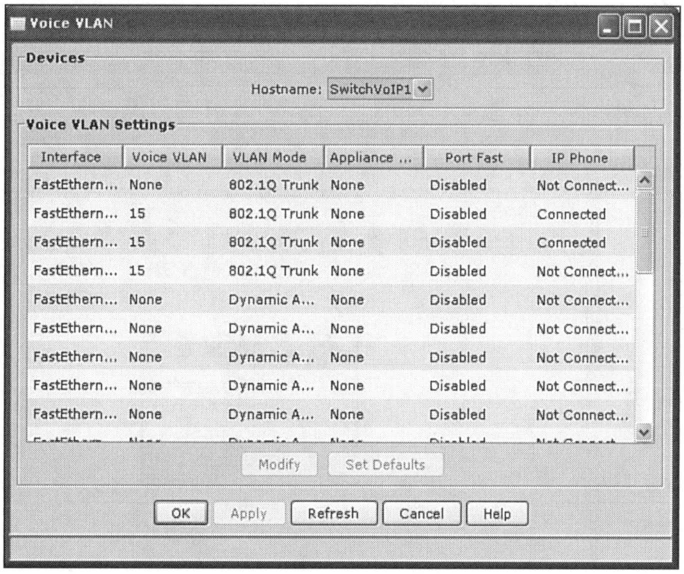

Step 12.   Select the second interface in the Interface column. You can expand the Interface column to be able to read the entire port name by placing the mouse pointer over the bar that separates the Interface column from the Voice VLAN column. The pointer turns into a double-arrowed pointer. Click and hold the left mouse button and drag to the right to expand the Interface column. Click the **Modify** button. Figure 3-22 shows the Voice VLAN options.

Figure 3-22   CNA Voice VLAN Options

Step 13.   In the Modify Voice VLAN window, click the **Voice VLAN** drop-down menu. If the VLAN ID is *not x*5, select the **New VLAN ID** option. In the [1 - 1001] textbox, enter *x***5** (where *x* is the pod number chosen in previous labs).

Step 14.   In the Port Fast drop-down menu, select the **Enable** option. Click the **OK** button. Notice how the VLAN Mode column is automatically set to trunk mode. In the Voice VLAN window, click **OK**.

Step 15.   Under the Configure menu in the Switching section, select the **VLANs** option. Click the **Configure VLANs** tab. Click the **Create** button. In the VLAN ID:[2 - 1001] textbox, enter the data VLAN used for your pod number—*x***0** (where *x* is the pod number chosen in previous labs). If *x*0 is already created, created VLAN *X*00.

Click the **OK** button. VLAN *x*0 appears as active in the VLANs window. From the VLANs window, click the **OK** button. Figure 3-23 shows the Create VLAN screen.

Figure 3-23   CNA Create VLAN Options

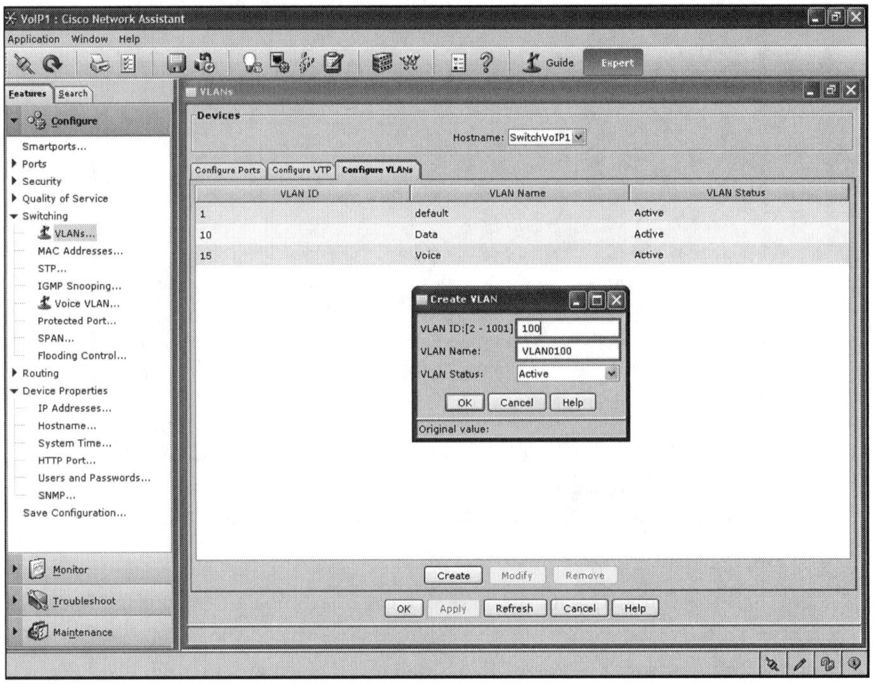

Expand the **Ports** section and click the **Port Settings** option. The Port Settings option can be used to view a link's status, to see and change the speed and duplex configuration, and to configure PortFast. Figure 3-24 shows the Port Settings menu.

Figure 3-24   CNA Port Settings Menu

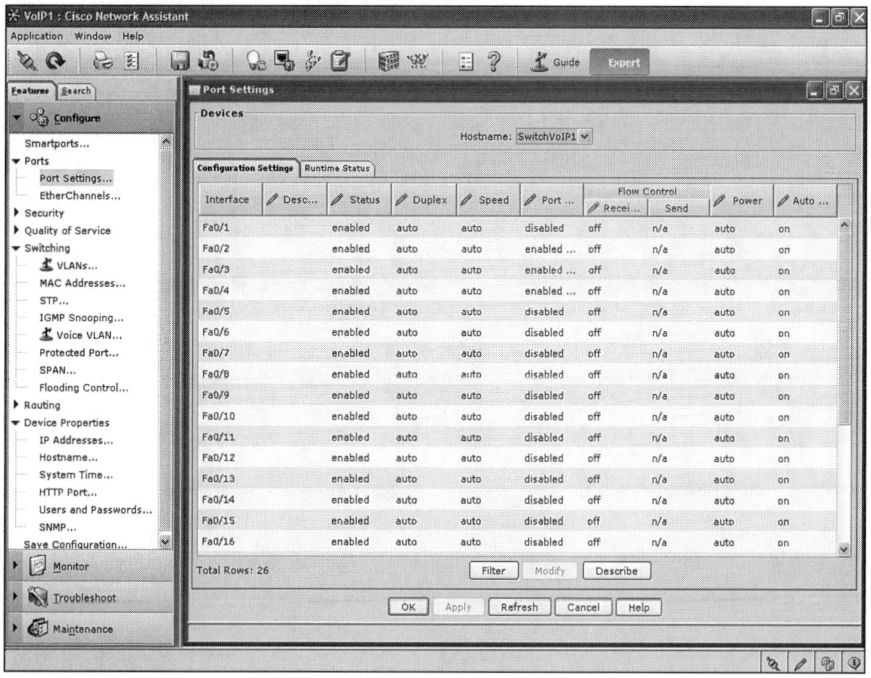

If an external switch is being used, click port **Fa0/1** and click the **Modify** button. Figure 3-25 shows the Modify Port Settings dialog box. Click inside the Description textbox and enter **Link to Router**. In the Port Fast drop-down menu, select the **enable** option. Click **OK** to close this window.

Figure 3-25   CNA Modify Port Settings Menu

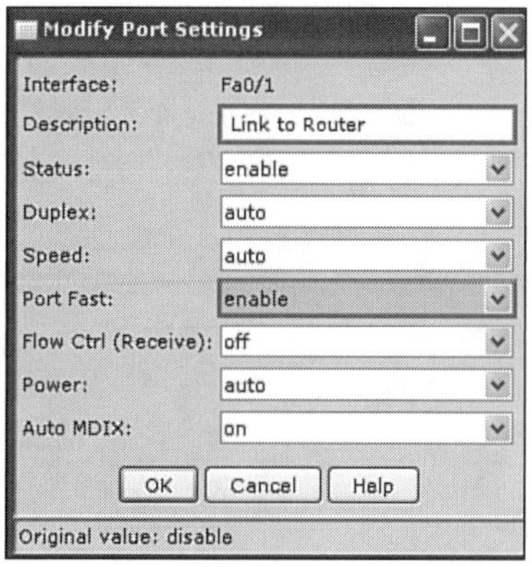

Step 16.   In the Port Settings window, click **OK**.

Step 17.   Explore the Monitor, Troubleshoot, and Maintenance tabs to determine the tools that can be used. When you're finished, click **Save Configuration** in the Configure section. Notice that the default setting is for all devices in the community to have their configuration saved. Click the **Save** button.

Step 18.   Close the Topology View window. When prompted to save the changed topology, click **Yes**.

Step 19.   Click the close box for Cisco Network Assistant. When asked if you are sure you want to exit, click the **Yes** button.

Step 20.   Manually clear from the router and switch the configuration information that was added from this lab.

CHAPTER 4

Dial Plans and Dial Peers

A dial plan allows people to call each other by dialing a number on the telephone. Dial plans include access codes, area codes, and specialized codes. The North American Public Switched Telephone Network (PSTN) uses a ten-digit dial plan that includes a three-digit area code and a seven-digit telephone number (that is, 904-555-4568). Most private branch exchanges (PBXs) support variable-length dial plans that use 3 to 11 digits. Dial plans must comply with the telephone networks to which they connect. Dial plans are similar to IP addressing in that only totally private voice networks that are not linked to the PSTN or to other PBXs can use any dial plan they choose.

Dial peers are used to configure dial plans and to identify call source and destination endpoints. They also define each call leg in the call connection. Dial peers are a critical component of VoIP.

Types of Dial Peers

The first basic command required to configure dial peers is **dial-peer**. The two types of dial peers used in these labs are Plain Old Telephone System (POTS) and voice over IP (VoIP) dial peers. Other dial peer options are multimedia over IP (MMoIP), voice over ATM (VoATM), and voice over Frame Relay (VoFR). The following examples show basic configurations for POTS and VoIP dial peers:

```
dial-peer voice 3 pots
 destination-pattern 5556123
 port 2/0/1


dial-peer voice 4 voip
 destination-pattern 5557000
 session target ipv4:12.91.0.1
```

The POTS dial peer maps a dial string to a voice port on a local router or gateway. A dial peer is configured using the **dial-peer voice** *tag* {**pots** | **vofr** | **voip**} command. The *tag* is a number between 1 and 2147483647 that identifies an individual dial peer. POTS dial peers are configured using the **dial-peer voice** *tag* **pots** command, and VoIP dial peers are configured using the **dial-peer voice** *tag* **voip** command. In most cases, POTS dial peers are used to connect a physical voice port to a PBX, a telephone, or the PSTN. VoIP a dial peers are used to define packet voice network attributes and map dial strings to a remote router or device. The following sample configurations provide basic examples of POTS and VoIP dial peers. The first example is a POTS dial peer, and the second is a VoIP dial peer.

```
dial-peer voice 3 pots  <--POTS dial peer
 destination-pattern 5556123
 port 2/0/1


dial-peer voice 4 voip  <--VoIP dial peer
 destination-pattern 5557000
 session target ipv4:12.91.0.1
```

Destination Patterns

Another command used with dial peers is **destination-pattern**. The destination pattern is used to associate a dial string with a particular telephony device. The call is routed when a dialed string matches a destination pattern. The POTS or VoIP voice port configuration determines the way the call is routed.

To provide flexibility in the configuration, a destination pattern can be either an entire telephone number or a partial number using wildcard digits. For example, a wildcard period character (.) represents a single telephone number digit. If a destination pattern were configured as **destination-pattern 28674..**, a telephone number starting with 28674 and ending with any two additional digits would be routed through this port.

Several wildcards are destination wildcards. These additional wildcards provide for a more granular configuration. To keep the labs at a basic level, only a few wildcards are discussed and used in these labs. The following sample configurations provide basic examples of destination patterns for POTS and VoIP dial peers. The first example is a destination pattern for a POTS dial peer, and the second is a destination pattern for a VoIP dial peer.

```
dial-peer voice 3 pots
 destination-pattern 5556123  <--Destination pattern
 port 2/0/1


dial-peer voice 4 voip
 destination-pattern 5557000  <--Destination pattern
 session target ipv4:12.91.0.1
```

Ports and Session Targets

Other important commands used to configure dial peers include the **port** and **session** commands. A port is configured using the **port** *voice interface slot* command. The **port** command associates a dial peer to a physical router port. When a call matches the destination pattern, the call is routed using the port defined with the **port** command.

The **session** command associates a dial peer to a network IP address of a remote router or device through which the call should be routed. The **session** command is used with a VoIP dial peer. When the call matches the destination pattern, the call is sent in the direction of the target IP address defined with the **session** command. The following sample configurations provide basic examples of the **port** and **session** commands for POTS and VoIP dial peers. The first example is a port configuration for a POTS dial peer, and the second is a session target configuration for a VoIP dial peer.

```
dial-peer voice 3 pots
 destination-pattern 5556123
 port 2/0/1  <--Port


dial-peer voice 4 voip
 destination-pattern 5557000
 session target ipv4:12.91.0.1 <--Session
```

Call Legs

A *call leg* is a logical connection (segment) between two routers or between a router and a telephony-capable device. A typical voice call might be composed of four call legs—two from the perspective of the originating router and two from the standpoint of the terminating router. Similar to static routes, dial peers must be configured for each call leg to complete the path.

The following examples show basic configurations for POTS and VoIP dial peers:

```
dial-peer voice 3 pots
 destination-pattern 5556123
 port 2/0/1


dial-peer voice 4 voip
 destination-pattern 5557000
 session target ipv4:12.91.0.1
```

Figure 4-1 illustrates a basic voice topology with PBXs and routers; it also shows the concept of call legs. A phone attached to PBX A places a call destined for a phone attached to PBX B. PBX A forwards the call to Router A using a POTS dial peer. Router A forwards the call to Router B using a VoIP dial peer. Router B forwards the call to PBX B using a POTS dial peer. PBX B connects the call to the destination phone.

Figure 4-1   Dial Peer Call Legs

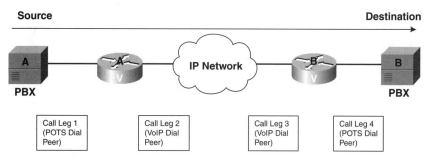

Lab 4-1: Single-Router Dial Peer Exercise

In this lab, the company OCSIC.org has decided to train its IT staff on dial peers in a single-router network.

Dial peers are used to forward calls to the destination telephony device. This lab exercise involves a single router with multiple POTS dial peers. It gives you a basic understanding of the POTS dial peer configuration.

This lab exercise provides practice scenarios with POTS dial peer concepts related to a single router.

The objective of this lab is to use the information provided in Figure 4-2 to complete Table 4-1.

You do not need equipment to perform this lab.

The procedure for this lab consists of one task: using the information found in Figure 4-2 to complete Table 4-1.

Note: The configuration in this figure is for instructional purposes only; it might not be appropriate for a production network. Some voice network devices were removed to simplify the figure.

Figure 4-2 illustrates the topology for this lab.

Figure 4-2   Lab Topology: A Basic Cisco Dial Plan with a Single Router

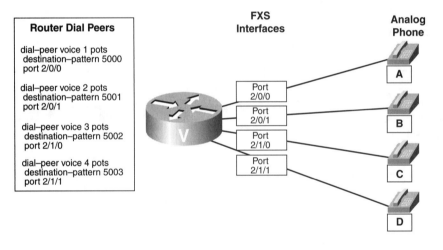

Complete Table 4-1 based on the information in Figure 4-2.

Table 4-1   **Dial Peer Configuration Table for a Single-Router Network**

Originating Phone	Destination Phone	Originating Phone Number	Destination Phone Number	Dial Peer Used to Reach the Destination Phone	Port Used to Reach the Destination Phone
A	B	5000	5001	2	2/0/1
B	C	5001	5002	3	2/1/0
C	D	____	____	_	____
D	A	____	____	_	____
A	C	____	____	_	____
B	D	____	____	_	____
C	A	____	____	_	____
D	B	____	____	_	____
A	D	____	____	_	____
C	B	____	____	_	____
D	C	____	____	_	____

Lab 4-2: Single-Router Wildcard Dial Peer Exercise

In this lab, OCSIC.org has decided to train its IT staff on wildcard dial peers in a single-router network.

Wildcard digits work in conjunction with dial peers to provide a more granular method of defining the destination pattern. This lab exercise uses a single router with multiple POTS dial peers. It gives you a basic understanding of wildcard digits.

This lab exercise provides practice scenarios with POTS dial peer wildcard concepts related to a single router.

The objective of this lab is to use the information provided in Table 4-2 and Figure 4-3 to complete Table 4-3.

You do not need equipment to perform this lab.

Destination Pattern Wildcard Digits

The destination pattern can be either a complete telephone number or a partial telephone number with wildcard digits, represented by the period (.) character. Each period represents a wildcard for a single digit that the originating router expects to match. For example, if the destination pattern for a dial peer is defined as 4701..., any dialed string beginning with 4701, plus any three additional digits, matches this dial peer.

In addition to the period, several other symbols are available to be used as wildcard characters in the destination pattern; some of them are provided in Table 4-2. For a complete list of destination wildcards, refer to the Cisco IOS Voice Command PDF at http://www.cisco.com/univercd/cc/td/doc/product/software/ios123/123tcr/123tvr/vrht_d1.pdf. These symbols are used to minimize the number of dial peers required in configuring telephone number ranges. Some wildcard symbols have been omitted from Table 4-2 and the labs. Dial plans can be complicated; the purpose of these labs is to provide basic configuration examples.

Table 4-2   Common Wildcard Symbols Used in Destination Patterns

Symbol	Description
.	The period indicates a single-digit placeholder. For example, 5551... (three periods) matches any dialed string beginning with 5551, plus three additional digits—555100, 555129, 555678, and so on.
[ ]	Brackets contain a range of digits. A consecutive range is indicated with a hyphen (-). For example, [1-5] indicates that the digits 1, 2, 3, 4, and 5 will be accepted. A nonconsecutive range is indicated with a comma (,). For example, [2,6] indicates that 2 or 6 will be accepted as dialed digits. Hyphens and commas can be used in combination. For example, [5-7,9] indicates that 5, 6, 7, and 9 will be accepted as dialed digits. Multiple brackets can be used within the same destination pattern.
	Note that only single-digit ranges are supported within destination patterns. For example, [43-207] is invalid.
T	Indicates the interdigit timeout value. The router waits a specified time to collect additional dialed digits.

Note: The configuration in Figure 4-3 is for instructional purposes only; it might not be appropriate for a production network. Some voice network devices were removed to simplify the figure.

Figure 4-3 illustrates the topology for this lab.

Figure 4-3   Lab Topology: A Cisco Dial Plan with a Single Router

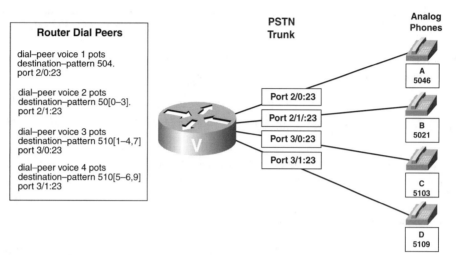

Complete Table 4-3 based on the information in Table 4-2 and Figure 4-3.

Table 4-3   Dial Peer Configuration Table for a Single-Router Network

Originating Phone	Destination Phone	Originating Phone Number	Dial Peer Used to Reach the Destination Phone	Port Used to Reach the Destination Phone	Range of Phone Numbers Accepted by the Dial Peer (List Several)
A	B	5046	2	2/1:23	5000–5009, 5010–5019, 5020–5029, 5030–5039
B	C	5021	3	3/0:23	5101, 5102, 5103, 5104, 5107
C	D	___	_	___	___
D	A	___	_	___	___
A	C	___	_	___	___
B	D	___	_	___	___
C	A	___	_	___	___
D	B	___	_	___	___
A	D	___	_	___	___
B	A	___	_	___	___
C	B	___	_	___	___
D	C	___	_	___	___

Lab 4-3: Two-Router Wildcard Dial Peer Exercise

In this lab, OCSIC.org has decided to train its IT staff on wildcard dial peers in a two-router network.

This lab exercise involves two routers with multiple POTS and VoIP dial peers. It gives you a basic understanding of voice dial peer configuration using wildcard digits.

This lab exercise provides practice scenarios for POTS and VoIP dial peer concepts related to a two-router network using wildcard digits.

The objective of this lab is to use the information provided in Figure 4-4 to complete Table 4-4.

You do not need equipment to perform this lab.

Note: The configuration in this figure is for instructional purposes only; it might not be appropriate for a production network. Some voice network devices were removed to simplify the figure.

Figure 4-4 illustrates the topology for this lab.

Figure 4-4   Lab Topology: A Cisco Dial Plan with a Two-Router Network Using Wildcards

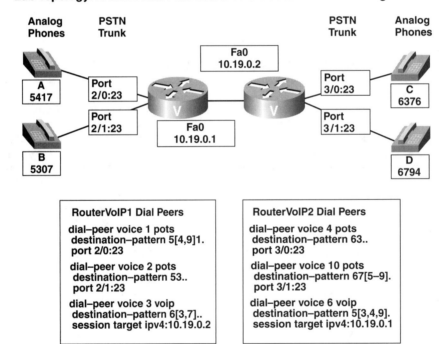

Complete Table 4-4 based on the information in Figure 4-4.

Table 4-4 Dial Peer Configuration Table for a Two-Router Network Using Wildcards

Originating Phone	Destination Phone	Originating Phone Number	VoIP Dial Peer (if Required) Used to Reach the Destination Phone	POTS Dial Peer Used to Reach the Destination Phone	Port Used to Reach the Destination Phone	Range of Phone Numbers Accepted by the Destination Dial Peer (List Several)
A	B	5417	N/A	2	2/1:23	5300–5309, 5310–5319, 5320–5329, 5330–5339, 5340–5349, 5350–5359, 5360–5369, 5370–5379, 5380–5389, 5390–5399
B	C	_____	____	____	_____	_____
C	D	_____	____	____	_____	_____
D	A	_____	____	____	_____	_____
A	C	_____	____	____	_____	_____

continues

Table 4-4   Dial Peer Configuration Table for a Two-Router Network Using Wildcards   *continued*

Originating Phone	Destination Phone	Originating Phone Number	VoIP Dial Peer (if Required) Used to Reach the Destination Phone	POTS Dial Peer Used to Reach the Destination Phone	Port Used to Reach the Destination Phone	Range of Phone Numbers Accepted by the Destination Dial Peer (List Several)
B	D	_____	_____	_____	_____	_____ _____ _____ _____ _____
C	A	_____	_____	_____	_____	_____ _____
D	B	_____	_____	_____	_____	_____ _____ _____ _____ _____ _____ _____ _____ _____ _____
A	D	_____	_____	_____	_____	_____ _____ _____ _____
C	B	_____	_____	_____	_____	_____ _____ _____ _____ _____ _____ _____ _____ _____
D	C	_____	_____	_____	_____	_____ _____ _____ _____ _____ _____ _____ _____ _____

Lab 4-4: Four-Router Wildcard Dial Peer Exercise

In this lab, OCSIC.org has decided to train its IT staff on wildcard dial peers in a four-router network.

This lab exercise involves four routers with multiple POTS and VoIP dial peers. It gives you a basic understanding of voice dial peer configuration using wildcard digits.

This lab exercise provides practice scenarios for POTS and VoIP dial peer concepts related to a four-router network using wildcard digits.

The objective of this lab is to use the information provided in Figure 4-5 to complete Table 4-2.

You do not need equipment to perform this lab.

Note: The configuration in this figure is for instructional purposes only; it might not be appropriate for a production network. Some voice network devices were removed to simplify the figure.

Figure 4-5 illustrates the topology for this lab.

Figure 4-5   Lab Topology: A Cisco Dial Plan with a Four-Router Network Using Wildcards

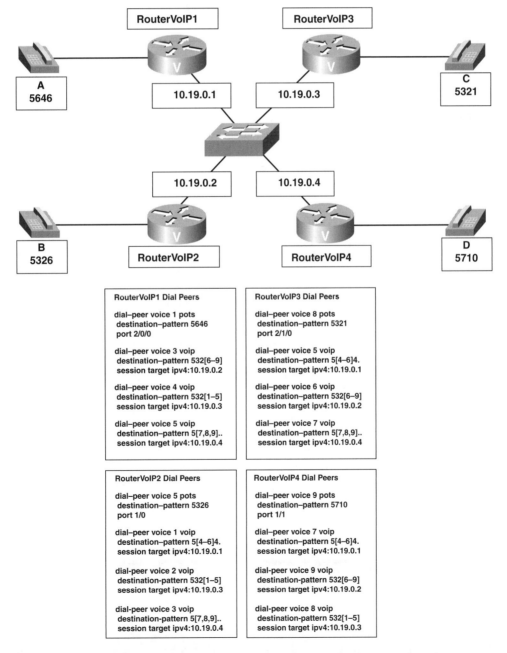

Complete Table 4-5 based on the information in Figure 4-5.

Table 4-5   Dial Peer Configuration Table for a Complex Four-Router Network

Originating Phone	Destination Phone	Originating Phone Number	VoIP Dial Peer Used to Reach the Destination Phone	Range of Phone Numbers Accepted by the VoIP Dial Peer (List Several)	POTS Dial Peer Used to Reach the Destination Phone	Port Used to Reach the Destination Phone
A	B	5646	3	5326, 5327, 5328, 5329	5	1/0
B	C	5326	2	5321, 5322, 5323, 5324, 5325	8	2/1/0
C	D	5321	____	____	_____	____
D	A	5710	____	____	_____	____
A	C	5646	____	____	_____	____
B	D	5326	____	____	_____	____
C	A	5321	____	____	_____	____
D	B	5710	____	____	_____	____
A	D	5646	____	____	_____	____
C	B	5321	____	____	_____	____
D	C	5710	____	____	_____	____

Lab 4-5: Complex Two-Router Wildcard Dial Peer Exercise

In this lab, OCSIC.org has decided to train its IT staff on wildcard dial peers in a two-router complex network.

This lab exercise uses two routers in a more-complex topology with multiple POTS and VoIP dial peers. It gives you a basic understanding of voice dial peer configuration using wildcard digits.

This lab exercise provides practice scenarios for POTS and VoIP dial peer concepts related to a complex two-router network using wildcard digits.

The objective of this lab is to use the information provided in Figure 4-6 and Table 4-6 to complete Table 4-7.

You do not need equipment to perform this lab.

Note: The configuration in this figure is for instructional purposes only; it might not be appropriate for a production network. Some voice network devices were removed to simplify the figure.

Figure 4-6 illustrates the topology for this lab.

Figure 4-6   Lab Topology: A Cisco Dial Plan with a Complex Two-Router Network Using Wildcards

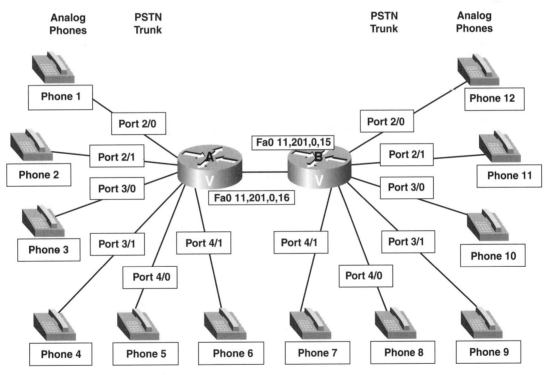

Table 4-6 shows the dial plan extension numbers associated with the phone ports that you need to know to complete Table 4-7.

Table 4-6   Dial Plan Extension Numbers

Phone	Extensions Associated with the Phone Port
1	1000, 1001, 1002, 1003, 1004
2	1015, 1016, 1017, 1019
3	1321, 1322, 1323, 1327, 1328
4	1324, 1325, 1326
5	1008
6	1200 through 1299
7	1400, 1401, 1402, 1403, 1404
8	1405, 1406, 1407, 1409, 1415, 1416, 1417, 1419
9	1521, 1522, 1523, 1527, 1528
10	1610 through 1655
11	1408, 1410
12	1656 through 1659

Complete Table 4-7 based on the information in Figure 4-6 and Table 4-6.

Table 4-7   Dial Peer Configuration Table: Complex Two-Router Wildcard Dial Peer Exercise

Phone	Phone Characteristic	Write the three basic router configuration lines for each phone using Figure 4-6 and Table 4-6 as a reference.
1	Dial peer	**dial-peer voice 1 pots**
	Destination pattern	**destination-pattern 100[0-4]**
	Port	**port 2/0**
2	Dial peer	_____
	Destination pattern	_____
	Port	_____
3	Dial peer	_____
	Destination pattern	_____
	Port	_____
4	Dial peer	_____
	Destination pattern	_____
	Port	_____
5	Dial peer	_____
	Destination pattern	_____
	Port	_____

Phone	Phone Characteristic	Write the three basic router configuration lines for each phone using Figure 4-6 and Table 4-6 as a reference.
6	Dial peer	_____
	Destination pattern	_____
	Port	_____
7	Dial peer	_____
	Destination pattern	_____
	Port	_____
8	Dial peer	_____
	Destination pattern	_____
	Port	_____
9	Dial peer	_____
	Destination pattern	_____
	Port	_____
10	Dial peer	_____
	Destination pattern	_____
	Port	_____
11	Dial peer	_____
	Destination pattern	_____
	Port	_____
12	Dial peer	_____
	Destination pattern	_____
	Port	_____

Router	Router Characteristic	Write the three basic router configuration lines to allow the routers to forward calls between the two networks. Use Figure 4-6 and Table 4-6 as a reference.
A to B	Dial peer	_____
	Destination pattern	_____
	Port	_____
B to A	Dial peer	_____
	Destination pattern	_____
	Port	_____

CHAPTER 5

Configuring VoIP Ports

This chapter focuses on configuring Foreign Exchange Station (FXS), Foreign Exchange Office (FXO), and T1 ports for transporting voice traffic. You will use the dial peer knowledge covered in the preceding chapter and apply it to the ports configured in this chapter. A single pod (one Cisco CallManager Express [CME] router) is the focus of the lab topology.

FXS and FXO Interfaces

As a review, an FXS interface is used to connect an analog device such as a fax machine, answering machine, or modem to the network. An FXS interface supplies ring, voltage, and dial tone for basic telephone equipment and PBXs.

FXO ports, on the other hand, are analog ports that connect office equipment such as a phone switch or PBX to the router. If a company orders an outside line from the phone company, it would connect the line to the FXO port. If the central office (CO) sends a ring down that line, the router could answer the call. That is because the device on the other end sees the FXO port as a telephone, but a real analog telephone should *never* be connected to the FXO port on the router.

A small-business office that requires only a small number of outside lines would most likely use multiple analog FXO connections to make calls to the PSTN. If more lines are needed, a T1 would be used. Each FXO port on the router would connect to a single PSTN line. This line can carry only one call at a time.

FXO and FXS interfaces indicate on-hook (a phone that is in the cradle) or off-hook (a phone that is picked up and emits a dial tone) status and seizure of telephone lines by one of two access signaling methods:

- **Loop start** signaling lets a phone switch know a phone went off-hook by current flowing through the local loop.

- **Ground start** signaling lets a phone switch know a phone went off-hook by applying a ground potential to the ring lead.

The service provider determines the type of signaling used. Normally, loop start signaling is used for home phones. Ground start signaling is commonly used for pay phones and for lines that connect to business PBXs.

In Lab 5-2, the **ring number** command is used to set the FXO port to answer after a certain number of rings. The default number of rings is one. Normally this default is fine so that incoming calls are answered quickly. Certain models of equipment systems might need to be set to a higher value to give the equipment sufficient time to respond.

Note: The **ring number** command is not applicable to FXS ports because these types of ports do not receive ringing on incoming calls.

T1 Interfaces

A T1 connection allows connectivity of 24 individual channels that support 64 kbps each to the router. You can configure each channel can be configured to carry voice (or data) traffic. A T1 line is a digital connection, whereas the FXS and FXO connections are analog.

In Lab 5-3, "Configuring T1/PRI Connectivity," the **direct-inward-dial** command is used to enable Direct Inward Dialing (DID) on a dial peer. DID is a service of the local phone company that provides a block of numbers used to call into a company's own PBX (which is simulated by the Adtran or a similar product). When DID is used, a company can assign a company employee a phone number without requiring a physical line into the PBX (Adtran) for each person. DID allows a caller to dial a phone extension directly.

Another command used within a dial peer is **port** $x/x/x$, where

- The first x is the slot.
- The second x is the voice interface subunit.
- The third x is the port number.

The **port** command associates a dial peer with a specific voice port. Another way of looking at this is that when someone dials the number listed in the **destination-pattern** command, the call is routed to the voice port referenced in this command. The slot, subunit, and port numbers are numbers researched in steps in the first part of the lab. It is important to document the findings when so noted in the lab.

Lab 5-1: Configuring FXS Connectivity

In this lab, the company OCSIC.org wants to be able to reuse an analog phone for emergency calls. The analog phone plugs into the router FXS port. You could use a similar configuration for an analog fax machine or another analog device.

Note: This lab relies on the two IP Phones being able to connect to one another *before* this lab is started.

The objective of this lab is to configure a router FXS port for an analog phone.

To perform this lab, you need the following equipment:

- Cisco CME-capable router (with digital signal processors [DSPs] to support voice channels) and an FXS port

- Switch/switch module

- One analog phone with an RJ-11 cable

- Two Cisco IP Phones (powered using any method)

Figure 5-1 shows the topology used for this lab. Keep in mind that you could use an integrated switch module in the router instead of the external switch.

Figure 5-1   Lab Topology: Cisco CME Network with FXS Capability

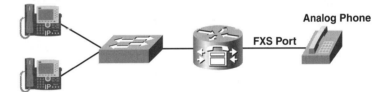

The procedure for this lab consists of the following tasks. The following sections describe each task in detail.

- **Task 1**—Verify FXS capability.

- **Task 2**—Connect and configure the analog phone.

Task 1: Verify FXS Capability

Step 1.   Power on the router and the external switch if it is being used.

Step 2.   Attach any cables necessary, and configure the router and switch/switch module appropriately until connectivity exists between the two Cisco IP Phones. Test the IP Phones by calling from one phone to another. Do not proceed until connectivity exists. Use the IP addressing scheme described in Table 5-1.

Table 5-1   IP Addressing Scheme with an Internal Switch

Pod	Hostname of Router or Switch	Ethernet IP Address	VLAN Type
Pod 1	RouterVoIP1	10.10.0.1/24	Data
		10.15.0.1/24	Voice
		10.1.0.1/24	Management
Pod 2	RouterVoIP2	10.20.0.1/24	Data
		10.25.0.1/24	Voice
		10.2.0.1/24	Management
Pod 3	RouterVoIP3	10.30.0.1/24	Data
		10.35.0.1/24	Voice
		10.3.0.1/24	Management
Pod 4	RouterVoIP4	10.40.0.1/24	Data
		10.45.0.1/24	Voice
		10.4.0.1/24	Management

Step 3.   Use the **show hardware** privileged mode command to verify that at least one FXS interface is installed in the router:

```
RouterVoIPX# show hardware
```

The following is sample output displayed by the **show hardware** command:

```
Cisco 2811 (revision 53.50) with 249856K/12288K bytes of memory.
Processor board ID FTX1004C3NJ
6 FastEthernet interfaces
2 Serial(sync/async) interfaces
2 Voice FXO interfaces
2 Voice FXS interfaces
DRAM configuration is 64 bits wide with parity enabled.
239K bytes of non-volatile configuration memory.
62720K bytes of ATA CompactFlash (Read/Write)

Configuration register is 0x2102
```

Step 4.   Look at the router and notice how the slots where the WAN interface cards (WICs) install are numbered. On a 2800 series router, the slots are numbered HWIC*x* (where *x* is the slot number) to the side of the cards. On a 1760 or 2600 series router, the slots are numbered below the WIC slot.

It is important to make a note of the router slot into which the FXS card is inserted.

Step 5.   Use the **show voice port summary** command to see a brief summary of the voice ports installed on a router, as demonstrated here:

```
RouterVoIPX# show voice port summary

                                    IN       OUT
PORT      Ch   SIG-TYPE   ADMIN  OPER  STATUS   STATUS    EC
========  ==   =========  =====  ====  ======   =====     ==
0/0/0     --   fxo-ls            dorm  idle     on-hook   y
0/0/1     --   fxo-ls            dorm  idle     on-hook   y
```

```
0/2/0      --   fxs-ls              dorm  on-hook  idle    y
0/2/1      --   fxs-ls              dorm  on-hook  idle    y
50/0/1     1    efxs                dorm  on-hook  idle    y
50/0/1     2    efxs                dorm  on-hook  idle    y
50/0/2     1    efxs                dorm  on-hook  idle    y
50/0/3     2    efxs                dorm  on-hook  idle    y
```

The PORT column shows in which slot the FXS WIC is installed in the router. The PORT column shows the WIC in a slot/subunit/port format.

Step 6. Use the **show voice port** *slot/subunit/port* command to see detailed information about the FXS card. For example, if the FXS WIC is listed as 0/3/0 and 0/3/1 in the PORT column, the command would be **show voice port 0/3/0** or **show voice port 0/3/1**:

```
RouterVoIPX# show voice port slot/subunit/port
```

Notice the port's operation state and administrative state.

Step 7. Use the **show running-config | begin voice-port** command to see the section of the configuration that deals with the voice ports.

Using the **show running-config** command, can you determine whether the card in the router is an FXS or FXO card?

Task 2: Connect and Configure the Analog Phone

Step 1. The FXS ports are labeled with a 0 or 1. Connect an analog phone to the router FXS port 0 using a phone cable.

Step 2. From global configuration mode on the router, configure a POTS dial peer for connectivity through the FXS port. Assign each dial peer a unique number. In this step, dial peer 1 is used:

```
RouterVoIPX(config)# dial-peer voice 1 pots
```

Step 3. The **destination-pattern** *number* command defines the phone number to reach the analog phone that connects to the FXS port. Use Table 5-2 (the Router FXS Port 0 column) to locate a number that corresponds to the appropriate pod. For example, Pod 3 would use the phone number 5555088.

```
RouterVoIPX(config-dial-peer)# destination-pattern number
```

Table 5-2   IP Telephony Dial Plan

Pod	Dial Plan—Extension Numbers	Voice Mail Extension	First E.164 DID Number	Router FXS Port 0
Pod 1	5000 to 5029	5555028	5105555000	5555028
Pod 2	5030 to 5059	5555058	5105555030	5555058
Pod 3	5060 to 5089	5555088	5105555060	5555088
Pod 4	5100 to 5129	5555128	5105555100	5555128

Step 4.   The **port** *x*/*x*/**0** command associates a dial peer with a specific voice port—in this case, FXS port 0. The first *x* is the slot, the second *x* is the voice interface subunit, and the 0 is the port number. These slot, subunit, and port numbers are the same numbers researched in previous steps. Refer to your notes for the format.

```
RouterVoIPX(config-dial-peer)# port x/x/0
```

Step 5.   From the analog phone, dial the four-digit extension number of one of the Cisco IP Phones. The IP Phone should ring. Troubleshoot if necessary until the IP Phone rings.

What number shows on the Cisco IP Phone when a call is made from the analog phone?

_____

_____

Step 6.   From the IP Phone, dial the seven-digit analog phone number. This is the same number that appeared on the Cisco IP Phone display in the preceding step. Ensure that the analog phone rings. Troubleshoot as necessary.

Step 7.   Save the router/and or switch configuration:

```
RouterVoIPX# copy running-config startup-config
```

Lab 5-2: Configuring FXO Connectivity

In this lab, OCSIC.org has configured the IP Phones, and now it wants to configure the analog connection to the PSTN.

Note: This lab allows an outbound call only.

This lab relies on two Cisco IP Phones being able to communicate with one another. Also, the phone that connects to the FXS port should be able to connect to the IP Phones (and vice versa), as demonstrated in the previous lab.

The objective of this lab is to configure and test a router FXO port.

To perform this lab, you need the following equipment:

- Cisco CME-capable router with an FXO port
- Switch/switch module
- Adtran unit or a similar device that simulates WAN connectivity
- Two Cisco IP Phones (powered using any method)
- Two analog phones

Figure 5-2 shows the topology used for this lab. Keep in mind that you could use an integrated switch module in the router instead of the external switch.

Figure 5-2   Lab Topology: Cisco CME Network with FXO Capability

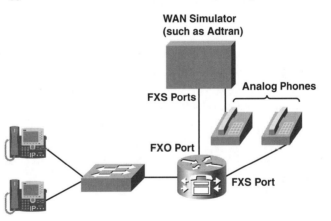

The procedure for this lab consists of the following tasks. The following sections describe each task in detail.

- **Task 1**—Configure the FXO interface.
- **Task 2**—Configure the dial peer.
- **Task 3**—Verify FXO connectivity.

Task 1: Configure the FXO Interface

Step 1.   Connect an RJ-11 phone cable from the lowest-numbered FXO port on the router to a port on the Adtran (or a similar WAN simulation unit) FXS card.

Step 2.   Connect an RJ-11 phone cable from an analog phone to another FXS port on the Adtran (or a similar unit).

What seven-digit phone number is used on the FXS port of the Adtran (or a similar unit) that has a phone attached?

_____

_____

Step 3.   The FXO router ports are shown in the output of the **show running-config** command as voice-port lines. Use the **show running-config | begin voice-p** command to verify that you cannot determine the FXO port using this command:

```
RouterVoIPX# show running-config | begin voice-p
```

Step 4.   Another useful command for identifying FXO ports is **show voice port**. The output lists the FXO ports and the slot/subunit/port number, as demonstrated here:

```
RouterVoIPX# show voice port

Foreign Exchange Office 0/0/0 Slot is 0, Sub-unit is 0, Port is 0
 Type of VoicePort is FXO
 Operation State is DORMANT
 Administrative State is UP
 No Interface Down Failure
 Description is not set
--More--
```

Write the format shown in the command output for FXO port 0. An example of a command output from an FXO card that inserts into slot 0 is voice-port 0/0/0 and voice-port 0/0/1.

_____

Step 5.   From global configuration mode, use the command **voice-port** *slot/subunit/port* to enter FXO port configuration mode. Use the *slot/subunit/port* parameters documented in the **show running-config** command output. An example of this command is **voice-port 0/0/0** for an FXO card that is inserted into slot 0 on the router.

```
RouterVoIPX(config)# voice-port slot/subunit/port
```

Step 6.   Enter the **ring number 2** command to set the FXO port to answer after two rings:

```
RouterVoIPX(config-voiceport)# ring number 2
```

Task 2: Configure the Dial Peer

Step 1.   From global configuration mode, create an analog dial peer with the command **dial-peer voice**:

```
RouterVoIPX(config)# dial-peer voice 5 pots
```

Step 2.   Use the command **destination-pattern 5556...** to set the digits that will match this dial peer. This command sets the pattern to any call that comes in destined for 5556XXX, where X is any number from 0 to 9. The periods shown in the command define the dial pattern digit as any number. You may have to change the destination pattern to match the phone number being used. The 5556... is used if an Adtran unit is programmed and being used:

```
RouterVoIPX(config-dial-peer)# destination-pattern 5556...
```

Step 3. Use the command **port** *slot/subunit/port* to associate the FXO port being used with the dial peer number. The *slot/subunit/port* numbers are the same as the numbers documented earlier in the lab.

```
RouterVoIPX(config-dial-peer)# port slot/subunit/port
```

Step 4. The router needs to know which phone number digits to forward for voice calls. Use the command **forward-digits all** to forward all the digits (the full length of the destination dial pattern) to the PSTN (the Adtran or WAN simulation unit being used):

```
RouterVoIPX(config-dial-peer)# forward-digits all
```

Task 3: Verify FXO Connectivity

Step 1. Ensure that a second analog phone connects to the router FXS port 0 and has the appropriate commands for it to work (see Lab 5-1).

Step 2. From the analog phone attached to the router FXS port, dial the seven-digit number associated with the analog phone attached to the Adtran. If an Adtran unit is being used, the phone numbers programmed on the Adtran Octal FXS ports are as follows: the port 1 phone number is 555-6001, port 2 is 555-6002, port 3 is 555-6003, and so on. The analog phone connected directly to the Adtran port should ring.

Does the called analog phone ring? If not, perform appropriate troubleshooting before proceeding.

Step 3. From enable mode on the router, debug the dial peer information. Make another call from the analog phone attached to the router FXS port to the other analog phone:

```
RouterVoIPX# debug voice dialpeer all
```

Step 4. While viewing the debug output, list the line that proves that the dial peer works correctly.

_____

_____

_____

_____

_____

_____

_____

Step 5. Turn off debugging.

Step 6. Test the configuration by calling from an IP Phone to the analog phone attached directly to the Adtran. Notice the output that is different when a Cisco IP Phone is being used to call an analog phone.

Did the call work? If not, perform appropriate troubleshooting before proceeding.

Step 7.   Turn off debugging:

```
RouterVoIPX# undebug all
```

Step 8.   Save the configuration:

```
RouterVoIPX# copy running-config startup-config
```

Lab 5-3: Configuring T1/PRI Connectivity

In this lab, OCSIC.org has decided that the analog connection to the PSTN is insufficient. As a result, a Primary Rate Interface (PRI) will be added to give additional capacity and to add DID capability. The analog connection will be kept for a secondary connection to the PSTN. Configure the PRI with the following settings.

Note: This lab uses the Adtran to simulate a PBX. Ensure that you have loaded the latest Adtran IP Telephony configuration for this lab. If you are using the four-port Quad T1/PRI card in the Adtran, ensure that the card is in slot 4 of the Adtran chassis.

You can use multiple types of network modules (NMs) for T1 connections. If the router has a network module it labeled NM-DHV2-1T1/E1, the special commands are provided in the lab.

This lab relies on two Cisco IP Phones working successfully, as well as the analog phone that connects to the FXS port.

Remove any FXO port connection to the Adtran before you begin this lab. This is so that a T1 connection (instead of the FXO port) will be used to get to an outside PSTN connection. If you have just finished the preceding lab (FXO connectivity), you should remove the FX0 dial peer by using the command **no no dial-peer voice 5 pots**.

The objective of this lab is to configure and test a PRI interface for voice connectivity.

To perform this lab, you need the following equipment:

- Cisco CME-capable router with a T1 PRI port
- Switch/switch module
- Two IP Phones (powered using any method)
- Two analog phones
- Adtran (or another WAN simulation device) with T1 capability
- Special T1 cable

Figure 5-3 shows the topology used for this lab. Keep in mind that an integrated switch module in the router could be used instead of the external switch.

Figure 5-3   Lab Topology: Cisco Network with T1 Capability

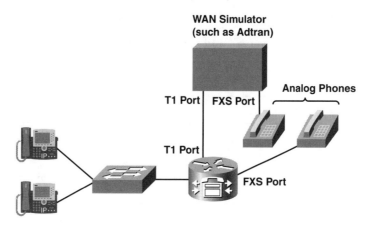

The procedure for this lab consists of the following tasks. The following sections describe each task in detail.

- **Task 1**—Verify that the router has T1 capability.
- **Task 2**—Configure the ISDN switch type.
- **Task 3**—Configure the T1 controller.
- **Task 4**—Configure the dial peers.
- **Task 5**—Test connectivity.

Task 1: Verify That the Router Has T1 Capability

Note: If the T1 interface does not appear in the output, use the global configuration command **card type t1** *x* (where *x* is the slot number documented previously) or **card type t1** *x* **1** (where 1 is the use of onboard controllers). Note that this command is needed only on the NM-HDV2-1T1/E1 module.

Step 1. Use the **show hardware** command to view the installed hardware. Verify that a T1 card is installed. If it is not installed, use the **card type** command as explained in the previous note.

```
RouterVoIPX# show hardware
```

Step 2. Use the **show diag** command to determine in which slot the T1 card is installed:

```
RouterVoIPX# show diag
```

Based on the command output shown, into what slot does the T1 card get inserted? It is important for you to write down exactly how it appears (WIC slot 1 and Slot 1 are examples). This information will be used in a later command.

Step 3. Perform a **show running-config** command from enable mode:

```
RouterVoIPX# show running-config
```

Based on the output shown, how is the T1 card listed?

_____

_____

_____

_____

_____

_____

_____

_____

_____

_____

_____

Note: The first number listed in the output is the slot number. This number is important in a later command.

Step 4.   Look at the router, and locate a port that is labeled CTRL T1/E1 or CTRLR T1. This is the T1 port. The T1 module is integrated into or inserted into the NM-HDV card.

Note: If you have a Quad T1/PRI card installed in the Adtran unit and you are using the configuration file provided by the authors, you *must* connect to the port number that corresponds to the pod number because of how the Adtran must be configured. When the Quad T1/PRI card is installed in an Adtran unit, do not use the integrated T1 network module port for the labs in this book.

Step 5.   Connect a cable from the router T1 port to a T1 port on the Adtran or a similar unit. The Adtran can have just one T1 port, or you can install an optional card that provides four more T1s. The optional card is labeled Quad T1/PRI. If the four-port T1 card is installed in the Adtran, connect to the port that corresponds to the pod number being used.

Note: The cable that is used to connect the router T1 port to any Adtran T1 port is a special cable. The pinouts are 1 to 4, 2 to 5, 4 to 1, and 5 to 2.

Task 2: Configure the ISDN Switch Type

Step 1.   From global configuration mode, use the command **isdn switch-type primary-ni** to set the PRI switch type. This type must be the same one that the provider is using. In this lab, the provider is the Adtran unit or a similar product. Ensure that whatever is being used has been configured with the primary-ni ISDN switch type. This is included in the Adtran configuration provided with this book.

```
RouterVoIPX(config)# isdn switch-type primary-ni
```

Note: If the **isdn switch-type** command does not work on the router, you most likely need to enable the T1 controller by using the command **card type t1** *x* (where *x* is the slot number documented previously) or **card type t1** *x* **1** (where 1 is the use of onboard controllers) from global configuration mode.

Task 3: Configure the T1 Controller

Step 1.   From privileged mode, look at the running configuration to determine the slot number for the T1 port, or look back to your previous step notes:

```
RouterVoIPX# show running-config
```

Step 2.   The **network-clock-participate** command allows the ports on a specific module or voice WAN interface card (VWIC) to use the network clock for timing. The alternative is to restrict a device to use its own clocking signals.

From global configuration mode, use the command **network-clock-participate wic | slot** *X* (where *X* is the physical slot where the T1 port is installed). Whether you use the **wic** parameter or the **slot** parameter is based on what was documented with the **show diag** command.

```
RouterVoIPX(config)# network-clock-participate wic X
```

or

```
RouterVoIPX(config)# network-clock-participate slot X
```

Note: In some versions of Cisco IOS Software (12.3T8 on the 1760 router), this command is unavailable and is not needed.

Note: The commands in Steps 3 through 6 may already be programmed (depending on the IOS version being used). Use the **show running-config** command to see if these commands are already present. Add any commands that are not seen in the output.

Step 3.   From global configuration mode, enter the mode to control the T1 port by using the **controller t1** *slot/port_or_subslot/port* command. The *slot/port_or_subslot/port* parameters are the same as what was researched earlier. An example in the 2811 router would be **controller t1 1/0/0** or **controller t1 1/0**, depending on the NM-HDV2-1T1 type.

```
RouterVoIPX(config)# controller t1 slot/port_or_subslot/port
```

Step 4.   In T1 controller mode, enter the command **framing esf** to set the type of framing used:

```
RouterVoIPX(config-controller)# framing esf
```

Step 5.   In T1 controller mode, enter the command **linecode b8zs** to set the line coding:

```
RouterVoIPX(config-controller)# linecode b8zs
```

Step 6.   Set the clocking to the line with the **clock source line** command:

```
RouterVoIPX(config-controller)# clock source line
```

Note: If an error appears that this command is unavailable, this is because the T1 controller is automatically clocking from internal (line).

Step 7.   From the T1 controller configuration mode, use the command **pri-group timeslots 1-12** to assign the first 12 channels to the PRI:

```
RouterVoIPX(config-controller)# pri-group timeslots 1-12
```

Note: If an error appears that there are not enough DSP resources, reduce the number of timeslots to eight (**1-8** in the command) or a lower number, depending on your DSP resources.

The B channels on the T1 controller should go up, and you should see messages to that effect.

Step 8.   Use the command **show isdn status**, and verify that Layer 1 is ACTIVE and that Layer 2 shows MULTIPLE_FRAME_ESTABLISHED:

```
RouterVoIPX# show isdn status
```

If the command output does not show ACTIVE and MULTIPLE_FRAME_ESTABLISHED, perform appropriate troubleshooting.

Step 9.   In the **show isdn status** command output, make a note of what serial port is listed on the second line of the output. This information is needed in the next step. An example of the serial output listing is ISDN Serial1/0/0:23 or Serial1/0:23.

Step 10. Use the **show interfaces serial** *mod/port_or_subslot/port***:23** command to verify that the interface status is up and up (spoofing). Examples of this command on a 2811 router are **show interfaces serial 1/0/0:23** and **show interfaces serial 1/0:23** (depending on the hardware being used).

```
RouterVoIPX# show interfaces serial mod/port_or_subslot/port:23
```

Task 4: Configure the Dial Peers

Step 1. Before configuring the dial peers, test standard phone configuration by calling one of the IP Phones from the analog phone attached to the router FXS port. Only four digits are needed to dial from the FXS analog phone to the Cisco IP Phone.

Also, from the Cisco IP Phone, dial the seven-digit number for the analog phone connected to the FXS router port. Do not proceed unless these connections work.

Step 2. Remove any connection that might exist between the router FX0 port and the Adtran FXS card or a similar unit.

Step 3. Connect a second analog phone to an FXS port on the Adtran or a similar unit.

Step 4. Place a call from one of the IP Phones to the analog phone connected directly to the Adtran or a similar unit. (The Adtran analog FXS port 1 phone number is 555-6001, port 2 is 555-6002, port 3 is 555-6003, and so on.) The call should *not* connect.

Step 5. From the analog phone connected to the FXS router port, dial the analog phone connected directly to the Adtran analog FXS port or a similar unit. (The Adtran analog FXS port 1 phone number is 555-6001, port 2 is 555-6002, port 3 is 555-6003, and so on.) The call should *not* connect.

Based on what you have learned thus far, why did the phone calls fail?

_____

_____

_____

Step 6. In Lab 5-1 you configured a dial peer for the local FXS port. The next four steps configure a dial peer for phone numbers that can be reached on the simulated PBX (Adtran or a similar unit). This dial peer will use the PRI port on the router to access the PSTN (the analog FXS port on the Adtran or a similar unit). The **dial-peer voice** command creates a POTS dial peer:

```
RouterVoIPX(config)# dial-peer voice 2 pots
```

Step 7. The **destination-pattern** command defines the phone number that will be forwarded. This command allows any call that starts with the numbers 5554, 5555, or 5556 to be sent out the port designated in the next step. The three periods that follow the command are part of the command.

```
RouterVoIPX(config-dial-peer)# destination-pattern 555[4,5,6]...
```

Step 8. The **port** command tells the router which port to forward the call through for a specific number that was defined with the **destination-pattern** command. The **port** *x/x/x***:23** or **port** *x/x***:23** command references the serial interface associated with the T1 controller configured earlier on the router. Use the **show running-config** command at the command line to verify the serial interface number, or refer to your notes. An example of a serial port interface number is **port 1/0/0:23** or **port 1/0:23** (depending on what model of NM-HDV2-1T1/E1 is being used).

```
RouterVoIPX(config-dial-peer)# port x/x/x:23
```

Step 9.   The router needs to know which phone number digits to forward for voice calls. Use the command **forward-digits all** to forward all the digits (the full length of the destination dial pattern) to the PSTN (the Adtran or a similar unit):

```
RouterVoIPX(config-dial-peer)# forward-digits all
```

Step 10.   Test the configuration by calling from the Cisco IP Phone to the analog phone attached to the Adtran analog FXS port (or a similar unit). The Adtran FXS port 1 phone number is 555-6001, port 2 is 555-6002, port 3 is 555-6003, and so on.

Was the call successful? If not, perform appropriate troubleshooting.

What message appears on the IP Phone when a call is successfully made to the analog phone connected directly to the Adtran FXS port? Does this same message appear if a call is made from one Cisco IP Phone to another IP Phone?

Step 11.   Make a call from the analog phone connected to the router FXS port to the analog phone attached to the Adtran analog FXS port (or a similar unit). The call should succeed.

Make another call from the analog phone connected to the Adtran or a similar unit to the analog phone connected directly to the router FXS port. This call fails, because a dial peer has not been configured for this situation.

Step 12.   Configure a new dial peer using the **dial-peer voice** command. This dial peer allows a call from an outside phone (such as the one connected directly to the Adtran or a similar unit) to call the analog device that connects to the FXS port on the router.

```
RouterVoIPX(config)# dial-peer voice 3 pots
```

Step 13.   Use the **incoming called-number** command to program the router with numbers that are allowed from the outside world. The three periods that follow the command are part of the command.

```
RouterVoIPX(config-dial-peer)# incoming called-number 5555...
```

Step 14.   Use the **direct-inward-dial** command to enable DID:

```
RouterVoIPX(config-dial-peer)# direct-inward-dial
```

Step 15.   Use the **port** *x/x/x*:**23** or **port** *x/x*:**23** command to apply the dial peer to a specific interface. This command allows calls that come in from the previously defined numbers (5555...) to be allowed through a particular router port. An example of this command is **port 1/0/0:23** or **port 1/0:23** (depending on what model of NM-HDV2-1T1/E1 is being used). Use the port parameters previously documented.

```
RouterVoIPX(config-dial-peer)# port x/x/x:23
```

Task 5: Test Connectivity

Step 1.   Test the configuration by calling from the analog phone attached to the Adtran (or a similar device) analog (FXS) port to the analog phone connected to the FXS port on the router. The call should be successful.

Did the call work properly? If not, perform appropriate troubleshooting.

Step 2. Test the configuration by calling from the analog phone connected to the router FXS port to the analog phone connected to the Adtran (or a similar device). The call should be successful.

Step 3. Test the configuration by calling from the analog phone connected to the Adtran (or a similar device) to the IP Phone. Use seven-digit dialing. The call fails. This is because the CME router ephone-dn has a four-digit number configured.

Step 4. Modify the router configuration in the ephone-dn that relates to the lowest phone number to allow the CME router to recognize the seven-digit number:

```
RouterVoIPX(config)# ephone-dn x
RouterVoIPX(config-ephone-dn)# number xxxx secondary 555xxxx
```

The four *x*s in the command represent the four digits in the lowest IP Phone number. An example of the command for pod 4 is **number 5100 secondary 5555100**.

Step 5. Test the configuration by calling from the analog phone connected to the Adtran (or a similar device) to the lowest-numbered IP Phone. Use seven-digit dialing (as you would if you were calling from a pay phone to an IP Phone at a company). The call succeeds. This is because the CME router ephone-dn now recognizes the lowest-numbered IP Phone as having a seven-digit extension as well as a four-digit extension.

Step 6. Save the router configuration:

```
RouterVoIPX# copy running-config startup-config
```

Digit Manipulation

Depending on the design of the voice network, you might need to manipulate the digits at different points throughout the voice network. Digits can be added, removed, or changed, depending on the dial plan. Several digit manipulation options are available, depending on the situation. This chapter discusses some common digit manipulation strategies:

- Digit stripping and prefixes

- Forward digits

- Number expansion

- Translation rules for VoIP

Digit Stripping and Prefixes

When a router matches a phone number (dial string) to an outbound plain old telephone service (POTS) dial peer, the default behavior strips the left-justified digits that explicitly match the destination pattern. The remaining digits (excess digits) are forwarded to the Private Branch Exchange (PBX), public switched telephone network (PSTN), or other telephony device. For example, the following dial peer matches any seven-digit number that starts with **555**. The four periods represent wildcards and can be any combination of numbers:

```
dial-peer voice 3 pots
destination-pattern 555....
port 2/0/0
```

If someone dialed 555-4539, this dial peer would be matched. The default behavior is for the router to strip the first three 5s from the number, because these are the numbers matched in the dial peer. The number 4539 would be forwarded to the destination.

You might need to modify this default behavior if the overall telephony design requires the stripped digits. Two commands used to modify this default behavior are **no digit-strip** and **prefix**.

The **no digit-strip** dial peer command disables the default digit-stripping behavior. When the **no digit-strip** command is added to a dial peer, all the digits are forwarded. If the dialed number is 555-4539 and it matches the destination pattern in the dial peer, no numbers are stripped, and all the numbers (**5554539**) are forwarded. The following dial peer illustrates the **no digit-strip** command:

```
dial-peer voice 3 pots
destination-pattern 555....
no digit-strip
port 1/0/1
```

The **prefix** dial peer command adds digits to the beginning of the dial string before it is forwarded to the PBX, PSTN, or other telephony device. Here's a sample dial peer:

```
dial-peer voice 3 pots
destination-pattern 1904678....
prefix 8
port 1/0/1
```

The dial peer in this example matches any number starting with **1904678** and any four digits. The terminating gateway might require five digits (a five-digit extension), but the default behavior is to forward only four digits. The **prefix** command can be used to add a digit (such as the number 8) to the beginning of the dial string. The example given adds an **8** to the four digits that are forwarded. Because of the default behavior, if the dialed number is **19046784539**, the numbers **1904678** are stripped, the number **8** is prepended, and the number **84539** is forwarded.

You can also use the **prefix** command to add a pause in dialing. You can insert a comma (,) after the **prefix** command to add a 1-second pause before dialing. Each comma causes the router to wait 1 second. This is useful if a secondary dial tone is required by a PBX or PSTN. For example, a pause for the secondary dial tone might be necessary when a company requires its employees to dial the number 9 to get an outside line. In the following example, the dialed number **1-904-678-4539** matches the dial peer. If the dialed number is **1-904-678-4539**, the numbers **1904** are stripped, the number **9** is prepended with a 1-second pause, and the number **96784539** is forwarded:

```
dial-peer voice 3 pots
destination-pattern 1904.......
prefix 9,
port 1/0/1
```

Forward Digits

Even though the router by default strips the digits on the left that match the dial peer destination pattern, you can control the number of stripped digits using the **forward-digits** command. The **forward-digits** command can forward all digits or a specified number of digits. This command is similar to the **no digit-strip** command, except the **forward-digits** command allows for a more granular approach to selecting the number digits. For example, the **forward-digits 5** command forwards the last five digits in the dialed string. The **forward-digits all** command forwards all digits in the dialed string. The **forward-digits** command is supported only in POTS dial peers.

In the following example, the router's default behavior would be to strip the numbers **65** and forward the remaining four digits. The **forward-digits 5** command instructs the router to forward the last five digits. If the dialed number is **657249**, the dial peer forwards the last five digits—**57249**.

```
dial-peer voice 3 pots
destination-pattern 65....
forward-digits 5
port 1/1
```

In the following example, the router's default behavior would be to strip the numbers **65** and forward the remaining four digits. The **forward-digits all** command instructs the router to forward all numbers. If the dialed number is **657249**, the dial peer forwards all the digits—**657249**.

```
dial-peer voice 3 pots
destination-pattern 65....
forward-digits all
port 1/1
```

Number Expansion

The **num-exp** (number expansion) command is executed from global configuration mode. It is used in conjunction with the **destination-pattern** dial peer configuration mode command. The number expansion rule allows you to prepend a set of digits to the beginning of a dialed string before it is forwarded to the next device. The **prefix** and **num-exp** commands are similar in their function. However, the **prefix** command is applied to and affects an individual dial peer, and **num-exp** is applied in global configuration mode and affects all dialed numbers.

Many companies use a four- or five-digit extension for internal calls. It is convenient for employees to remember just the four- or five-digit extension, but the full ten-digit number might be required to route the number through the corporate network. For example, the extension number **5650** is easier to remember and quicker to enter than the full telephone number, 1-904-555-5650.

The **num-exp** command expands the extension number and adds the digits necessary to reach the destination. The syntax for this command is **num-exp** *extension-number expanded-number*. The following example shows the configuration for an extension number of **5650** with an expanded number of **19045555650**. This configuration prepends the numbers **1904555** when the extension number **5650** is dialed.

```
Router(config)# num-exp 5650 19045555650
```

Table 6-1 provides number expansion examples. The period (.) is a wildcard character that represents a single character in a telephone number.

Table 6-1   Using the num-exp Command

Extension	Destination Pattern	num-exp Command Entry	Description
4369	5153764369	**num-exp 4369 5153764369**	Expands the extension number of 4369 to 5153764369
4...	515376....	**num-exp 4... 515376....**	Expands a four-digit extension that begins with the number 4 and prepends the numbers 515376 to it
....	515376....	**num-exp .... 515376....**	Expands any dialed string of four digits by prepending the digits 515376 (515376....)

You can use the **show num-exp** and **show dialplan number** commands to verify number expansion and verify how the telephone number maps to a dial peer.

The **show num-exp** command displays the number expansion information:

```
RouterVoIPX# show num-exp [dialed-number]
```

The following example provides output for the **show num-exp** command using the dialed number 5650. The output shows that the number 5650 is expanded to 19045555650.

```
RouterVoIP1#sh num-exp 5650
Dest Digit Pattern = '5650'     Translation =
                                '19045555650'
```

The **show dialplan number** command displays the telephone number and dial peer information:

```
RouterVoIPX# show dialplan number [dialed-number]
```

The following example provides output for the **show dialplan number** command using the number 5555650. The last statement shows that the number 5555650 was matched by a dial peer.

```
RouterVoIP1#show dialplan number 5555650
Macro Exp.: 5555650
VoiceEncapPeer3
        peer type = voice, information type = voice,
        description = '',
        tag = 3, destination-pattern = '5555650',
        answer-address = '', preference=0,
        CLID Restriction = None
        CLID Network Number = ''
        CLID Second Number sent
        CLID Override RDNIS = disabled,
        source carrier-id = '', target carrier-id = '',
        source trunk-group-label = '',  target trunk-group-label = '',
        numbering Type = 'unknown'
        group = 3, Admin state is up, Operation state is up,
        Outbound state is up,
        incoming called-number = '', connections/maximum = 0/unlimited,
        DTMF Relay = disabled,
        URI classes:
        Destination =
        huntstop = disabled,
        in bound application associated: 'DEFAULT'
        out bound application associated: ''
        dnis-map =
        permission :both
        incoming COR list:maximum capability
        outgoing COR list:minimum requirement
        Translation profile (Incoming):
        Translation profile (Outgoing):
        incoming call blocking:
        translation-profile = ''
        disconnect-cause = 'no-service'
        advertise 0x40 capacity_update_timer 25 addrFamily 4 oldAddrFamily 4
        type = pots, prefix = '',
        forward-digits default
        session-target = '', voice-port = '0/2/1',
        direct-inward-dial = disabled,
        digit_strip = enabled,
        register E.164 number with H323 GK and/or SIP Registrar = TRUE
        fax rate = system,   payload size =  20 bytes
        supported-language = ''
        Time elapsed since last clearing of voice call statistics never
```

```
          Connect Time = 0, Charged Units = 0,
          Successful Calls = 0, Failed Calls = 0, Incomplete Calls = 0
          Accepted Calls = 0, Refused Calls = 0,
          Last Disconnect Cause is "",
          Last Disconnect Text is "",
          Last Setup Time = 0.
Matched: 5555650    Digits: 7
```

Translation Rules

You can use translation rules to convert or manipulate a telephone number. You can also use translation rules to modify an incoming or outgoing telephone number before it reaches the matched dial peer. For example, many companies use a four- or five-digit dial extension internally, but numbers must be added to the extension to allow the number to be recognized by the PSTN when dialing an external number. You can also use translation rules to convert a four-digit extension number into the ten-digit number that the PSTN expects, or you can use a translation rule to convert the dialed number into a completely different number.

Using the translation-rule Command

Two basic methods exist to manipulate input numbers and translate them into other numbers:

- The **translation-rule** command

- The **voice translation-rule** command

Although they sound similar, they are created and applied slightly differently.

When an input number matches the translation rule, it is replaced with the matched string. The **translation-rule** command has been superseded by the newer **voice translation-rule** command. The **voice translation-rule** command was introduced in Cisco IOS Software Release 12.2(11)T. The **translation-rule** command is still supported in the latest versions of the Cisco voice IOS. This chapter provides the information to configure both commands. A few differences exist between the translation rule and voice translation rule, including support for a maximum of ten translation statements per translation rule, as opposed to a maximum of 15 translation statements per voice translation rule. Voice translation rule also supports translation of redirect numbers, such as when digits are forwarded to voice mail. This is not supported with regular translation rules. The **translation-rule** command is easier to understand and configure. The labs in this chapter focus on this command, but the theory can be directly applied to the **voice translation-rule**. The basic command structure for the two types of translation rules are as follows:

translation-rule *number*

  rule *precedence match-pattern replace-pattern*

translate {**called** | **calling**} *translation-rule-tag*

voice translation-rule *number*

  rule *precedence /match-pattern/ /replace-pattern/*

voice translation-profile *name*

translate {**called** | **calling** | **redirect-called**} *voice-translation-rule-tag*

Table 6-2 describes the syntax used with the **rule** command to configure voice translation rules.

Table 6-2   Syntax Used in the rule Command

Syntax	Description
precedence	Sets the priority of the translation rule. The range is 1 to 15.
/match-pattern/	An expression that is used to match incoming call information. The slash (/) is part of the command and is a delimiter in the pattern.
/replace-pattern/	The expression used to replace the matched pattern in the call information. The slash (/) is part of the command and is a delimiter in the pattern.
reject	The *match-pattern* that is used for call reject purposes.

Table 6-3 describes the pattern matched with wildcard characters used to configure the voice translation rules.

Table 6-3   Characters Used in the rule Command

Voice Translation Rule Character	Description
.	Any single digit.
0 to 9, *, or #	Any specific character.
[0-9]	Any sequence of numbers in a range or in consecutive order.
*	Repeat the preceding regular expression zero or more times.
?	Repeat the preceding regular expression zero times or one time. (Use Ctrl-V followed by the question mark (?) character to enter this character in IOS.)
.*	Any digit (including null) followed by one or more occurrences.
.+	Any digit (except null) followed by one or more occurrences.
^$	No digits.
/	A delimiter that marks the start and end of both the matched and replaced strings.
^	Matched digits must occur at the beginning of the digit string.
+	Repeat the expression (digit) just prior to this symbol. The digit can be repeated one or more times.
\	Escape the meaning of the next character.

The first step of configuring a translation rule is to create a translation rule number using the **translation-rule** *number* command or the **voice translation-rule** *number* command. The *number* can be any number from 1 to 2,147,483,647 and is simply used to uniquely identify the translation rule. The **translation-rule** and **voice translation-rule** commands are applied in global configuration mode.

After you configure the **translation-rule** or **voice translation-rule** command, you need to apply the **rule** command. The **rule** command defines a number pattern and then the parameters that are applied when the number pattern is dialed. There are two types of rules:

- The match and replace rule defines a number pattern that is "matched." The number(s) are replaced with a different set of digits.

- The reject rule type specifies a dial pattern that prevents the call from being placed.

The slash (/) and backslash (\) characters are used with the **voice translation-rule** *number* command. The **translation-rule** *number* command does not use the slash character. Depending on where it is used, the slash could indicate when to slice or replace a number.

Note: The **voice translation-rule** command requires additional configuration steps but is not discussed further in this chapter. The remaining sections focus on understanding the rules. The basic rules apply to both kinds of translation rules. The router configuration examples in this chapter use the **translation-rule** command and not the **voice translation-rule** command.

The following example shows a dial peer that is configured to use translation rule number 2, which contains one translation rule:

```
translation-rule 2
 rule 0 ^7 1904
ephone-dn 3  dual-line
 number 5002
 call-forward busy 5555028
 call-forward noan 5555028 timeout 18
 translate called 2
dial-peer voice 4 pots
 destination-pattern 1904.......
 port 0/2/1
```

The rule defined is rule 0, in which **7** is the pattern that must be matched and replaced. The **1904** in the command is the pattern that is substituted for the number **7**. Notice in the **ephone-dn 3** section how the **translate called** command is used to associate a translation rule with a specific extension number (directory number). The **translate called 2** command under **ephone-dn 3** references the **translation-rule 2** command.

The called number is **75555029**. The previous configuration strips the leading digit **7** from any called number that begins with 7 (dialed from extension 5002) before the number is forwarded by the outbound POTS dial peer (dial peer 4).

The caret (^) symbol used in the **rule** command specifies that the matched digits must occur at the start of a dial string. Some companies use 7 to acquire an outside long-distance line. This translation rule strips the 7 and replaces it with a 1904 to dial a long-distance phone number to a particular area code.

A translation rule set can have multiple translation rules (there is a maximum of 11). For example, the following translation rule set has ten translation rules:

```
translation-rule 3
rule 0 ^710 0
rule 1 ^711 1
rule 2 ^712 2
rule 3 ^713 3
rule 4 ^714 4
rule 5 ^715 5
rule 6 ^716 6
rule 7 ^717 7
rule 8 ^718 8
rule 9 ^719 9
!
dial-peer voice 2 voip
```

```
destination-pattern 7..........
translate-outgoing called 3
session target ipv4:12.91.0.1
```

This example could apply to companies that use the number 7 to acquire a long-distance outside line. When applied to the dial peer, each rule would evaluate the telephone number dialed until a match is found.

Two examples based on the preceding translation rule show that if someone dials **710** as the first three digits, the numbers **710** are replaced with a **0**. If someone dials **719**, these three digits are replaced with a **9**.

The following example provides the basic steps for configuring a simple translation rule. This simple configuration translates a number that is not part of a dial peer into a number that is assigned to a dial peer.

```
translation-rule 2
 rule 0 1234567 5555028
```

The **translation-rule 2** command creates the translation rule with the number 2. (Any number from 1 to 2147483647 can be used.) The **rule 0** in this example translates the dialed numbers **1234567** into the numbers **5555028** when applied to an ephone-dn.

The following configuration shows **translation-rule 2** being applied to **ephone-d 2**.

```
ephone-dn 2  dual-line
 number 5031
 call-forward busy 6900
 call-forward noan 6900 timeout 3
 translate called 2
```

In this case, ephone-dn 2's extension is 5031. The **translate called 2** command references **translation-rule 2**. Because you are applying this translation rule to only one ephone-dn (extension 5031), only this phone is affected by the translation rule. Other ephone-dns will not translate the numbers. If this rule wasn't applied to any **ephone-dn**, the numbers **1234567** would cause the phone to ring fast busy as soon as the number **1** was dialed if no other dial peer matched the number **1**.

The following **dial-peer voice 1 pots** is configured to forward the numbers **5555028** (to port 0/2/0):

```
dial-peer voice 1 pots
 destination-pattern 5555028
 port 0/2/0
```

This dial peer forwards only the numbers **5555028**; it does not forward the numbers **1234567**. This dial peer never "sees" the numbers **1234567** because they are translated into the numbers **5555028** before they reach this dial peer.

Table 6-4 provides examples for voice translation rules. The Match String and Replace String are applied to the Dialed String column to create the Replaced String Value (the actual telephone number forwarded).

Table 6-4   Simple Translation Rule Examples

Rule	Match String	Replace String	Dialed String	Replaced String Value	Comments
rule 1 123 456	123	456	123	456	Replaces the number pattern 123 located anywhere in the called number with 456.

Rule	Match String	Replace String	Dialed String	Replaced String Value	Comments
rule 33 123 456	123	456	6123	6456	Replaces the number pattern 123 anywhere in the called number with 456.
rule 126 123 456	123	456	99123	99456	Replaces the number pattern 123 anywhere in the called number with 456.
rule 29 ^123 456	^123	456	1238	4568	Replaces the number pattern 123 only at the beginning of the called number with 456.
rule 9 ^123 456	^123	456	1236870	4566870	Replaces the number pattern 123 only at the beginning of the called number with 456.
rule 35 ^123 456	^123	456	99123	99123	Replaces the number pattern 123 only at the beginning of the called number with 456. Because the dialed string does not start with 123, no match (and therefore no replacement) occurs.
rule 57 ^123.. 5551050	^123..	5551050	12389	5551050	Replaces the called number beginning with 123 and any other two digits with the number 5551050.
rule 62 ^12... 8562344	^12...	8562344	1237409	856234437409	Replaces the called number that begins with 12 and any other three digits with the number 8562344.
rule 48 /^1..../ /7561491/	/^1..../	/7561491/	18745	7561491	Replaces the called number beginning with 1 and any other four digits with 7561491. The slashes are used only with the **voice translation-rule** command.
rule 83 /.+/ /2890116/	/.+/	/2890116/	123740	2890116	Replaces all called numbers (except null) with 2890116.

continues

Table 6-4   Simple Translation Rule Examples   *continued*

Rule	Match String	Replace String	Dialed String	Replaced String Value	Comments
rule 99 /^0+/ /813/	/^0+/	/813/	04567145	8134567145	Replaces all called numbers starting with any combination of zero(s)— 0, 00, 000, and so on— with 813.
rule 71 /^0+/ /555/	/^0+/	/555/	0009644	5559644	Replaces all called numbers starting with any combination of zero(s)— 0, 00, 000, and so on— with 555.

Number Slice

You can use a technique called *number slice* to copy one or more parts of a matched pattern to a replaced pattern. You do this by "slicing" the number into sets that you can either keep or ignore.

Table 6-5 describes the number slice characters used when copying parts of a matched number to the replacement number.

Table 6-5   Characters Used in Number Slice

Voice Translation Rule Character	Description
()	The characters within parentheses are kept as part of the replacement number.
\	Indicates where to slice the number in the match or replacement.
(a\)	Keeps the expression represented by *a*.
a\	Ignores the expression represented by *a*.
\1	Copies the first set into the replacement number.

The following translation rule is an example of the slice process:

```
/ (a\) b\ (c\) / /p\1\2/
```

This example splits the matched number into three sets—*a*, *b*, and *c*. The backslashes (after the *a*, *b*, *c*) indicate where to slice the number. The parentheses indicate the sets that are reused in the replacement pattern. The *p* indicates the additional digits to be inserted into the replacement number:

- Set 1 becomes expression *a*.

- Set 2 becomes expression *c*.

- Expression *b* is ignored, because it is not contained in parentheses.

The replacement number is the value of *pac*.

The following translation rule uses the format from the previous example:

```
voice translation-rule 1
 rule 1 /^\(35\)6\(72\)$/ /9\1\2/
```

where:

- Set 1 is 35.
- Set 2 is 72.
- The 6 is ignored.

In this example, a dialed string of **35672** would result in a replaced string of **93572**. The **6** is not in parentheses and is ignored.

Lab 6-1: Translation Rule Exercise 1

This lab exercise provides practice translation rules and the steps to test the rules on the router.

The objective of this lab is to become more familiar with translation rules by logically determining the replaced string values based on a provided rule.

This lab does not require any equipment to perform.

The procedure for this lab consists of a single task—completing Table 6-6.

Task 1: Complete Table 6-6

Table 6-6 lists translation rules. Complete Table 6-6 by filling in the Replaced String Value column. Compare the Rule column to the Dialed String column. Determine the value to enter into the Replaced String Value column.

Table 6-6   Translation Rules Practice Table 1

Rule	Dialed String	Replaced String Value	Comments
rule 1 748 287	748	_____	_____
rule 1 748 287	6748	_____	_____
rule 1 748 287	99748	_____	_____
rule 1 ^748 287	7488	_____	_____
rule 1 ^748 287	7486870	_____	_____
rule 1 ^748 287	74899	_____	_____
rule 1 ^748.. 5551050	74889	_____	_____
rule 1 ^12... 8562344	7487409	_____	_____

Lab 6-2: Translation Rule Exercise 2

In this lab, the company OCSIC.org has decided to train the IT staff on translation rules in a single-router network.

This lab exercise provides practice translation rules and the steps to test the rules on the router.

The objective of this lab is to become more familiar with translation rules by logically determining the replaced values and testing on a CME router.

To perform this lab, you need a Cisco CME-capable router.

Figure 6-1 shows an example of the topology used for this lab. Keep in mind that an integrated switch module in the router could be used instead of the external switch.

Figure 6-1   Lab Topology: Cisco CME Network with FXS Capability

**Workstation with Console
Connection to Router**

The procedure for this lab consists of the following tasks, as described in detail in the following sections:

- **Task 1**—Complete Table 6-7.

- **Task 2**—Verify the translation rules in Table 6-7.

- **Task 3**—Complete Table 6-8.

- **Task 4**—Verify the translation rules in Table 6-8.

Task 1: Complete Table 6-7

Table 6-7 lists eight translation rules. Each rule shows the rule syntax and what number has been dialed (the value in the Dialed String column). Make a note of what the replaced value should be based on the translation rule given in the Replaced String Value column.

Table 6-7   Translation Rules Practice Table 2

Rule	Dialed String	Replaced String Value	Comments
rule 1 769 381	769	_____	_____
rule 1 769 381	6769	_____	_____
rule 1 705 212	99705	_____	_____

continues

Table 6-7   Translation Rules Practice Table 2   *continued*

Rule	Dialed String	Replaced String Value	Comments
rule 1 // //	8135554620	_____	_____
rule 1 /^589\(.*\)/ /555\1/	5891672	_____	_____
rule 1 /^\(289\)\(....\)/ /601\2/	2896438	_____	_____
rule 1 /^601\(....\)/ /444\1/	6016438	_____	_____
rule 1 /\(^...\)754\(.... \)/ /\1444\2/	9197541212	_____	_____

Task 2: Verify the Translation Rules in Table 6-7

Step 1.   Now that you have "guessed" what you think the replaced value will be, you need to create and test the translation rule on the router.

Because there are two types of translation rules, you will create either a translation rule or a voice translation rule. The command syntax for each option is as follows:

```
RouterVoIPX(config)# translation-rule number
RouterVoIPX(config-translate)# rule precedence match-pattern replace-pattern
RouterVoIPX(config)# voice translation-rule number
RouterVoIPX(cf-translation-rule)# rule number /match-pattern/ /replace-pattern/
```

Step 2.   You can use two commands to test a translation rule after it has been entered. The command used depends on if you created the translation rule using the **translation-rule** command or the **voice translation-rule** command:

```
RouterVoIPX# test translation-rule number pattern
RouterVoIPX# test voice translation-rule number pattern
```

Task 3: Complete Table 6-8

Table 6-8 lists more translation rules. Each rule shows the rule syntax and what number has been dialed (the value in the Dialed String column).

Make a note of what the replaced value should be based on the translation rule given in the Replaced String Value column.

Table 6-8   Translation Rules Practice Table 3

Rule	Dialed String	Replaced String Value	Comments
rule 1 ^705 212	7058	_____	_____
rule 1 ^433 179	4336870	_____	_____
rule 1 ^433 179	43399	_____	_____
rule 1 /\(^...\)\(647\)\ (....\)/ /\1444\3/	9196471212	_____	_____
rule 1 /\(.*\)3828$/ /\13434/	2234853828 9048083828	_____ _____	_____ _____
rule 1 /^[456]/ /9/	42345 22345 72345	_____ _____ _____	_____ _____ _____
rule 1 /^[1-40]/ /9/	2234	_____	_____

Task 4: Verify the Translation Rules in Table 6-8

Step 1. Now that you have "guessed" what you think the replaced value will be in Table 6-8, you will again create and test the translation rules on the router:

```
RouterVoIPX(config)# translation-rule number
RouterVoIPX(config-translate)# rule precedence match-pattern replace-pattern
RouterVoIPX(config)# voice translation-rule number
RouterVoIPX(cf-translation-rule)# rule number /match-pattern/ /replace-pattern/
```

Step 2. You can use two commands to test a translation rule after it has been entered. The command used depends on whether you created the translation rule using the **translation-rule** command or the **voice translation-rule** command:

```
RouterVoIPX# test translation-rule number
RouterVoIPX# test voice translation-rule number
```

Lab 6-3: Configure Translation Rules for the Help Desk

In this lab, OCSIC.org has decided to use translation rules to provide an easy-to-remember help desk number for employees. The company has chosen to use the word HELP, which translates to the numbers 4357. The help desk phone number is actually a different number, so translation needs to occur.

Note: This lab relies on the two IP phones being able to connect to one another *before* you start this lab. Also, the IP phones must be able to call two analog phones connected to the router. Troubleshoot as necessary. Do not proceed unless the two phones that connect to the same CME router can call one another and the two analog phones. Refer to previous labs for more information.

The objective of this lab is to configure a translation rule for the help desk.

To perform this lab, you need the following equipment:

- Cisco CME-capable router

- Switch/switch module

- Workstation with an Ethernet 10/100 NIC installed

- Two Cisco IP Phones (powered using any method)

- Two analog phones

Figure 6-2 shows the topology used with this lab.

Figure 6-2   Lab Topology: Translation Rules

The procedure for this lab consists of the following tasks, as described in detail in the following sections:

- **Task 1**—Verify phone connectivity.

- **Task 2**—Configure translation rules for the help desk.

Task 1: Verify Phone Connectivity

Step 1.   On one pod, verify the connectivity between the two Cisco IP Phones. Do not proceed unless the call succeeds.

Step 2.   Verify the connectivity between the analog phone connected to the router FXS port and the two Cisco IP Phones. Each phone should be able to call all the others. From each Cisco IP Phone, use seven digits to call the analog phone that connects to the FXS port. From the analog phones, dial each of the IP phones. Do not proceed unless the calls are successful.

Task 2: Configure Translation Rules for the Help Desk

Step 1. View the running configuration file so that you can make a note of the analog phone numbers associated with the analog FXS port dial peer:

```
RouterVoIPX# show running-config
```

Based on the output shown, write down the phone numbers for the analog phone.

Analog phone number:

Write down the ephone-dn and extension numbers for both Cisco IP Phones.

ephone-dn number:

Cisco IP Phone extension number:

---

ephone-dn number:

Cisco IP Phone extension number:

Step 2. From global configuration mode, use the **translation-rule** command to create a new translation rule. This translation rule will be given the number 2:

```
RouterVoIPX(config)# translation-rule 2
```

Step 3. Create the actual rule or rules that will be applied under **translation-rule 2**. The **rule** command is used to define the rules.

In this lab, OCSIC.org wants to create an easy number for employees to use to dial the help desk. The company has decided to use 4357 (HELP) as the new number. The actual help number is the analog phone number you recorded earlier in this lab. For example, if you listed 555-5028 for analog phone number 1, that will be your original help desk number for this lab.

The 0 in the rule is the precedence, the 4357 is the number that employees can dial for the help desk, and the 5555028 is the number that is translated and passed to the appropriate dial peer. Substitute your help desk number for the one in this example.

```
RouterVoIPX(config-translate)# rule 0 4357 555XXXX
```

Step 4. Apply the rule to an ephone-dn using the **translate** command. Use the first ephone-dn you recorded earlier in this lab for this configuration.

```
RouterVoIPX(config)# ephone-dn X
RouterVoIPX(config-ephone-dn)# translate called 2
```

Step 5.   Verify the configuration by dialing the phone number 4357 from the IP phone that is the extension associated to the ephone-dn that you just configured in the previous step. The associated analog phone should ring when you dial 4357.

Did the phone ring?

_____

If not, troubleshoot as necessary.

Step 6.   From the same Cisco IP Phone, dial the same analog phone using the original seven-digit number (the number used in the **rule 0** command). The seven-digit number still dials the analog phone, because no translation is required, and the dial peer was unaffected.

Step 7.   Dial 4357 from the other Cisco IP Phone. This phone emits a fast busy tone as soon as the number 4 is dialed, because this phone's ephone-dn does not have a translation rule or a dial peer applied to allow the number 4357 to be translated.

Step 8.   Save this router configuration for the next lab:

```
RouterVoIPX# copy running-config startup-config
```

Lab 6-4: Configure Translation Rules for 1-800 Numbers

In this lab, OCSIC.org has decided to provide a 1-800 number. The company will use a translation rule to convert the 1-800 number to an actual PSTN number.

1-800 numbers used to call companies are translated at some point into local PSTN numbers. The 1-800 numbers are usually assigned to trunk lines. For example, you may call a 1-800 number that connects to a T1 trunk line. The T1 trunk can have up to 24 channels. Each of the channels (phone lines) can have a separate PSTN phone number. The phone numbers are local numbers to the company. For example, the PSTN phone numbers on the T1 could range from 906-555-5000 to 906-555-5023. When customers call the 1-800 number, the phone company translates the 1-800 number into one of the many local numbers. This occurs in a round-robin fashion—if one number is busy, it rolls over to the next open line. This lab simulates this process using the analog and IP phones.

Note   This lab relies on the two IP phones being able to connect to one another *before* you start this lab. Also, the IP phones must be able to call the analog phone connected to the router FXS port. Troubleshoot as necessary. Do not proceed unless connectivity can occur. Refer to previous labs for more information.

The objective of this lab is to configure a translation rule for a 1-800 number.

To perform this lab, you need the following equipment:

- Cisco CME-capable router

- Switch/switch module

- Workstation with an Ethernet 10/100 NIC installed

- Two Cisco IP Phones (powered using any method)

- Two analog phones

Figure 6-3 shows the topology used with this lab. Keep in mind that an integrated switch module in the router could be used instead of the external switch.

Figure 6-3   Lab Topology: Translation Rule for the Help Desk

The procedure for this lab consists of the following tasks, described in detail in the following sections:

- **Task 1**—Verify phone connectivity.

- **Task 2**—Configure and test the second FXS port.

- **Task 3**—Configure a translation rule for 1-800 numbers.

Task 1: Verify Phone Connectivity

Step 1.   On one pod, verify the connectivity between the two Cisco IP Phones. Do not proceed unless the call succeeds.

Step 2.   Verify the connectivity between the analog phone connected to the router FXS port and the two Cisco IP Phones. Each phone should be able to call all the others. From each Cisco IP Phone, use seven digits to call the analog phone that connects to the FXS port. From the analog phones, dial each of the IP phones. Do not proceed unless the calls are successful.

Task 2: Configure and Test the Second FXS Port

Step 1.   On one pod, connect a second analog phone to the second FXS port using an RJ-11 cable.

Step 2.   From global configuration mode, create a new dial peer for this analog phone. To create this dial peer, you must know two pieces of information:

- The phone number used for the second FXS port (the phone number for the phone lists in Table 6-9)
- The port number syntax for the second FXS port (use the **show voice port summary** command)

```
RouterVoIPX# show voice port summary

RouterVoIPX(config)# dial-peer voice 12 pots

RouterVoIPX(config-dial-peer)# destination-pattern 555XXXX

RouterVoIPX(config-dial-peer)# port X/X/X
```

Table 6-9   FXS Phone Numbers

Pod	Extension Numbers	Router FXS 0 Port	Router FXS 1 Port
Pod 1	5000 to 5029	5555028	5555029
Pod 2	5030 to 5059	5555058	5555059
Pod 3	5060 to 5089	5555088	5555089
Pod 4	5100 to 5129	5555128	5555129

Step 3.   From a Cisco IP Phone, dial the seven-digit phone number for the analog phone you have just connected to the second FXS port.

Did the call succeed?

_____

Do not proceed until it does.

Step 4.   From the analog phone connected to the first FXS router port, dial the seven-digit phone number of the analog phone connected to the second FXS port.

Did the call succeed?

_____

Do not proceed until it does.

Task 3: Configure a Translation Rule for 1-800 Numbers

Step 1.   View the running configuration file to verify the analog phone numbers associated with the two analog FXS dial peers. Answer the questions based on the output shown and information configured in the preceding task.

```
RouterVoIPX# show running-config
```

Write down the phone numbers for both analog phones that connect to the router FXS ports.

Analog phone 1:

_____

Analog phone 2:

_____

Document the ephone-dn numbers associated with both Cisco IP Phones.

ephone-dn number:

_____

Cisco IP Phone extension number:

_____

ephone-dn number:

_____

Cisco IP Phone extension number:

_____

Step 2.   From global configuration mode, use the **translation-rule** command to create a new translation rule. This translation rule is given the number 3:

```
RouterVoIPX(config)# translation-rule 3
```

Step 3.   Create the rule (it could be more than one, but you will do just one) that will be applied under **translation-rule 3**. The **rule** command is used to define the rules.

In this lab, OCSIC.org wants to create a 1-800 number. The full 1-800 number is 1-800-476-3988. The local PSTN number that the 1-800 will translate to is the number for the second analog phone number (the one that connects to the second FXS port. Replace the x's in the command with the phone number for the second analog phone number:

```
RouterVoIPX(config-translate)# rule 0 18004763988 555xxxx
```

Step 4.   Apply the rule to an ephone-dn using the **translate** command. Use the second ephone-dn listed in your notes from a previous step:

```
RouterVoIPX(config)# ephone-dn x
RouterVoIPX(config-ephone-dn)# translate called 3
```

Step 5.   Verify the configuration by dialing the phone number 1-800-476-3988 from the Cisco IP Phone configured in a previous step and the one that is associated with the ephone-dn configured in the preceding step. The analog phone should ring.

Did the phone ring?

_____

If not, troubleshoot as necessary.

Step 6.   From the same IP phone, place a call to the analog phone using the original seven-digit number (the actual number of the analog phone). The seven-digit number still dials the analog phone, because no translation is required, and the dial peer was unaffected.

Step 7.   Dial 1-800-476-3988 from the other IP Phone. This phone goes to fast busy as soon as the number 1 is dialed, because the ephone-dn does not have a matching translation rule or dial peer applied to allow the number 1-800-476-3988 to be translated.

Step 8.   Save the configuration for the next lab:

```
RouterVoIPX# copy running-config startup-config
```

Lab 6-5: Testing and Troubleshooting Translation Rules

In this lab, OCSIC.org has decided to train the technical staff on testing and troubleshooting translation rules.

Note   This lab relies on the two IP phones being able to connect to one another *before* you start this lab. Also, the IP phones must be able to call two analog phones connected to the router. Troubleshoot as necessary. Do not proceed unless the two phones that connect to the same CME router can call one another and the two analog phones. Refer to previous labs for more information.

The two translation rules created during the two previous labs are needed for this lab to function properly.

The objectives of this lab are as follows:

- Test translation rules.

- Debug translation rules.

To perform this lab, you need the following equipment:

- Cisco CME-capable router

- Switch/switch module

- Workstation with an Ethernet 10/100 NIC installed

- Two Cisco IP Phones (powered using any method)

- Two analog phones

Figure 6-4 shows the topology used with this lab. Keep in mind that an integrated switch module in the router could be used instead of the external switch.

Figure 6-4   Lab Topology: Translation Rule Troubleshooting

The procedure for this lab consists of the following tasks, as described in detail in the following sections:

- **Task 1**—Verify phone connectivity.

- **Task 2**—Test translation rules.

- **Task 3**—Debug translation rules.

Task 1: Verify Phone Connectivity

Step 1.   On one pod, verify the connectivity between the two Cisco IP Phones. Do not proceed unless the call succeeds.

Step 2.   Verify the connectivity between the analog phone connected to both router FXS ports and the two Cisco IP Phones. Each phone should be able to call all the others. From each Cisco IP Phone, use seven digits to call each analog phone. From the analog phones, dial each of the IP phones. Do not proceed unless the calls are successful.

Task 2: Test Translation Rules

Step 1. Although the translation rules in these labs are at a basic level in more complicated environments, it may be difficult to identify the problem. Tools are available to test and troubleshoot translation rules. Two commands that you can use to test translation rules are **show translation-rule** and **test translation-rule**. These commands allow for a number to be tested to verify whether it is associated with a specific translation rule. The format for the **test translation-rule** command is **test translation-rule** *number* **input-test-string** [**type** *match-type* [**plan** *match-type*]].

From enable mode, use the **show translation-rule** command to view information about all the translation rules on the router. The **show translation-rule** *tag* command allows you to specify a particular translation rule. The tag is the number of the translation rule. View basic information about the translation rules with the **show translation-rule** command:

```
RouterVoIPX# show translation-rule
```

The output of the **show translation-rule** command looks similar to the following. It displays the translation rule, the match pattern, and the replacement (sub) pattern.

```
RouterVoIP1#show translation-rule
Translation rule address: 0x45B75A38
Tag name: 2
Translation rule in_used 1
**** Xrule rule table *******
        Rule : 0
        in_used state: 1
        Match pattern: 4357
        Sub  pattern: 5555028
Translation rule address: 0x454C02F8
Tag name: 3
Translation rule in_used 1
**** Xrule rule table *******
        Rule : 0
        in_used state: 1
        Match pattern: 18004763988
        Sub  pattern: 5555029
```

Step 2. From enable mode, use the **test translation-rule** command to view information about all the translation rules on the router. The command syntax is **test translation-rule** *tag word*. The *tag* is the number of the translation rule you want to test. The *word* allows you to input different numbers to test whether they match a translation rule. View basic information about the translation rules with the **show translation-rule** command.

```
RouterVoIPX(config)# test translation-rule 2 4357
```

The output of the **test translation-rule** command will look similar to the following output. If the test number matches, it displays the replaced number. If the test number does not match, the output states that it does not match.

```
RouterVoIP1# test translation-rule 2 4357
The replaced number: 5555028
```

Step 3.   Redo the **test translation-rule** with a set of digits that will not match the translation pattern:

RouterVoIPX(config)# **test translation-rule 2 9999**

Does the output show that the 999 pattern does not match any translation rules?

Task 3: Debug Translation Rules

Step 1.   The **debug** command is a useful tool when problems arise that need a more in-depth method of troubleshooting. Input the **debug translation detail** command. No output is displayed until a call is made:

RouterVoIPX# **debug translation detail**

Step 2.   Using the translation rule defined earlier in this lab, dial 4357 from the IP phone configured for this translation rule. After the number is dialed, the router displays large amounts of output. Hang up the phone. Review the output to verify the basic process the router uses when a translation rule match is found.

Step 3.   From the same Cisco IP Phone, call the number 4222. This number does not match a defined translation rule. Review the router output. Compare the output from the preceding step with the output from a number that does not match a translation rule. Like most debug outputs, you may not be able to understand each line of the output, but you can scan it for error messages and research as appropriate.

Step 4.   Turn off all debugging. You do not need to save your configurations from this lab.

RouterVoIPX# **undebug all**

CHAPTER 7

Configuring Inter-Pod Connectivity

This chapter focuses on connecting two pods via a T1 connection as well as a serial port connection. T1 connectivity simulates connectivity between two different companies. A serial connection is more indicative of connectivity between two sites of the same company. Lab 7-2 introduces the idea of class of restriction (COR).

Digit Manipulation

Phone digits sometimes need to be translated or manipulated to create communication between different sites. Reasons for digit manipulation include the following:

- Allow Cisco IP Phone users to call each other by simply dialing an extension number

- Allow IP Phone users to access the public switched telephone network (PSTN)

- Allow for variable-length external (outside the company) dialing

- Block certain numbers

- Redirect calls to a particular number

In the labs, using the dial plan provided, a phone that has an extension of 5030 has an E.164 DID number of 510-555-5030. Without some form of digit manipulation, a call coming from the outside (the PSTN) that dials 510-555-5030 does not match the ephone-dn defined in the router configuration for that phone. The configuration is for the extension number—5030. A method needs to be used to translate the called number of 510-555-5030 to the extension number of 5030.

The three Cisco IOS Software methods to manipulate telephony digits in these labs are as follows:

- **dial-peer** commands, which have been used in previous chapters as well as this chapter

- **dialplan-pattern** command, which is demonstrated in this chapter

- Translation rules, which are covered in Chapter 8, "GUI and IOS Intermediate Administration"

Being able to manipulate digits and understanding when to do so is important in IP telephony. More digit manipulation concepts are covered in the next chapter, but the labs in this chapter introduce these concepts.

Class of Restriction (COR)

The class of restriction (COR) router feature allows you to apply rules on calls that originate and terminate on a router. COR is applied to voice dial peers. Because dial peers are a subcomponent of the CME ephone-dn configuration, COR configurations can also be applied under the ephone-dn configuration.

COR rules or restrictions always apply in one direction. This is a very important concept. A COR configuration is needed for an incoming call, and a different COR configuration is needed for an outgoing call. For example, suppose that two IP Phones connect to a CallManager Express (CME) router. If a restriction were needed to stop each phone from calling the other phone, two configurations would be needed:

- A restriction stopping the first phone from calling the second phone

- A restriction stopping the second phone from calling the first phone

COR configuration involves creating a dial peer specifically for the COR. The **dial-peer cor custom** command is used to name the voice capabilities before specifying the COR rules and then applying them to dial peers. An example follows. Names usually indicate the rules that will be applied later: **local** for local calls, **longdist** for long-distance calls, **1800** for 1-800-xxx-xxxx toll calls, **1900** for 1-900-xxx-xxxx toll calls, and **911** for emergency calls:

```
dial-peer cor custom
 name local
 name longdist
 name 911
 name 1800
 name 1900
```

This dial peer is made specifically to restrict (or allow) certain types of calls. The types of calls are specified on individual lines under the dial peer, and they are given a name. The four types of calls in this example are

- Local (**local**)

- Long-distance (**longdist**)

- Emergency (**911**)

- Toll-free (**1800**)

After the custom COR dial peer is created that specifies the types of calls, other dial peers are created that allow members to be created. These dial peers are named so that they will be easy to apply. An example follows:

```
dial-peer cor list Staff
 member 911
 member local
 member 1800
dial-peer cor list Admin
 member 911
 member local
 member 1800
 member longdist
 member 1900
dial-peer cor list Student
 member 911
 member local
dial-peer cor list Use911
 member 911
dial-peer cor list Use1800
 member 1800
```

```
dial-peer cor list Uselocal
 member local
dial-peer cor list Use1900
 member 1900
dial-peer cor list Uselongdist
 member longdist
```

After these dial peers are created, they are applied to a specific dial peer or ephone-dn:

```
dial-peer voice 1 voip
 destination-pattern 904&
 session target ipv4:192.168.1.1
 corlist outgoing Uselocal
dial-peer voice 2 voip
 destination-pattern 1800&
 session target ipv4:192.168.1.1
 corlist outgoing use1800
dial-peer voice 3 ports
 destination-pattern 1900&
 port 1/1/0
 corlist outgoing Use1900
dial-peer voice 4 pots
 destination-pattern 911
 port 1/1/0
 corlist outgoing Use911
ephone-dn 1
 number 5030
 cor incoming Staff
```

Whoever has the Cisco IP Phone with the phone number 5030 belongs to the list called Staff. Looking back at the configuration, the Staff list has members called 911, local, and 1800. Now look at the dial peers.

Dial peer 1 has a destination pattern of any calls that begin with 904 and a COR list of Uselocal. The Uselocal COR list has a member called local. Staff belongs to local, so anyone who is in the Staff group (such as ephone-dn 1) is allowed to make local calls.

Dial peer 2 has a destination pattern of any calls that begin with 1800 and a COR list of Use1800. The Use1800 COR list has a member called 1800. Staff belongs to 1800, so any phone that is in the Staff group (such as phone number 5030) is allowed to make 1-800-xxx-xxxx calls.

Dial peer 3 has a destination pattern of any calls that begin with 1900 and a COR list of Use1900. The Use1900 COR list has a member called 1900. The Staff group does *not* belong to 1900, so any phone that is in the Staff group (such as ephone dn-1) is *not* allowed to make 1-900-xxx-xxxx calls.

Note: ephone-dns without an incoming COR list are allowed to dial from any dial peer (that is, free from any dial restrictions). Similarly, any dial peer without an outgoing COR list applied can be dialed from any phone.

Lab 7-1: Configuring T1/PRI Connectivity Between Two Pods

In this lab, the company OCSIC.org has decided to connect two sites that communicate via a T1 connection. These sites need to be able to dial from one Cisco IP Phone to an IP Phone at the other site.

Note: This lab requires that two Cisco IP Phones and an analog phone be able to call each other. Also, the pod should have connectivity to the "WAN" (Adtran or a similar unit) via a T1 connection. An analog phone that connects to the Adtran (or a similar unit) can call the IP Phones or the other analog phone. All of this *must* be working before you begin this lab. Refer to the labs in Chapter 2, "Router, Integrated Switch, and IP Phone Basic Configuration," to configure the router and switch. Select a method in Chapter 3, "Managing and Configuring Cisco VoIP Devices," to configure CallManager Express. Complete Lab 5-1, "Configuring FXS Connectivity," and Lab 5-3, "Configuring T1/PRI Connectivity," to configure the FXS and T1 ports.

You can use the same two Cisco IP Phones to check communications for a single pod. Then, after you begin this lab, you can connect a single Cisco IP Phone to each pod.

The objective of this lab is to have two pods communicate with each other's analog and Cisco IP Phones using T1 connectivity.

To perform this lab, you need the following equipment:

- Two Cisco CME-capable routers with T1 PRI ports installed
- Two switches/switch modules
- Two Cisco IP Phones (powered using any method)
- Three analog phones
- Adtran (or another WAN simulation device) with two T1-capable ports
- Two T1 cables

Figure 7-1 shows the topology used for this lab. Keep in mind that an integrated switch module in the router could be used instead of the external switch.

Figure 7-1   Lab Topology: Two Pods with T1 Capability

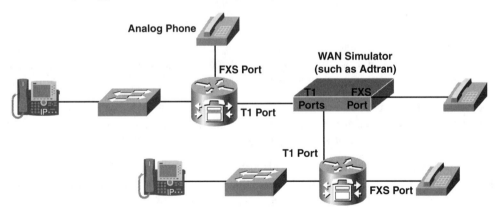

The procedure for this lab consists of the following tasks, which are described in detail in the following sections:

- **Task 1**—Verify connectivity between phones.

- **Task 2**—Verify inter-router connectivity.

- **Task 3**—Verify Cisco IP Phone connectivity between sites.

Task 1: Verify Connectivity Between Phones

Step 1.   On one router pod, dial between the Cisco IP Phone and the analog phone to verify connectivity. Do not proceed if the phones do not connect. Troubleshoot as necessary until the call connects.

Step 2.   On one router pod, dial from the Cisco IP Phone to the Cisco IP Phone connected to the remote router (refer to Table 7-1). Do not proceed if the phone call fails. Troubleshoot as necessary until the call connects.

Table 7-1   IP Telephony Dial Plan

Pod	Dial Plan—Extension Numbers	Voice Mail Extension	First E.164 DID Number	Router FXS Port 0	Router FXS Port 1
Pod 1	5000 to 5029	5555028	5105555000	5555028	5555029
Pod 2	5030 to 5059	5555058	5105555030	5555058	5555059
Pod 3	5060 to 5089	5555088	5105555060	5555088	5555089
Pod 4	5100 to 5129	5555128	5105555100	5555128	5555129

Step 3.   On one router pod from the analog phone connected to the FXS port, dial the analog phone on the remote router. Do not proceed if the phone call fails. Troubleshoot as necessary until the call connects.

Step 4.   Do the same testing from the second router pod.

Task 2: Verify Inter-Router Connectivity

Step 1.   In Lab 5-3, Task 5, Step 4 you added a command to the IP Phone to allow the CME router to recognize a seven-digit number. The command was applied under the lowest ephone-dn. The four x's in the command represent the four digits in the lowest IP Phone number. An example of the command for pod 4 is **number 5100 secondary 5555100**. The command applied is

```
RouterVoIPX(config)# ephone-dn 1
RouterVoIPX(config-ephone-dn)# number 5100 secondary 5555100
```

This command can be applied to each ephone-dn, or you can use another command (**dialplan-pattern 1 555.... extension-length 4**) to accomplish the same thing at the global level for all IP Phones. If you have 20 to 40 phones, you may not want to apply the **number** *xxxx* **secondary 555***xxxx* command to each ephone-dn. This task provides the steps to allow seven-digit dialing for all IP Phones at the global level. The **number** *xxxx* **secondary 555***xxxx* command must be removed from all ephone-dns (if applied) before you complete the following steps. Issue the following command to remove the **number** *xxxx* **secondary 555***xxxx* command from the lowest ephone-dn on each router:

```
RouterVoIPX(config)# ephone-dn x
RouterVoIPX(config-ephone-dn)#no number xxxx secondary 555xxxx
```

Step 2. From privileged mode on both routers, use the command **debug voip dialpeer all** to see how a phone call is handled between routers that connect via T1:

```
RouterVoIPX# debug voip dialpeer all
```

Step 3. From one Cisco IP Phone, use seven digits to dial the analog phone that connects to the remote router's FXS port. Use Table 7-1 for the exact number to dial. The phone call connects.

From the output on the router that has the attached phone that originated the call, is a dial peer matched? If so, which dial peer is matched, and why? If not, why did no dial peer match?

_____

_____

Coordinate with the partner pod to determine the matching dial peer. From the output on the other router, is a dial peer matched? If so, which dial peer matched, and why was it a match?

_____

_____

Step 4. From a Cisco IP Phone on one router, use seven digits to dial the Cisco IP Phone on the other router. For example, if the Cisco IP Phone shows 5031 as the extension number, the number dialed would be 555-5031. The call should fail.

Notice the outputs on both of the routers. On the router that originated the call, which dial peer was matched?

_____

On the router that originated the call, what number is displayed as the "Called number" in the debug output?

_____

Step 5. On the router with the lowest pod number (that is, if pods 3 and 4 are connected, apply this to pod 3), use the **dialplan-pattern** command to manipulate the digits to match the ephone-dn entry for the Cisco IP Phone. The **dialplan-pattern** command is used in telephony-service mode. The four periods are part of the command:

```
RouterVoIPX(config)# telephony-service
RouterVoIPX(config-telephony)# dialplan-pattern 1 555.... extension-length 4
```

Step 6. On the router with the highest pod number (that is, if pods 3 and 4 are connected, apply this to pod 4), use the IP Phone and dial the seven-digit number to call the other router's Cisco IP Phone. The call should succeed. Notice the debug output when the call succeeds.

Step 7. Turn off all debugging:

```
RouterVoIPX# no debug all
```

Step 8. On the router with the lowest pod number (that is, if pods 3 and 4 are connected, apply this to pod 3), try dialing (using seven digits) the IP Phone connected to the other router. The call should fail.

Why did the call fail?

_____

_____

Step 9. Add the **dialplan-pattern** command to the router with the highest pod number so that calls can dial in both directions. The four periods are part of the command:

```
RouterVoIPX(config)# telephony-service
RouterVoIPX(config-telephony)# dialplan-pattern 1 555.... extension-length 4
```

Task 3: Verify Cisco IP Phone Connectivity Between Sites

Step 1. From privileged mode on both routers, use the command **debug voip dialpeer all** to see how a phone call is handled between the routers:

```
RouterVoIPX# debug voip dialpeer all
```

Step 2. Using seven digits, dial from one IP Phone to the other IP Phone.

Step 3. Disconnect the call and reverse the process—dial from the opposite IP Phone. All calls should be successful. Notice in the output how the dial peers are processed.

Step 4. Remove all debugging:

```
RouterVoIPX# no debug all
```

Step 5. Save the router configurations:

```
RouterVoIPX# copy running-config startup-config
```

Lab 7-2: Configuring COR

In this lab, OCSIC.org wants to implement COR to limit access to where certain IP Phones can call.

The objective of this lab is to configure COR on the IP telephony network.

To perform this lab, you need the following equipment:

- Two Cisco CME-capable routers with specific files for an IP Phone (basic CME .tar file)

- Two switches/switch modules

- Workstation with an Ethernet 10/100 network interface card (NIC) installed

- Two Cisco IP Phones (powered using any method)

- Two analog phones

- Adtran (or a similar device)

Figure 7-2 shows the topology used for this lab. Keep in mind that an integrated switch module in the router could be used instead of the external switch.

Figure 7-2   COR Lab Topology

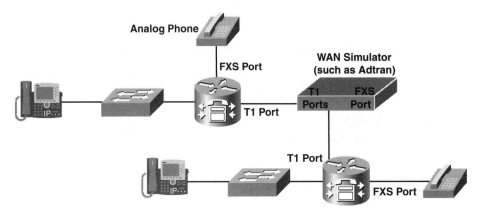

The procedure for this lab consists of the following tasks, which are described in detail in the following sections:

- **Task 1**—Configure COR parameters.

- **Task 2**—Apply the COR with a dial peer or directory number.

- **Task 3**—Test the COR.

This lab requires connectivity between the two pods' Cisco IP Phones, connectivity between any IP Phone and the analog phone connected to the FXS port (using the same router), and connectivity between any IP Phones. All of this *must* be working before you begin this lab. Use appropriate labs for assistance in configuring the router, or manually configure the router to ensure that the connectivity is working properly. Refer to the labs in Chapter 2 to configure the router and switch, select a method in Chapter 3 to configure CME, complete Lab 5-1 to configure the FXS ports, and complete Lab 5-3 to configure the T1.

Task 1: Configure COR Parameters

Note: COR is used to determine which incoming dial peer can use which outgoing dial peer to make a call. A dial peer can have one incoming and one outgoing COR list. This lab creates a COR that prevents the local IP Phone from calling the remote router's IP Phone and analog phone (local calls only). At the same time, the COR allows the analog phone to dial the local IP Phone, remote IP Phone, and remote analog phone.

Step 1. On one router's pod, dial between the Cisco IP Phone and the analog phone to verify connectivity. Do not proceed if the phones do not connect. Troubleshoot as necessary until the call connects.

Step 2. On one router pod, dial from the Cisco IP Phone to the Cisco IP Phone connected to the remote router (refer to Table 7-1). Do not proceed if the phone call fails. Troubleshoot as necessary until the call connects.

Step 3. On one router pod from the analog phone connected to the FXS port, dial the analog phone on the remote router. Do not proceed if the phone call fails. Troubleshoot as necessary until the call connects.

This verifies T1 connectivity. Do not proceed if the phone calls fail. Troubleshoot as necessary until the call connects.

Step 4. From global configuration mode, use the **dial-peer cor custom** command to enter COR configuration mode:

```
RouterVoIPX(config)# dial-peer cor custom
```

Step 5. The names associated with this class of restriction are local and longdistance. The **name** command is used to create these different CORs:

```
RouterVoIPX(config-dp-cor)# name local
RouterVoIPX(config-dp-cor)# name longdistance
```

Step 6. Return to global configuration mode:

```
RouterVoIPX(config-dp-cor)# exit
```

Step 7. Define a dial peer COR list called calllocal using the **dial-peer cor list** command:

```
RouterVoIPX(config)# dial-peer cor list calllocal
```

Step 8. Put the local member in the COR list:

```
RouterVoIPX(config-dp-corlist)# member local
```

Step 9. Return to global configuration mode:

```
RouterVoIPX(config-dp-corlist)# exit
```

Step 10. Define a COR list named calllongdistance:

```
RouterVoIPX(config)# dial-peer cor list calllongdistance
```

Step 11. Put the longdistance member in the COR list:

```
RouterVoIPX(config-dp-corlist)# member longdistance
```

Step 12. Return to global configuration mode:

```
RouterVoIPX(config-dp-corlist)# exit
```

Task 2: Apply the COR with a Dial Peer or Directory Number

Step 1. Apply the COR to POTS voice dial peer number 2:

```
RouterVoIPX(config)# dial-peer voice 2 pots
```

Step 2. Assign an outbound COR list to the dial peer:

```
RouterVoIPX(config-dial-peer)# corlist outgoing calllongdistance
```

Step 3. Use the **exit** command to return to global configuration mode:

```
RouterVoIPX(config-dial-peer)# exit
```

Step 4. The next two steps apply the calllocal COR to the lowest-numbered IP Phone. The calllocal COR has "local" as its member. The purpose of this COR is to prevent the phone with the lowest phone number from calling any number across the T1 (such as the other pod's analog phone or IP Phone).

Enter ephone directory number mode by using the **ephone-dn** *x* command. The *x* in the command is the directory number used for the lowest phone number. Normally it is 1, but it could be another number.

```
RouterVoIPX(config)# ephone-dn x
```

Use the **show running-config** command to verify before completing this step. The output is similar to the following:

```
ephone-dn 1 dual-line

 number 5030
 name Cheryl Schmidt
```

Step 5. In ephone-dn mode, apply the calllocal COR in the incoming direction. Notice that the **cor** command (not the **corlist** command) is used when applying a COR to an ephone-dn:

```
RouterVoIPX(config-ephone-dn)# cor incoming calllocal
```

Step 6. Use the **exit** command to go to global configuration mode:

```
RouterVoIPX(config-ephone-dn)#exit
```

Task 3: Test the COR

Step 1. Test this COR by using the IP Phone with the lowest phone number and by dialing a phone number associated with a remote pod (either the phone connected to the other pod's FXS port or one of the Cisco IP Phones). The phone call should fail because the IP Phone on the initiating router is not part of the longdistance COR. Use the analog phone to call the same numbers. These calls should work, because the analog phone's dial peer is part of the longdistance COR, and the longdistance COR is also applied to the dial peer associated with the T1 port.

Step 2. Test the COR by attempting to dial the phone that connects to the FXS ports from the IP Phones. The call should fail because of the COR. Test the COR by dialing from one analog phone to the other analog phone and both IP Phones. The analog phones should connect to all other phones, because the analog phone's dial peer is part of the longdistance COR, and the longdistance COR is also applied to the dial peer associated with the T1 port.

Step 3. Do *not* save the changes made to the router for this lab. When the test is successful, reload the router, making sure you do not save the configuration. These CORs are not needed for future labs.

```
RouterVoIPX# reload
```

Lab 7-3: Configuring Inter-Pod Serial Connectivity

In this lab, OCSIC.org has added another site with its own CallManager Express router. A WAN connection to the other site needs to be configured and tested.

The objective of this lab is to configure the VoIP dial peers across a WAN serial link.

To perform this lab, you need the following equipment:

- Two Cisco CME-capable routers with specific files for the Cisco IP Phone (basic CME .tar file)

- Two switches/switch modules

- Workstation with an Ethernet 10/100 NIC installed

- Four Cisco IP Phones (powered using any method)

- Adtran

- Router serial cables

Note: This lab requires that you have two IP Phones connected to one router. The two IP Phones should be able to call each other before you start this lab. Use the appropriate labs for help with configuring the router, or manually configure the router to ensure that the connectivity is working properly.

Figure 7-3 shows the topology used for this lab. Keep in mind that an integrated switch module in the router could be used instead of the external switch.

Figure 7-3   Lab Topology: Two Pods with Serial Connectivity

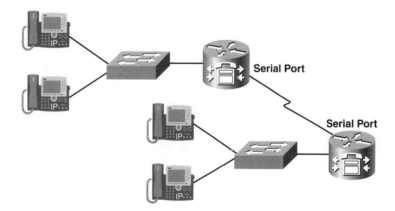

The procedure for this lab consists of the following tasks, which are described in detail in the following sections:

- **Task 1**—Configure serial interface connectivity.

- **Task 2**—Configure the dial peer.

- **Task 3**—Test the configuration.

- **Task 4**—Reconfigure the codec.

Task 1: Configure Serial Interface Connectivity

Note: In this lab, Pod 1 and Pod 2 partner, and Pod 3 and Pod 4 partner.

Step 1.   Ensure that the proper phone numbers are assigned to the Cisco IP Phones and that connectivity exists between the two phones that connect to the same router. Refer to Table 7-2 for the proper phone number assignment.

Table 7-2   IP Telephony Dial Plan

Pod	Extension Numbers
Pod 1	5000 to 5029
Pod 2	5030 to 5059
Pod 3	5060 to 5089
Pod 4	5100 to 5129

Step 2.   If it's present, remove the T1 cable from the router. Connect a serial cable to the lowest-numbered serial interface on the router to the other pod's lowest-numbered serial interface.

Step 3.   On both pods, use the **show ip interface brief** command to verify that a serial interface is installed and to verify the number associated with the serial interface.

```
RouterVoIPX# show ip interface brief
```

Make a note of the port/slot number assigned to the lowest-numbered serial interface.

Step 4.   On both pods, use the **show controllers serial** command for the lowest serial interface and verify if the cable is a DCE or DTE. Examples of this command are **show controllers serial 0/0** and **show controllers serial 0/3/0**.

```
RouterVoIPX# show controllers serial mod/port
```

The output of the **show controllers serial** command will look similar to the following output. The fourth line shows that this router is the DCE and will require the clock rate to be set. The remote router in this case is the DTE.

```
RouterVoIP2#show controllers serial 0/3/0

Interface Serial0/3/0

Hardware is GT96K

DCE V.35, clock rate 2000000

idb at 0x44EEA478, driver data structure at 0x44EF228C

wic_info 0x44EF2880

Physical Port 7, SCC Num 7
```

Step 5.   From global configuration mode, use the **interface serial** command to access the serial interface. Examples of this command are **interface serial 0/0** and **interface serial 0/3/0**.

```
RouterVoIPX(config)# interface serial mod/port
```

Step 6. On the pod that has the DCE end of the cable, use the **clock rate** command to set the clock rate on the lowest serial interface. This step artificially sets the clock rate to a low value to simulate a low-bandwidth WAN connection.

```
RouterVoIPX(config-if)# clock rate 64000
```

Step 7. On both routers, use the **encapsulation** command to configure the serial link encapsulation to HDLC.

```
RouterVoIPX(config-if)# encapsulation hdlc
```

Step 8. Refer to Table 7-3 to determine the appropriate IP address to apply on the serial interface.

Table 7-3   Serial Interface IP Address

Pod	Hostname of Router or Switch	Serial Interface IP Address
Pod 1	RouterVoIP1	10.19.0.1/24
Pod 2	RouterVoIP2	10.19.0.2/24
Pod 3	RouterVoIP3	10.39.0.1/24
Pod 4	RouterVoIP4	10.39.0.2/24

```
RouterVoIPX(config-if)# ip address 10.x.0.x 255.255.255.0
```

Step 9. Enable the serial interface.

```
RouterVoIPX(config-if)# no shutdown
```

Step 10. Wait for the other pod to complete the previous steps. Verify connectivity by using **ping** to test the serial connection. Ping the address of your partner pod's serial interface. Refer to Table 7-3 for the IP address.

```
RouterVoIPX# ping 10.x.0.x
```

Step 11. From an IP Phone connected to the pod, attempt to dial a four-digit extension number of one of the partner pod IP Phones. The call should fail.

Why does the call fail?

What message appears on the Cisco IP Phone when the call does not go through?

Task 2: Configure the Dial Peer

Step 1. From global configuration mode on both router pods, create a new dial peer using the **dial-peer voice** command:

```
RouterVoIPX(config)# dial-peer voice 6 voip
```

Step 2. Associate a pattern to the dial peer by using the global configuration mode **destination-pattern** command. Refer to Table 7-4 for the destination patterns being used. Depending on the pod number, use one of the commands shown in the table to configure a destination pattern. Note that the period at the end of the command is part of the command. For example, on pod 1, the command would be **destination-pattern 50[3,4,5].** (with only one period at the end to designate the fourth digit).

```
RouterVoIPX(config-dial-peer)# destination-pattern number
```

Table 7-4   Dial Peer Destination Pattern

Pod	destination-pattern Command
Pod 1	**destination-pattern 50[3,4,5].**
Pod 2	**destination-pattern 50[0,1,2].**
Pod 3	**destination-pattern 51[0,1].**
Pod 4	**destination-pattern 50[6,7,8].**

Step 3.   Use the **session target ipv4:10.*x*.0.*x*** command (where the IP address is the partner pod router's serial interface address):

```
RouterVoIPX(config-dial-peer)# session target ipv4:10.x.0.x
```

Step 4.   The G711 codec is used to translate analog voice data into a digital format. Use the **codec** command to manually configure what codec is being used. This codec will be used by any call that matches this dial peer.

```
RouterVoIPX(config-dial-peer)# codec g711ulaw
```

Task 3: Test the Configuration

Step 1.   From a Cisco IP Phone on one pod, dial the four-digit extension number of one of the Cisco IP Phones in the other pod, and keep the phone call active. The phone call should be successful. Troubleshoot as necessary if the phone call fails.

Step 2.   Have the lowest-numbered pod partner slowly say aloud the numbers one through ten into the phone.

How is the voice call quality? Is it acceptable?

Step 3.   Place a second simultaneous call between the pods using the other two Cisco IP Phones. Use the four-digit extension to make the call. This forces two calls on the WAN link. Have the highest-numbered pod partner count aloud from one through ten. After the counting, remain connected.

How is the voice quality? Is it the same, better, or worse?

Step 4.   Verify the codec being used by quickly pressing the blue **i** or **?** (question mark) button twice while the calls are connected.

What does the IP Phone display to indicate the codec being used?

Step 5.   Keep talking on both calls while monitoring the call statistics output.

Were any packets lost? If so, how many?

Step 6.   Hang up both calls.

The poor audio quality occurs because you are attempting to make a G.711 call, which requires 80 kbps per call, over a WAN connection that can support only 64 kbps.

Task 4: Reconfigure the Codec

Step 1.   From global configuration mode on both pods, access the dial peer:

RouterVoIPX(config)# **dial-peer voice 6 voip**

Step 2.   The G729 codec uses an 8-kbps data rate; the G711 codec used previously uses a 64-kbps data rate. Reconfigure the codec to use the G729 codec:

RouterVoIPX(config-dial-peer)# **codec g729br8**

Step 3.   Coordinate with the partner pod to place two simultaneous calls across the WAN link by dialing the four-digit extensions. Remain connected.

How is the voice quality?

Step 4.   On the Cisco IP Phone, press the blue **i** or **?** button twice while the calls are still connected.

Are any packets lost? If so, are there more packets or fewer packets than with the previous conversation?

The voice quality is improved because G.729 requires approximately 30 kbps, which is lower than the 64 kbps allocated for WAN bandwidth.

Step 5.   Save the configuration by using the command **copy running-config startup-config**:

RouterVoIPX# **copy running-config startup-config**

CHAPTER 8

GUI and IOS Intermediate Administration

This chapter focuses on using the graphical user interface (GUI) and command-line interface (CLI) to manage the Cisco CallManager Express (CME) router and the Cisco IP Phones. For the most part, the GUI is used, but the router is constantly examined to see the results of these changes, because some of these commands are not detailed in other chapters. This is a good way for those who prefer the CLI to see some new commands and for those who prefer using the GUI to see a new method of configuration.

Web Administrators

The main administrative account used for the web-based GUI is the *System administrator*. The System administrator, by default, has access to all the web-based menus.

Another type of administrative account is the Customer administrator. The *Customer administrator* lets people such as those who work on a help desk or who are on site manage some common features on the phones.

By default, the Customer administrator account can change the same features as the System administrator. Some companies may want to limit the features available to help desk or tech support staff. The Customer administrator account can be customized to remove various functions. An example is provided later in this chapter in Lab 8-2.

Phone User Accounts

Lab 8-3 shows how to create accounts for users to allow them to manage their own phone through a web interface. This type of account is called a *phone user*. This is useful if an employee is out sick and needs to forward his or her phone to another location. Users can also create their own speed dials using this method.

ephone Versus ephone-dn

CallManager Express calls a physical IP Phone an *ephone*, which is short for Ethernet phone. A phone line associated with an ephone is called an *ephone-dn*, which is short for Ethernet phone directory number.

ephones have characteristics associated with them such as model numbers, button configuration, MAC address, speed dials, and usernames/passwords. The usernames and passwords are so that the users can manage them remotely.

ephone-dns have phone numbers associated with them. You can also see configuration features such as call forwarding and timing settings associated with them.

Blind Transfers and Consultative Transfers

Lab 8-4 deals with transferring calls. Two new terms are associated with call transfers:

- A **blind transfer** is the default. The phone that receives a transferred call cannot see the phone number from which the call was transferred—only the number where the call originated.

  Some companies do not like this default behavior. They want to know the phone number of the person who transferred the call. This would be the case if you want to receive calls transferred from your secretary, but not calls from the general switchboard.

- A **consultative transfer** is done when the transferring person either connects the caller to a ringing phone (the ringback is heard) or speaks with the third party before being allowed to connect the caller to the third phone.

Cisco CallManager Express supports configuring blind or consultative transfers on a system-wide basis. Then, this default setting for all phones that connect to the router can be overridden for individual phone lines if that configuration is desired. This setting can be done only from the router CLI, not through the web GUI.

Call Park

Lab 8-5 introduces a feature called *call park*. This feature is also called "parking a call" or "the call is parked to an extension." Call park in telephony is the ability to put a call on hold at one telephone and pick up the call from another telephone. The call is transferred to an extension number that is used for call parking.

The call park function has many uses. A common use is when a call is answered by an employee who is not the person the caller wanted to speak to. The person who answers the call can park the call and use the public address system to let the employee know that he or she has a call (and, optionally, the extension used to park the call).

Another is if a person in a small company receives a call and needs to walk to another room (such as the warehouse or a receiving/shipping area) to verify inventory or check on an order's status. The person receiving the call could park the call and then pick it up when he or she goes into the other room. A third solution is that someone takes a call in his or her office and wants the boss to hear what the caller is saying. The employee can park the call and pick it back up in the supervisor's office.

Imagine that a hardware store has multiple lines coming into the store. Not every phone in every department needs all the external phone lines assigned to the phone. Instead, the call park feature can be used. When the main office tells a department to pick up on a particular number, it could be the call park feature that is being used. As you can see, the call park feature is handy for many types of businesses.

System Message

A *system message* is used in CallManager Express to display a message on every phone. The system message can be set using the GUI or from the router CLI. The number of characters that can be used in the system message varies because the Cisco IP Phone uses a proportional font rather than a fixed font. A general rule of thumb is that approximately 30 characters (including spaces) can be used with the system message.

Intercom Feature

Cisco CME supports an intercom by creating a pair of ephone-dns that are dedicated to being used by the intercom feature. Then, the two phones can speed-dial each other and have an intercom. Two connection methods are used to create an intercom—one-way and press-to-answer.

When an intercom speed-dial button is pressed, a call is placed to the ephone-dn that is one of the dedicated pair of ephone-dns for the intercom function. The ephone-dn that is being called automatically answers the call in speakerphone mode with the mute feature activated. This provides a one-way voice path from the person who started the call to the recipient. A beep is sounded when the call is auto-answered to alert the recipient of the incoming call.

To respond to an intercom and open a two-way voice path, the person who responds to the message over the intercom system deactivates the mute function by pressing the **Mute** button (in the lower-right corner of the Cisco IP Phone).

To prevent an unauthorized phone from dialing the intercom line, you can assign both of the intercom ephone-dns a dialing string with an alphabetic character. No one can dial the alphabetic character from a normal phone, but the phone at the other end of the intercom can be configured to dial the number that contains the alphabetic character through the Cisco CME router. Look at this sample configuration:

```
ephone-dn  1   dual-line
 number 5030
 label Line 1 5030
 description Ernie's Phone
ephone-dn  2   dual-line
 number 5031
 description 5105555031
ephone-dn 12
 number A9990
 name "Intercom"
 intercom A9991
ephone-dn 13
 number A9991
 name "Intercom"
 intercom A9990
ephone  1
 username "EFriend" password cisco
 mac-address 0008.A3D2.02BA
 type 7960
 button  1f1 2:12
ephone  2
 username "CSchmidt" password cisco
 mac-address 0006.2825.DBBB
 speed-dial 1 5030 label "Ernie Friend"
 type 7960
 button  1:2 2:13
```

Notice in the sample configuration how two ephone-dns were created (ephone-dns 12 and 13) to create the intercom between two phones. The **number** command under these two ephone-dns is used to assign a virtual phone number to this intercom session. Both ephone-dns must have a virtual phone number. This virtual phone number can include an alphabetic character to prevent unauthorized access. The **intercom** command must reference the other ephone-dn's extension (including the alphabetic character).

Now look at the ephone configurations. Notice the change in the **button** commands. On the first ephone, the button type is 1:1. This means that the first button is using a feature ring. This parameter was set in Lab 3-1 (or using one of the other methods shown in Lab 3-2 or Lab 3-3). The part that must be added for the intercom is the 2:12. The **12** in the command references the ephone-dn to use. The second ephone uses 2:13 to reference the other ephone-dn that is part of the intercom.

Cisco CME supports a *dialable intercom*. This feature creates an intercom that is set to one phone such as the switchboard, a secretary, a receptionist, or security. Any employee can dial the intercom to reach the person at that phone.

Paging Group

Another useful Cisco CME feature is paging group. A *paging group* is created using an ephone-dn. This paging ephone-dn can be dialed from anywhere, including on-net (from within your own network) and off-net (from a location other than the business). The paging group feature broadcasts unicast audio paging to a single group of Cisco IP Phones that have been associated with that paging ephone-dn used for the paging group.

A paging group is useful when you have a group of people who do the same function, such as help desk staff, sales staff, a technical support group, a secretarial pool, and so on. A call sent to the paging group causes all IP Phones associated with the paging group to ring. Multiple paging groups can be created, and two or more groups can be joined into a single, combined group.

Modifying the Customer Administrator Account with XML

You customize the Customer administrator account by modifying the XML template file and saving it with a new name. The new filename must have .xml as the filename extension. To change the settings, the XML file is downloaded from the router flash memory, modified, renamed, and then uploaded to the router flash memory. A command is issued to let the router know to use the customized file.

In the XML template, each line that starts with a title enclosed in angle brackets describes an XML object. For example, <AddExtension> refers to the Add Extension capability through the web interface. Here's a sample XML template:

```
<Presentation>
  <MainMenu>
      <!-- Take Higher Precedence over CLI "dn-wed-edit" -->
      <AddExtension> [Hide | Show] </AddExtension>
      <DeleteExtension> [Hide | Show] </DeleteExtension>
      <AddPhone> [Hide | Show] </AddPhone>
      <DeletePhone> [Hide | Show] </DeletePhone>
  </MainMenu>
  <Extension>
      <!-- Control both view and change, and possible add or delete -->
      <SequenceNumber> [Hide | Show] </SequenceNumber>
      <Type> [Hide | Show] </Type>
      <Huntstop> [Hide | Show] </Huntstop>
      <Preference> [Hide | Show] </Preference>
      <HoldAlert> [Hide | Show] </HoldAlert>
```

```
        <TranslationRules> [Hide | Show] </TranslationRules>
        <Paging> [Hide | Show] </Paging>
        <Intercom> [Hide | Show] </Intercom>
        <MWI> [Hide | Show] </MWI>
        <MoH> [Hide | Show] </MoH>
        <LBDN> [Hide | Show] </LBDN>
        <DualLine> [Hide | Show] </DualLine>
        <Reg> [Hide | Show] </Reg>
        <PGroup> [Hide | Show] </PGroup>
        <CallPark> [Hide | Show] </CallPark>
        <CFNA> [Hide | Show] </CFNA>
        <CFB> [Hide | Show] </CFB>
        <CFA> [Hide | Show] </CFA>
        <Label> [Hide | Show] </Label>
        <SecondaryN attr=[Both | Change]> [Hide | Show] </SecondaryN>
        <Overlay> [Hide | Show] </Overlay>
    </Extension>
    <Phone>
        <!-- control both view and change, and possible add and delete --->
        <SequenceNumber> [Hide | Show] </SequenceNumber>
        <CallBlockExpt> [Hide | Show] </CallBlockExpt>
        <AutoLineSel> [Hide | Show] </AutoLineSel>
        <LoginPin> [Hide | Show] </LoginPin>
        <RecNightBell> [Hide | Show] </RecNightBell>
        <ExtAssign> [Hide | Show] </ExtAssign>
    </Phone>
    <System>
        <!-- Control View Only -->
        <PhoneURL> [Hide | Show] </PhoneURL>
        <PhoneLoad> [Hide | Show]</PhoneLoad>
        <CallHistory> [Hide | Show] </CallHistory>
        <MWIServer> [Hide | Show] </MWIServer>

        <!-- Control Either View and Change or Change Only -->
        <TransferPattern attr=[Both | Change]> [Hide | Show] </TransferPattern>
        <VoiceMailNumber attr=[Both | Change]> [Hide | Show] </VoiceMailNumber>
        <MaxNumberPhone attr=[Both | Change]> [Hide | Show] </MaxNumberPhone>
        <DialplanPattern attr=[Both | Change]> [Hide | Show] </DialplanPattern>
        <SecDialTone attr=[Both | Change]> [Hide | Show] </SecDialTone>
        <Timeouts attr=[Both | Change]> [Hide | Show] </Timeouts>
        <CallBlock attr=[Both | Change]> [Hide | Show] </CallBlock>
        <HuntGroup attr=[Both | Change]> [Hide | Show] </HuntGroup>
        <NightSerBell attr=[Both | Change]> [Hide | Show] </NightSerBell>
        <DateTime attr=[Both | Change]> [Hide | Show] </DateTime>
        <DirService attr=[Both | Change]> [Hide | Show] </DirService>
        <ExtLoginClr attr=[Both | Change]> [Hide | Show] </ExtLoginClr>
        <SysMessage attr=[Both | Change]> [Hide | Show] </SysMessage>
```

```
      <MoHFile attr=[Both | Change]> [Hide | Show] </MoHFile>
      <!-- Control Change Only -->
      <!-- Take Higher Precedence over CLI "time-web-edit" -->
      <Time> [Hide | Show] </Time>
    </System>
    <Function>
      <AddLineToPhone> [No | Yes] </AddLineToPhone>
      <DeleteLineFromPhone> [No | Yes] </DeleteLineFromPhone>
      <NewDnDpCheck> [No | Yes] </DpDnCrossCheck>
      <MaxLinePerPhone> [1-6] </MaxLinePerPhone>
    </Function>
  </Presentation>
```

For each object in the template, you have a choice of actions; the choices appear in brackets. For example, some choices appear as [Hide | Show] or as [No | Yes]. The choice is what is shown to a Customer administrator when he or she logs into the GUI interface. Delete the action that you do not want, as well as the vertical bar and brackets around the actions. You must make a choice for each object. The following sample configuration file shows where the Add Extension option will be hidden from the main menu and the Type and Paging options will be removed from the Extension menu:

```
<Presentation>
  <MainMenu>
      <!-- Take Higher Precedence over CLI "dn-wed-edit" -->
      <AddExtension> Hide </AddExtension>
      <DeleteExtension> Show </DeleteExtension>
      <AddPhone> Show </AddPhone>
      <DeletePhone> Show </DeletePhone>
  </MainMenu>
  <Extension>
      <!-- Control both view and change, and possible add or delete -->
      <SequenceNumber> Show </SequenceNumber>
      <Type> Hide </Type>
      <Huntstop> Show </Huntstop>
      <Preference> Show </Preference>
      <HoldAlert> Show </HoldAlert>
      <TranslationRules> Show </TranslationRules>
      <Paging> Hide </Paging>
      <Intercom> Hide </Intercom>
      <MWI> Show </MWI>
      <MoH> Show </MoH>
      <LBDN> Show </LBDN>
      <DualLine> Show </DualLine>
      <Reg> Show </Reg>
      <PGroup> Show </PGroup>
      <CallPark> Show </CallPark>
      <CFNA> Show </CFNA>
      <CFB> Show </CFB>
      <CFA> Show </CFA>
```

```
            <Label> Show </Label>
            <SecondaryN attr=Both> Show </SecondaryN>
            <Overlay> Show </Overlay>
    </Extension>
    <Phone>
        <!-- control both view and change, and possible add and delete --->
        <SequenceNumber> Show </SequenceNumber>
        <CallBlockExpt> Show </CallBlockExpt>
        <AutoLineSel> Show </AutoLineSel>
        <LoginPin> Show </LoginPin>
        <RecNightBell> Show </RecNightBell>
        <ExtAssign> Show </ExtAssign>
    </Phone>
    <System>
        <!-- Control View Only -->
        <PhoneURL> Show </PhoneURL>
        <PhoneLoad> Show</PhoneLoad>
        <CallHistory> Show </CallHistory>
        <MWIServer> Show </MWIServer>

        <!-- Control Either View and Change or Change Only -->
        <TransferPattern attr=Both> Show </TransferPattern>
        <VoiceMailNumber attr=Both> Show </VoiceMailNumber>
        <MaxNumberPhone attr=Both> Show </MaxNumberPhone>
        <DialplanPattern attr=Both> Show </DialplanPattern>
        <SecDialTone attr=Both> Show </SecDialTone>
        <Timeouts attr=Both> Show </Timeouts>
        <CallBlock attr=Both> Show </CallBlock>
        <HuntGroup attr=Both> Show </HuntGroup>
        <NightSerBell attr=Both> Show </NightSerBell>
        <DateTime attr=Both> Show </DateTime>
        <DirService attr=Both> Show </DirService>
        <ExtLoginClr attr=Both> Show </ExtLoginClr>
        <SysMessage attr=Both> Show </SysMessage>
        <MoHFile attr=Both> Show </MoHFile>
        <!-- Control Change Only -->
        <!-- Take Higher Precedence over CLI "time-web-edit" -->
        <Time> Show </Time>
    </System>
    <Function>
        <AddLineToPhone> Yes </AddLineToPhone>
        <DeleteLineFromPhone> Yes </DeleteLineFromPhone>
        <NewDnDpCheck> Yes </DpDnCrossCheck>
        <MaxLinePerPhone> 6 </MaxLinePerPhone>
    </Function>
</Presentation>
```

Lab 8-1: Configure the GUI for the System Administrator

In this lab, the company OCSIC.org wants to use a web-based GUI instead of the router CLI for Cisco IP Phone adds, moves, and changes. Currently the GUI is not installed or configured.

Note: This lab relies on the two IP Phones being able to connect to one another *before* you start this lab.

The objectives of this lab are as follows:

- Install the Cisco IOS files that are necessary for GUI administration.

- Configure and use the GUI System administrator interface to configure Cisco IP Phones.

To perform this lab, you need the following equipment:

- Cisco CME-capable router

- Appropriate .tar file obtained from the instructor and/or Cisco.com and loaded on the router

- Switch/switch module

- Workstation with an Ethernet 10/100 network interface card (NIC) installed

- Two Cisco IP Phones (powered using any method)

- TFTP server application

Figure 8-1 shows the topology used for this lab. Keep in mind that an integrated switch module in the router could be used instead of the external switch.

Figure 8-1   Lab Topology: GUI Administration

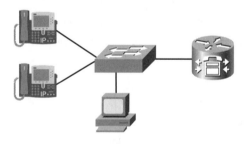

The procedure for this lab consists of the following tasks, described in detail in the following sections:

- **Task 1**—Install the GUI Cisco IOS files.

- **Task 2**—Configure the GUI.

- **Task 3**—Configure a speed dial.

- **Task 4**—Configure the system time.

Task 1: Install the GUI Cisco IOS Files

Step 1.   Power on the router and the external switch if it is being used. The router and switch/switch module should be configured with the basic configuration. The IP Phones should be plugged into the switch and configured with a basic configuration. From one Cisco IP Phone, call the other IP Phone. The call should succeed. Do not proceed until the IP Phones are configured.

Step 2.   From privileged mode, use the **show flash:** command to verify that the Cisco IOS files to perform GUI phone administration are present. The files have the .html extension. Some common
ones are admin_user.html, ephone_admin.html, and telephony_service.html. These files are
extracted from a file that begins with the letters cme-gui; they have a file extension of .tar. An
example of the filename is cme-gui-123-11T.tar.

```
RouterVoIPX# show flash:
```

Some routers come with the correct .tar file loaded in flash, but the HTML files still have to be
extracted.

If the files are not present, you must download a file from Cisco.com and have a Cisco CCO
account to access the file needed. The filename begins with the letters cme-gui and has a file
extension of .tar. An example of a filename is cme-gui-123-11T.tar. At press time, the URL for
this is www.cisco.com/cgi-bin/tablebuild.pl/ip-iostsp. On the Cisco home page, point to
Products & Solutions, followed by Voice and Unified Communications. Click the IP Telephony
option. From the Product Portfolio section, select the Cisco Unified IP Phones 7900 Series
link. In the Technical Documentation & Tools section, select Download Software. Select Cisco
IOS Software on the resulting page, and select Voice Software from the menu on the left bar.
Select the CCME/SRST link (Cisco CallManager Express/Survivable Remote Site Telephony).
In the Select a File to Download section, select a link that matches the IOS already loaded on
the CME router.

Note: The .tar IOS file *must* match the IOS version on the CME router.

Some older versions of the IOS do not combine these GUI administration files into a separate .tar file.

Step 3.   After they are downloaded, the GUI administration files must be extracted from the .tar file and
uploaded to the router flash memory using a TFTP server application or just extracted from the
.tar file that is already located in memory.

If you downloaded the .tar file, copy the file into the appropriate TFTP server folder. Ensure
that the PC connects to the router via Ethernet, is on the same network, has a proper IP address
and default gateway as the Ethernet port on the router, and has the TFTP server application
active. Ensure that the PC can ping the router before attempting the next step.

If the files are already extracted in flash memory, you can skip this step and the next one.

Step 4.   The **archive** command is used to extract the .tar files to the router. This command is used in
two cases:

- The files are on a PC in the TFTP folder. The **archive** command is used to extract the
  HTML files to flash memory on the router. This is the first command shown.

  ```
  RouterVoIPX# archive tar /xtract tftp://tftp_server_ip_address/filename flash:
  ```

- *tftp_server_ip_address* is the IP address of the PC that holds the .tar file and is functioning
  as the TFTP server. The *filename* parameter is the name of the file that starts with the letters
  cme-gui and has an extension of .tar.

- Here's an example:

  ```
  RouterVoIPX# archive tar /xtract tftp://10.20.0.33/cme-gui-123-11T.tar flash:
  ```

- If the .tar file is already in flash memory on the router, the HTML files can be extracted
  using the following command:

  ```
  RouterVoIPX# archive tar /xtract filename flash:
  ```

- The *filename* parameter is the name of the file that starts with the letters cme-gui and has an
  extension of .tar.

- A successful extraction shows an output similar to the following:

```
RouterVoIPX# archive tar /xtract cme-gui-123-11T.tar flash:
Loading cme-gui-123-11T.tar from 10.3.0.33 (via GigabitEthernet0/0.3): !
extracting CiscoLogo.gif (1602 bytes)
extracting Delete.gif (953 bytes)
extracting Plus.gif (1347 bytes)!
extracting Tab.gif (174 bytes)
extracting admin_user.html (3845 bytes)!
extracting admin_user.js (641134 bytes) !!!!!!!!!!!!!!!!!!!!!!!!!!!!!!!!!!!!!!!!!!
!!!!!!!!!!!!!!!!!!!!!!!!!!!!!!!!!!!!!!!!!!!!!!!!!!!!!!!!!!!!!!!!!!!!!!!!!!!!!!!!!!!!!
!!!!
extracting dom.js (16344 bytes)!!!!
extracting downarrow.gif (864 bytes)
extracting ephone_admin.html (6146 bytes)!
extracting logohome.gif (4658 bytes)!
extracting normal_user.html (3724 bytes)!
extracting normal_user.js (76732 bytes)!!!!!!!!!!!!!!!!
extracting sxiconad.gif (843 bytes)!
extracting telephony_service.html (2357 bytes)
extracting uparrow.gif (870 bytes)!
extracting xml-test.html (9968 bytes)!!
extracting xml.template (3311 bytes)!
[OK - 788992 bytes]
```

Do not proceed until the files have been successfully extracted. Use the **show flash:** command as necessary.

Task 2: Configure the GUI

Step 1.   The CME GUI allows administrators to configure Cisco IP Phones using the web interface rather than a router console or Telnet connection. The HTTP service must be enabled on the router to allow web connectivity:

```
RouterVoIPX(config)# ip http server
```

Step 2.   The **ip http path** command defines the location of the HTML files. In this case, the HTML files are located in the router's flash memory:

```
RouterVoIPX(config)# ip http path flash:
```

Step 3.   The **ip http authentication** command defines what userid and password are used when a web connection is being made. Without this command, the default authentication is the **enable secret** command on the router. In Step 5, you define a username and password to be used with the web interface.

```
RouterVoIPX(config)# ip http authentication local
```

Step 4.   Move to telephony service configuration mode:

```
RouterVoIPX(config)# telephony-service
```

Step 5.   Define a userid and password to be used when performing web-based configurations. Later, when performing web-based access, use the userid of **webadmin** and a password of **cisco**:

```
RouterVoIPX(config-telephony)# web admin system name webadmin password cisco
```

Step 6.   The **dn-webedit** command allows directory number changes to be made via the web interface:

```
RouterVoIPX(config-telephony)# dn-webedit
```

Step 7.   The **time-webedit** command allows the Cisco CallManager Express time to be configured through the web interface:

```
RouterVoIPX(config-telephony)# time-webedit
```

The only changes that can now be made through the web interface are directory number changes and time changes because of the commands that have been entered.

Step 8.   Return to privileged mode and save the router configuration:

```
RouterVoIPX# copy running-config startup-config
```

Task 3: Configure a Speed Dial

Step 1.   A PC is needed to access the CMI GUI. The PC must do one of the following:

- Connect to a switch/switch module port that has been configured for access mode and the Data VLAN (*X*0, where *X* is the pod number).
- Connect to the 10/100 PC port on one of the Cisco IP Phones.

    In either case, the PC needs to be configured with an IP address on the Data VLAN. This can be done through a DHCP pool for the Data VLAN configured on the CME router or by manually assigning an IP address to the PC. Table 8-1 shows the Data VLAN IP addressing scheme.

Table 8-1   IP Addressing Scheme for the Data VLAN

Pod	Hostname of Router or Switch	Router Ethernet IP Address	VLAN Type
Pod 1	RouterVoIP1	10.10.0.1/24	Data
Pod 2	RouterVoIP2	10.20.0.1/24	Data
Pod 3	RouterVoIP3	10.30.0.1/24	Data
Pod 4	RouterVoIP4	10.40.0.1/24	Data

Step 2.   From the PC, ping the Ethernet IP address on the router (the PC default gateway) that has been assigned. Do not proceed unless the ping succeeds.

Step 3.   From the PC, open a web browser, and enter the following URL:

```
http://10.X0.0.1/ccme.html
```

The *X* in the command is the pod number that is being used.

A username and password prompt appear.

Step 4.   Attempt to log in using a blank username and the enable secret password. This attempt should fail because of the use of the **ip http authentication local** command.

Attempt to log in using the username of **webadmin** and a password of **cisco**. The CCME web interface should appear, as shown in Figure 8-2.

Figure 8-2   CCME Web Interface

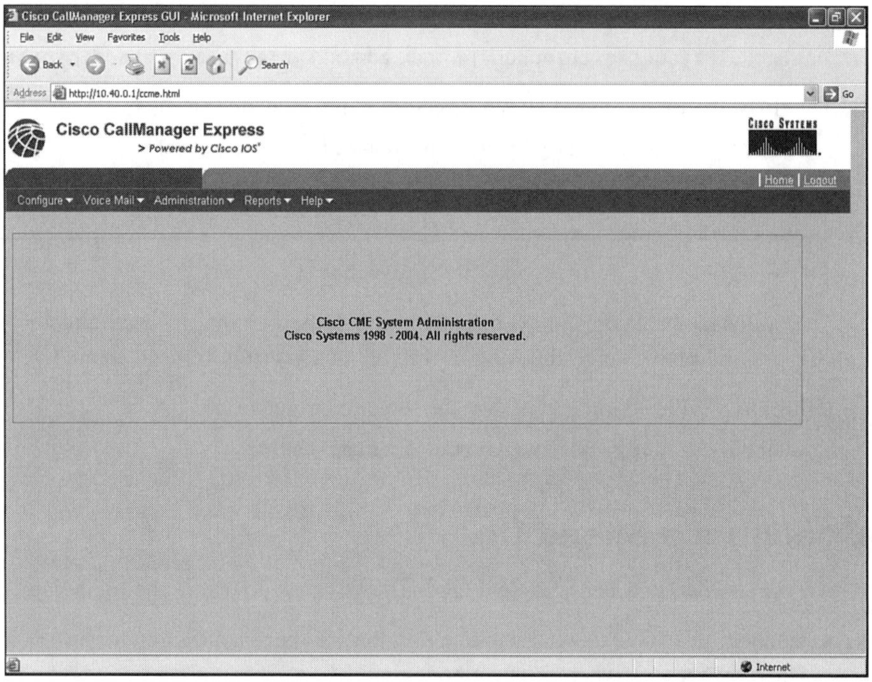

Step 5.   From the **Configure** menu option, select **Extensions**. At least two currently configured extensions should appear on the screen. If no extensions appear, the Cisco IP Phones have not been configured properly. Troubleshoot the phones and start this lab over.

Step 6.   From the **Configure** menu option, select **Phones**. The two configured Cisco IP Phones should be listed. If none is listed, the phones are not configured correctly. Start this lab over and connect and configure the phones properly.

Step 7.   In the Phone Physical ID (Mac Address) column, click the first MAC address listed. The MAC address is a link and therefore is underlined. The phone line buttons appear in a separate window in a table. Note that you might need to enable popups through your browser to see this window. Also, you might have to change security settings to a lower setting to perform these steps.

The number of buttons that appear on the screen should correspond to the correct number of buttons located to the right of the Cisco IP Phone's LCD display.

Note: If you click the MAC address and a window opens but nothing appears in the window, you might need to download a more recent version of the cme-gui .tar file.

Step 8.   Notice how the first button on the phone lists the Cisco IP Phone's own four-digit extension number. In this step, you create a speed dial button for the other Cisco IP Phone. For example, if the current phone has an extension of 5030, the speed dial number that will be used in this step will probably be 5031 for the other IP Phone.

Scroll down to locate the Speed Dial Information section. In the Speed Dial 1 textbox, enter the four-digit extension of the *other* Cisco IP Phone.

In the Label textbox, enter a name or description that will appear beside the speed dial button.

Step 9.   Click the **Change** button at the bottom of the screen. When you're asked whether you want to save the changes, click **OK**. In the message that appears on the screen, click the **OK** button to clear the message. The Cisco IP Phone reboots and appears with the changes.

Step 10.   Verify the changes on the Cisco IP Phone. Use the speed dial button by simply pressing the second button on the IP Phone that had the speed dial created. The second phone should ring immediately. Troubleshoot as necessary.

Task 4: Configure the System Time

Step 1.   From the **Configure** menu, select **System Parameters**. Use the **System Time** option to change the date or time to a different time than is currently defined, as shown in Figure 8-3. Notice that the current time is the computer's time, not the router's. Click the **Set** button to use the currently configured settings. Click **OK** to save the changes, and click **OK** again to acknowledge the save.

Figure 8-3   **CCME Web Interface: System Time**

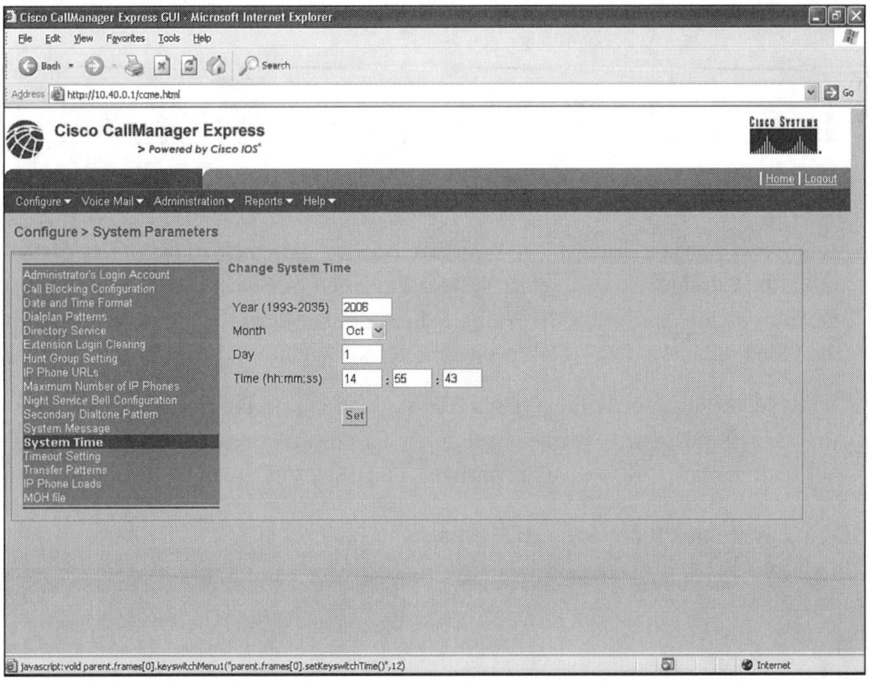

Step 2.   Select the **Date and Time Format** option from the left column. Change the format to a different selection. Click the **Set** button. Click **OK** to save the changes. Click **OK** again to acknowledge the save.

Step 3.   Reset the two IP Phones by selecting the **Configure** menu option and then **Phones**. Use the **Reset All** link, shown in Figure 8-4, to reset both phones. Click **OK** to reset the phones. Click **OK** again to acknowledge the save.

Figure 8-4   CCME Web Interface: Phones Reset All Link

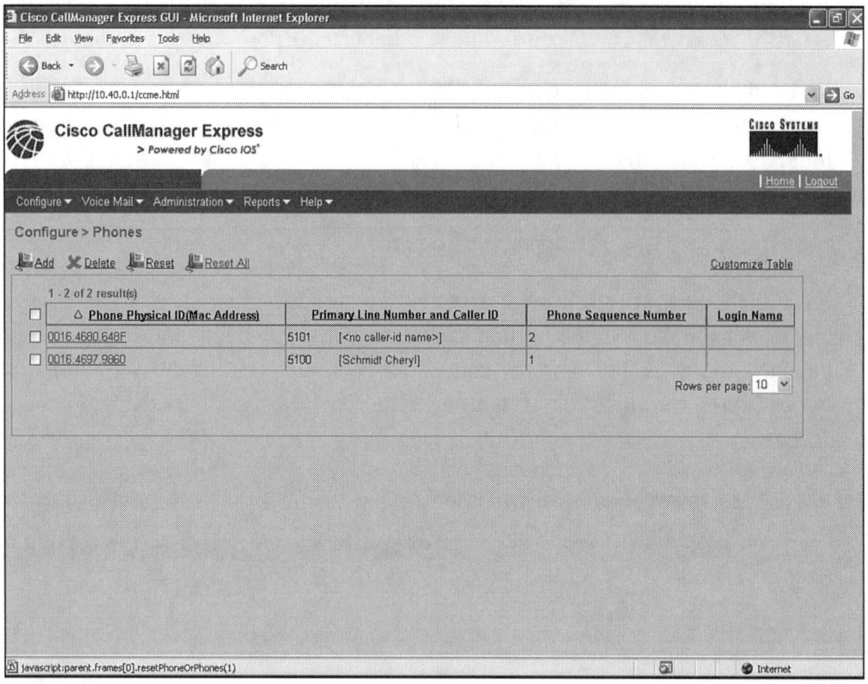

Step 4.   View the changes as they occur on the Cisco IP Phones as the phones reboot. Notice the change in the time format on the phones.

Step 5.   From the **Configure** menu, select **System Parameters**. Select the **Directory Service** option from the left column, and select the **Name Schema** link. Select the other name schema option. Click the **Change** button. Click **OK** to save the changes. Click **OK** again to acknowledge the change.

Step 6.   In the left column, click the **System Message** option. In the System Message textbox, enter a short message that will be displayed on the Cisco IP Phones, as shown in Figure 8-5. Click the **Set** button, click **OK** to save the changes, and click **OK** again to acknowledge the save.

Figure 8-5   CCME Web Interface: System Message

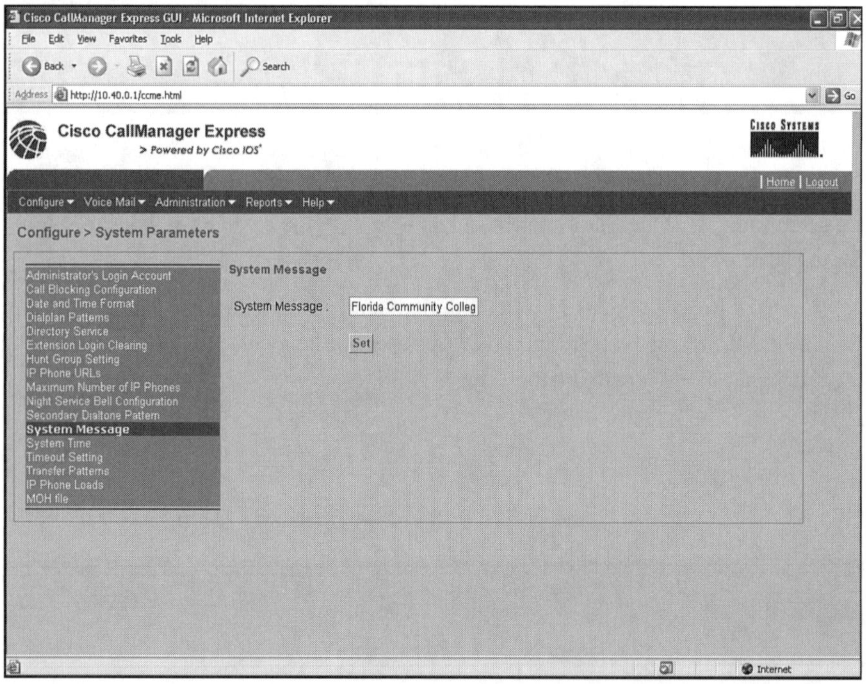

Notice the change on the Cisco IP Phones.

When might a System administrator use this option?

Step 7.   Log out of the GUI web administration page by clicking the **Logout** link in the upper-right portion of the window.

From the router CLI, look at how the GUI changes are converted into commands by looking at the running configuration.

How did your configuration change?

Step 8.   Save the router configuration:

```
RouterVoIPX# copy running-config startup-config
```

Lab 8-2: Configure the GUI for the Customer Administrator

In this lab, OCSIC.org wants an administrative assistant to be able to perform a subset of the tasks that the System administrator can perform in the GUI web interface. The Customer administrator feature in CallManager Express can be used for this function.

Note: This lab relies on the two IP Phones being able to connect to one another *before* you start this lab. Also, the PC should be able to access the CME GUI Administrator (http://10.*X*0.0.1/ccme.html) before you start this lab. Repeat Lab 8-1 if the PC cannot browse to this address.

The objective of this lab is to configure and use the GUI for the Customer administrator.

To perform this lab, you need the following equipment:

■ CME-capable router

■ Switch/switch module

■ Workstation with an Ethernet 10/100 NIC installed

■ Two Cisco IP Phones (powered using any method)

■ TFTP server application

Figure 8-6 shows the topology used for this lab. Keep in mind that an integrated switch module in the router could be used instead of the external switch.

Figure 8-6   Lab Topology: Customer Administrator GUI Administration

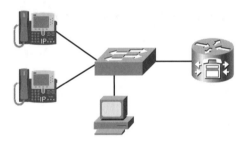

The procedure for this lab consists of the following tasks, described in detail in the following sections:

■ **Task 1**—Create a customer GUI administrator.

■ **Task 2**—Review changes to the router configuration.

■ **Task 3**—Test the new account.

■ **Task 4**—Optionally, modify the new account.

■ **Task 5**—Optionally, test the modified account.

Task 1: Create a Customer GUI Administrator

Step 1. Ensure that the two Cisco IP Phones connected to the CME router can call one another. If they cannot, troubleshoot as necessary.

Ensure that the PC can ping the router Data VLAN interface (10.X0.0.1, where X is the pod number) and can access the CME GUI Administrator (http://10.X0.0.1/ccme.html). Repeat Lab 8-1 and troubleshoot as necessary if connectivity is an issue.

Step 2. Open the web browser on the student PC, and enter the URL of **http://10.X0.0.1/ccme.html** (where X is the pod number). Use **webadmin** for the username and **cisco** for the password. This gives you access to the GUI as the System administrator.

Step 3. From the **Configure** menu, select **System Parameters**. Ensure that the Administrator's Login Account option (the first menu option on the left) is selected, as shown in Figure 8-7.

Figure 8-7   **System Parameters: Administrator's Login Account**

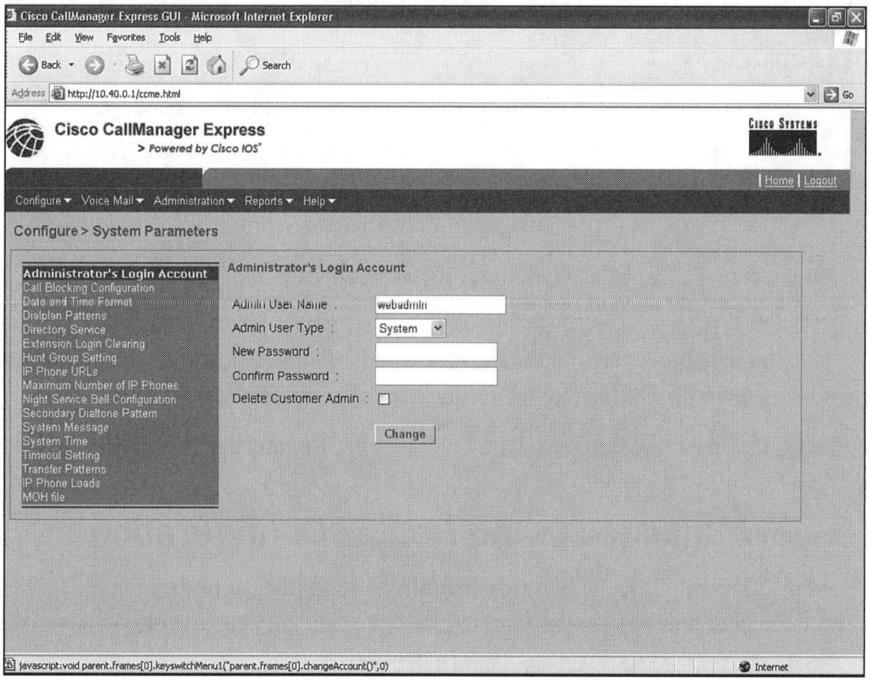

The list on the left of this window shows all the features that can be set by the System administrator account. How many options are available for the System administrator account?

Step 4. In the Admin User Type box, select **Customer**, as shown in Figure 8-8. In the Admin User Name textbox, enter **webcust**. Note that usernames are case-sensitive in Call Manager Express.

Figure 8-8   System Parameters: Customer Account

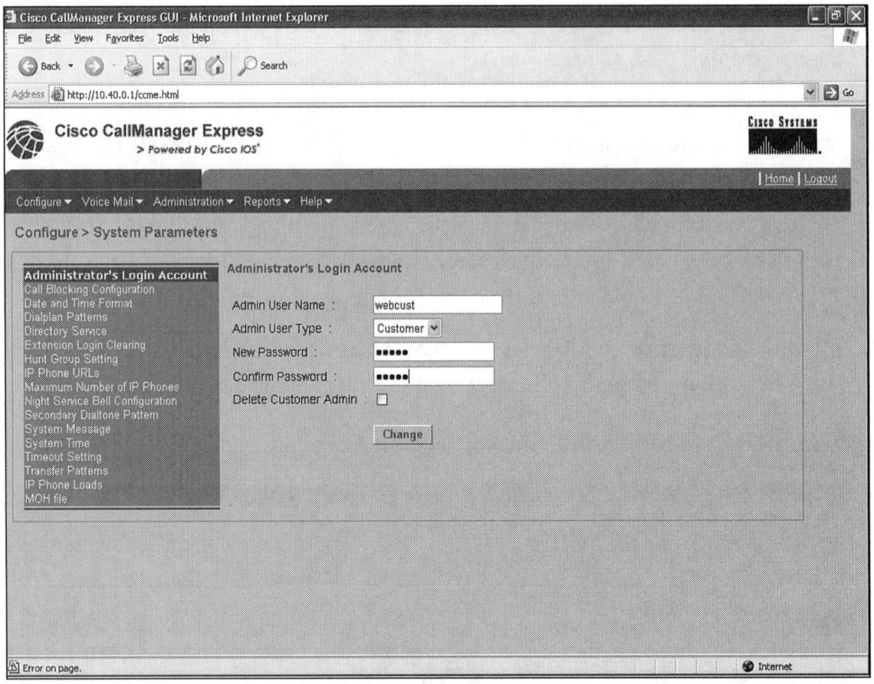

Set the New Password and Confirm Password to **cisco** in both textboxes. Passwords are also case-sensitive.

Step 5.   Click the **Change** button and select **OK** when asked to confirm the change. A confirmation window pops up, stating that the change has been implemented. Click **OK**.

Step 6.   Log out of the CallManager GUI by clicking the **Logout** link in the upper-right corner.

Task 2: Review Changes to the Router Configuration

Step 1.   From the router CLI, use the **show running-config | begin tele** command to view the changes to the configuration:

```
RouterVoIPX# show running-config | begin tele
```

What changes to the router configuration are evident?

_____

_____

Task 3: Test the New Account

Step 1.   Return to the GUI CME web page by entering the URL **http://10.X0.0.1/ccme.html** (where *X* is the pod number) in a web browser.

Step 2.   When prompted for a username and password, use the newly created Customer administrator account (**webcust** for the username and **cisco** for the password).

Step 3.   From the **Configure** menu, select **System Parameters**.

How many System Parameters options are available for the Customer administrator account?

Step 4. Note that by default, the Customer administrator and System administrator have the same level of access. Log out of the CallManager GUI by clicking the **Logout** link in the upper-right corner.

Task 4: Optionally, Modify the New Account

Step 1. Return to the router CLI. Use the **show flash:** command to verify that a file called xml. template exists. This file is used and modified to limit the Customer administrator account.

```
RouterVoIPX# show flash:
```

Step 2. On the PC that has access to the web interface, start the TFTP server application.

Step 3. From privileged mode on the router, copy the xml.template file from flash memory to the PC:

```
RouterVoIPX# copy flash:xml.template tftp:
```

At the Address or name of remote host prompt, enter the IP address of the PC with the TFTP server application.

At the Destination filename prompt, press **Enter** to accept the default.

The transfer should be successful. Troubleshoot as necessary until the file is transferred to the local PC. Note that the file is copied to the default folder for the TFTP server.

Step 4. Using a text editor such as Word, open the downloaded file, called xml.template.

Step 5. Modify the template using the parameters explained at the beginning of this chapter, or use the example given that hides the Add extension option from the main menu as well as the Type and Paging options from the Extension window. Be sure to make a choice for all objects in the template.

Step 6. Save the modified template with a new name. The file must have an extension of .xml. One way to accomplish this task is to save the file with a new name, such as custxml. The text editor will want to add an extension such as .txt or .doc. This is fine. Save the file again with another new name, such as custxml2.txt. Use Explorer to rename custxml2.txt to custxml.xml.

Step 7. Copy the modified file with the .xml extension to the TFTP application's default folder.

Step 8. From privileged mode on the router, use the **copy** command to upload the file to the router:

```
RouterVoIPX# copy tftp: flash:
```

When prompted for the address or name of the remote host, enter the PC's IP address with the TFTP server application.

When prompted for the source filename, enter the name of the modified file that has a file extension of .xml.

When prompted for the destination filename, press **Enter** to accept the default of using the same name.

Step 9. Ensure that the file transfers into flash memory on the router.

Step 10. Move to telephony service configuration mode on the router:

```
RouterVoIPX(config)# telephony-service
```

Step 11. The **web customize load** command is used to specify the new XML file to be used with the Customer administrator when using the GUI interface. The *filename* parameter is the name of the file transferred to flash from the TFTP server.

```
RouterVoIPX(config-telephony)# web customize load filename.xml
```

Step 12. Save the router configuration:

```
RouterVoIPX# copy running-config startup-config
```

Task 5: Optionally, Test the Modified Account

Step 1.   From the PC, access the CME GUI interface using the following URL, where *X* is the pod number being used:

`http://10.X0.0.1/ccme.html`

Note: If the web interface does not appear, the XML file is probably not formatted correctly. Modify the XML file again, and reload it to flash memory on the router. Otherwise, from the telephony-service configuration mode on the router, simply remove the **web customize load** command.

Step 2.   Log in as the Customer administrator. The userid is **webcust** and the password is **cisco**.

Step 3.   Click various options to see how the menu options have changed based on the changes to the XML file.

Step 4.   Log out of the web interface by clicking the **Logout** link in the upper-right corner.

Lab 8-3: Configure the GUI for the Phone User

In this lab, OCSIC.org needs to configure user credentials so that the users can change some settings on their assigned phones through the GUI web interface. Configure two users and test their levels of access.

Note: This lab relies on the two IP Phones being able to connect to one another *before* you start this lab. Also, the PC should be able to access the CME GUI Administrator (http://10.X0.0.1/ccme.html) before you start this lab. Troubleshoot as necessary.

The objectives of this lab are as follows:

- Configure the GUI for Phone users.

- Manage the Cisco IP Phone using the Phone user account.

To perform this lab, you need the following equipment:

- CME-capable router

- Switch/switch module

- Workstation with an Ethernet 10/100 NIC installed

- Two Cisco IP Phones (powered using any method)

Figure 8-9 shows the topology used for this lab. Keep in mind that an integrated switch module in the router could be used instead of the external switch.

Figure 8-9   Lab Topology: Phone User GUI Administration

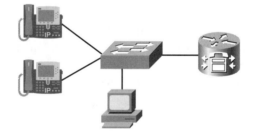

The procedure for this lab consists of the following tasks, described in detail in the following sections:

- **Task 1**—Create a Phone user account.

- **Task 2**—Manage the IP Phone using a Phone user account.

Task 1: Create a Phone User Account

Step 1.   From the PC, access the CME GUI using the following URL, where *X* is the pod number being used:

`http://10.X0.0.1/ccme.html`

Step 2.   Log in as the System administrator using the userid **webadmin** and a password of **cisco**.

Step 3.   From the **Configure** menu, select the **Phones** option. Figure 8-10 shows that the second MAC address is the one that has the Phone Sequence Number of 1 on this CME router.

Figure 8-10   Configure Phones Menu Option

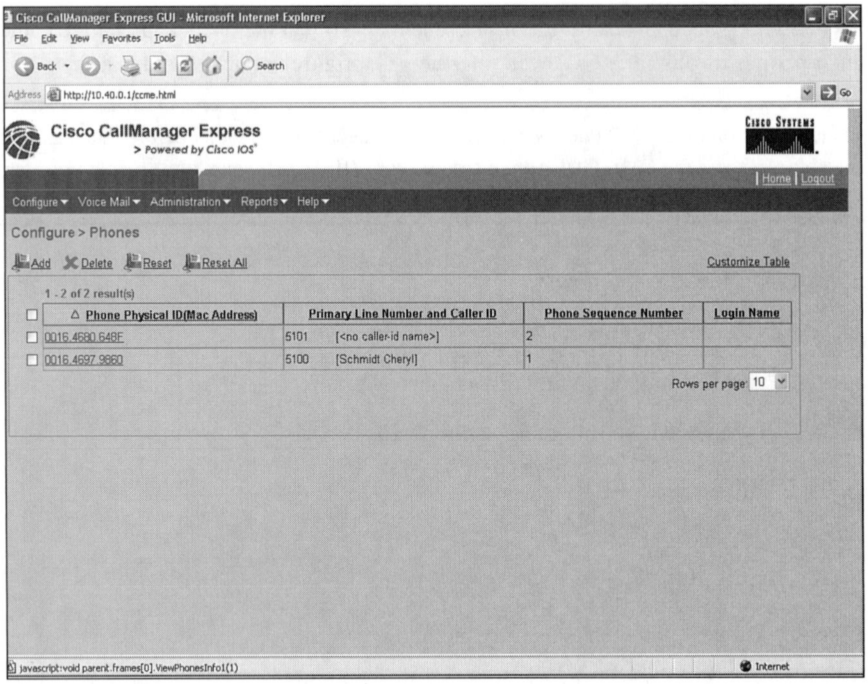

Locate the Phone Sequence Number column. Select the link for the IP Phone with a sequence number of 1 by clicking the MAC address of that phone located in the first column (Phone Physical ID) of that same row. You might need to disable popup blocking to access this site.

Step 4.   Scroll to the Login Account section. In the Login Username textbox, add a username of **EFriend** and a password of **cisco**. Reenter the password in the Re-enter Password textbox. Note that the username and password are case-sensitive. Click the **Change** button. When prompted to save the change, click **OK**. When the confirmation message appears, click **OK**.

Step 5.   From the **Administration** menu, select **Save Router Config**. When prompted to save the change, click the **OK** button.

A message may appear that the change is delayed because a Telnet session is active. This occurs only when a HyperTerminal session is active at the same time as a web session. Whether or not this message is displayed, proceed to the next step.

At the confirmation message that the router configuration was saved, click **OK**.

Step 6.   Log out of the GUI web interface by clicking the **Logout** link in the upper-right portion of the screen.

Step 7.   From the router CLI privileged mode, view the changes made through the GUI web interface:

```
RouterVoIPX# show running-config | begin ephone
```

Which ephone has the additional commands?

_____

_____

What commands have been added?

_____

_____

Step 8. From global configuration mode, use the command **ephone 2** to enter ephone configuration mode:

```
RouterVoIPX(config)# ephone 2
```

Step 9. Enter the command **username CSchmidt password cisco** to configure a phone user for the second phone:

```
RouterVoIPX(config-ephone)# username CSchmidt password cisco
```

Step 10. View the changes and notice how the router automatically encloses the username in quotation marks.

Step 11. Save the router changes:

```
RouterVoIPX# copy running-config startup-config
```

Task 2: Manage the IP Phone Using a Phone User Account

Step 1. From the PC, open a web browser and enter the following URL, where *X* is the pod number:

```
http://10.X0.0.1/ccme.html
```

Authenticate with the **EFriend** account and a password of **cisco**. Notice that the userid and password are case-sensitive in Cisco CME web administration.

Step 2. Point to the **Configure** menu. Figure 8-11 shows the option available to a Phone user.

Figure 8-11   Phone User Account: Configure Option

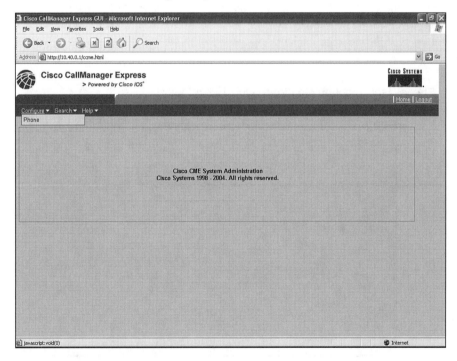

What is different from the other web accounts that have been used thus far?

_____

_____

Step 3. From the Configure menu, choose the **Phone** option. Figure 8-12 shows the Phone configuration window.

Figure 8-12   Phone User Account: Phone Window

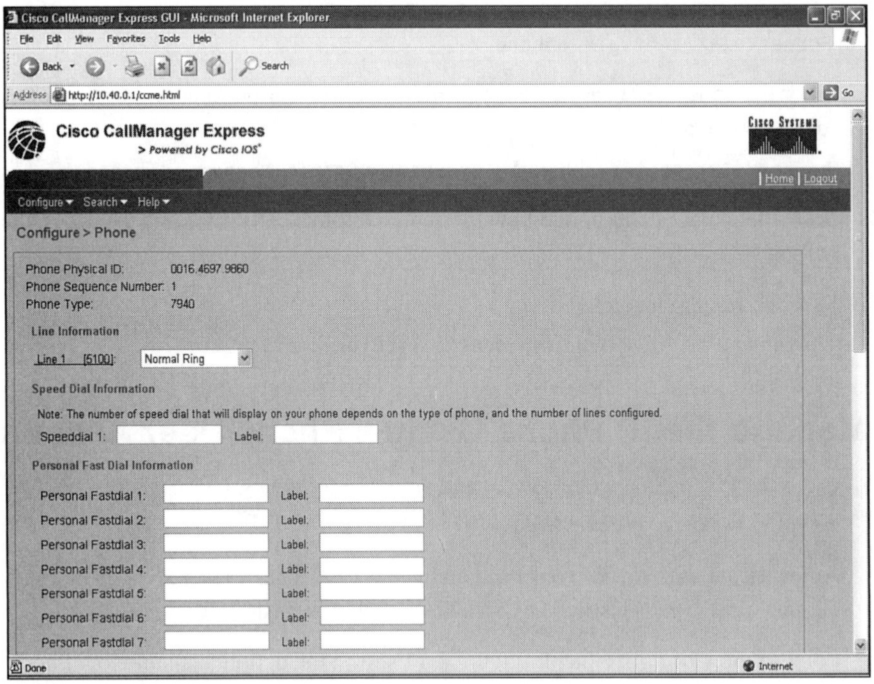

Does the system allow any phone except this phone to be configured?

Step 4.   In the Line Information section, click the **Line 1** link. Figure 8-13 shows the resulting window.

Figure 8-13   Phone User Account: Configure Line 1 Window

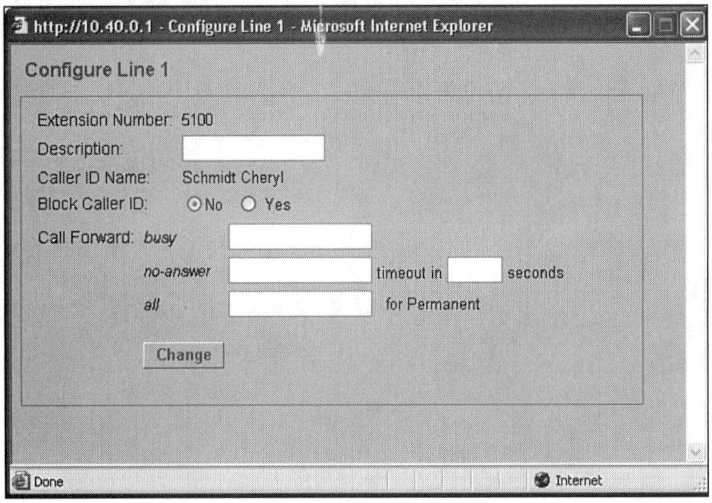

Step 5.   In the no-answer textbox, enter the other Cisco IP Phone's extension number so that any calls to this phone are forwarded to the other phone.

Step 6.   In the timeout in textbox, enter **3** for 3 seconds. Click the **Change** button.

Step 7.   In the Line Information section, use the drop-down menu to change the ring to **Feature Ring**, as shown in Figure 8-14.

Figure 8-14   Phone User Account: Feature Ring Option

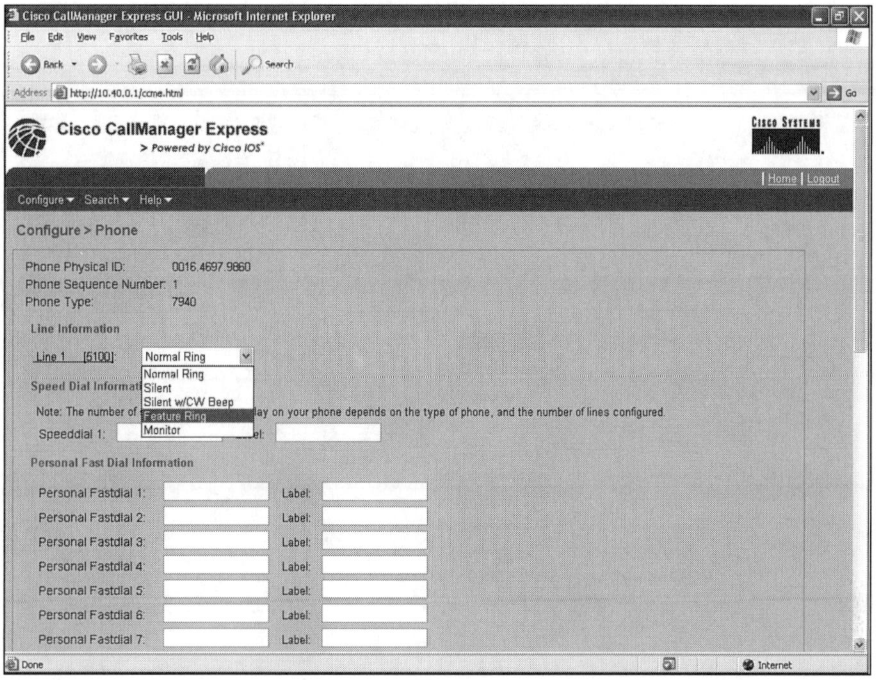

At the bottom of the window, notice how the user can change his or her password. Click the **Save Change** button. Click **OK** to save the changes, and click **OK** again to confirm the change.

Step 8.   From the Cisco IP Phone that was *not* configured for call forwarding, call the other IP Phone. Do not answer the call. Notice how the call is routed back to the phone that originated the call after 3 seconds.

Step 9.   Log out of the web GUI.

Step 10.   Log back into the web GUI with a username of **CSchmidt** and a password of **cisco**.

Step 11.   From the **Configure** menu, select **Phone**. Notice that the phone that is being managed is the opposite phone. Also notice that the speed dial previously configured is already configured in the Speed Dial Information section. Figure 8-15 shows how these parameters have already been entered.

Figure 8-15   Phone User Account: Speed Dial Information

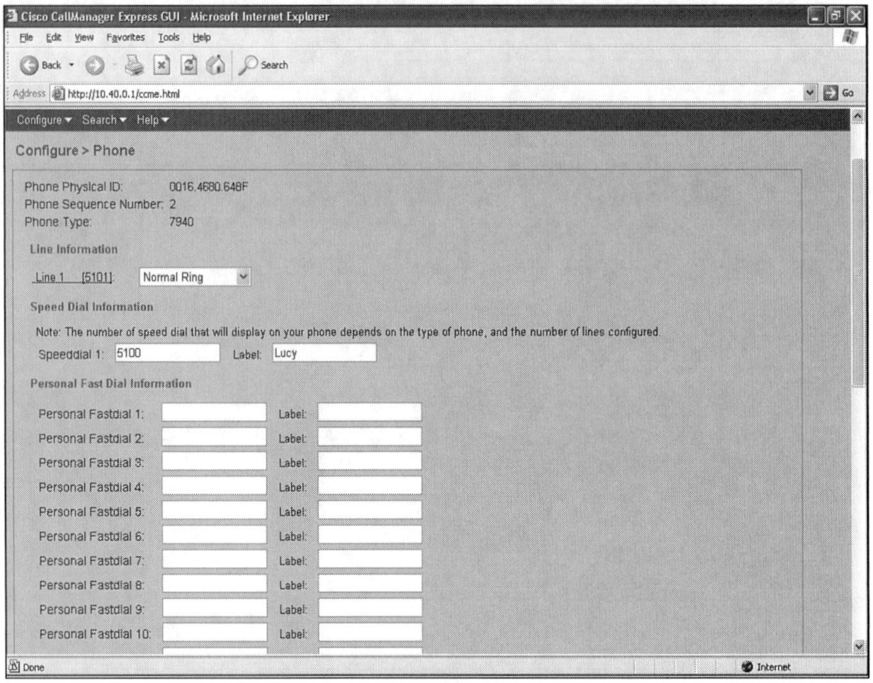

Step 12.   Log out of the web GUI.

Step 13.   From the router CLI, view the running configuration, and make notes about the commands that were modified due to the GUI interface.

```
RouterVoIPX# copy running-config startup-config
```

Why do you think the configuration changes were made under the ephone directory number (ephone-dn) rather than the ephone (ephone 1)?

Lab 8-4: Configure Call Transfer and Call Forward

In this lab, OCSIC.org currently has the system default of blind transfers. It wants to change to consultative transfers on a system-wide basis. To accomplish this, you need to configure CallManager Express to use consultative transfers. However, the ability to forward calls should be restricted in some instances, and the user should not be able to forward calls from the IP Phones.

Note: This lab relies on the two IP Phones being able to connect to one another *before* you start this lab. An analog phone connected to the FXS port on the router and both Cisco IP Phones should be able to successfully call this analog phone. Table 8-2 shows the phone number used for the FXS port phones. Also, the PC should be able to access the CME GUI Administrator (http://10.X0.0.1/ccme.html) before you start this lab. Troubleshoot as necessary.

Table 8-2   FXS Analog Phone Numbers

Pod	Extension Numbers	Router FXS 0 Port
Pod 1	5000 to 5029	5555028
Pod 2	5030 to 5059	5555058
Pod 3	5060 to 5089	5555088
Pod 4	5100 to 5129	5555128

The objectives of this lab are as follows:

- Transfer calls and set up call forwarding.

- Configure consultative transfer.

- Use the IP Phone to configure call forwarding to the other IP Phone.

- Restrict the ability to forward calls from the IP Phone using IOS commands.

To perform this lab, you need the following equipment:

- CME-capable router

- Switch/switch module

- Workstation with an Ethernet 10/100 NIC installed

- Two Cisco IP Phones (powered using any method)

- One analog phone connected to the FXS port

Figure 8-16 shows the topology used for this lab. Keep in mind that an integrated switch module in the router could be used instead of the external switch.

Figure 8-16   Lab Topology: Call Transfer

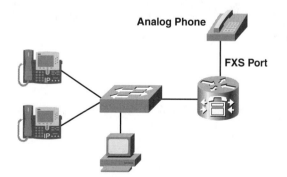

The procedure for this lab consists of the following tasks, described in detail in the following sections:

- **Task 1**—Configure call transfer and call forward.

- **Task 2**—Examine call forward features.

Task 1: Configure Call Transfer and Call Forward

Step 1.   Check connectivity between the analog phone and one of the IP Phones. From the Cisco IP Phone, use seven digits to call the analog phone that connects to the FXS port. From the analog phone, dial one of the IP Phones using four-digit dialing. Do not proceed unless the calls are successful.

Step 2.   Using the router CLI from privileged mode, verify that there is no **transfer-system** command in the telephony-service section. By default, the phone transfer from one IP Phone to the other is blind.

Step 3.   Using the **show run | begin ephone-dn** command, verify that no **call-forward** commands are configured under any ephone-dns in the running configuration. If any **call-forward** commands exist, remove them before completing any other steps. The *x* in the second command is any parameter listed after **call-forward**.

```
RouterVoIPX# show run | begin ephone-dn
RouterVoIPX(config-ephone-dn)# no call-forward x
```

Step 4.   Notice that the bottom of the Cisco IP Phone display has four buttons, as shown in Figure 8-17. These are called softkeys. A softkey button has a specific option associated with it and can be modified.

Figure 8-17   Cisco IP Phone Softkeys

From the analog phone, call one of the Cisco IP Phones, but do not answer. On the IP Phone, press the **Answer** softkey followed by the **Trnsfer** softkey. You hear a dial tone. Enter the extension of the other IP Phone. The other IP Phone should ring. Answer the call. The two IP Phones are now connected. This is where the IP Phone that answered the first call says, "A call just came in for you. I'm transferring it to you now." Then you must press the **Trnsfer** softkey again to transfer the call. The two Cisco IP Phones are disconnected, but the one Cisco IP Phone and the analog phone are now connected as a result of the transfer.

Step 5.   From global configuration mode, enter telephony service mode:

```
RouterVoIPX(config)# telephony-service
```

Step 6.   Use the **transfer-system ?** command to see all the options available. Use the **transfer-system full-consult** to enable consultative transfers:

```
RouterVoIPX(config-telephony)# transfer-system ?
RouterVoIPX(config-telephony)# transfer-system full-consult
```

Step 7.   From the analog phone, dial one of the IP Phones. When the IP Phone starts ringing, press the **Answer** softkey followed by the **Trnsfer** softkey. You hear a dial tone. Enter the extension of the other IP Phone. The other IP Phone should ring.

On the other IP Phone (the target IP Phone), press the **Answer** softkey. Notice that the call is not automatically transferred and that the only connection where a conversation can occur is between the two IP Phones. In fact, the caller on the analog phone is on hold. Even if the analog phone is hung up (don't try this until you complete the next step), the call transfer between the two IP Phones continues.

From the IP Phone that initiated the transfer, press the **Trnsfer** softkey a second time to complete the transfer. Now the analog phone and the second IP Phone have a connection. Hang up all phones.

You can try this again and hang up the analog phone after the **Trnsfer** softkey is pressed once and see how the connection between the two Cisco IP Phones still exists.

Step 8.   From one Cisco IP Phone, press the **CFwdAll** softkey. Then enter the number of the other IP Phone, followed by the pound symbol (the # key). This forwards all calls to the other IP Phone.

What message appears when all calls have been forwarded to another IP Phone?

_____

_____

Step 9.   From the analog phone, call the number of the IP Phone that has been forwarded. The call should be forwarded to the other IP Phone.

Step 10.   On the phone that has all calls forwarded, press the **CFwdAll** softkey to disable call forwarding.

Task 2: Examine Call Forward Features

Step 1.   From privileged mode, view the configuration and verify which ephone-dn has the lowest-numbered telephone number. For example, if you're using pod 4, the lowest-numbered telephone number would be 5100 (as opposed to 5101).

```
RouterVoIPX# show run | begin ephone-dn
```

Step 2.   From global configuration mode, enter **ephone-dn** *x* (where *x* is the ephone-dn that has the lowest-numbered phone number) to enter ephone-dn mode:

```
RouterVoIPX(config)# ephone-dn x
```

Step 3.   Enter the command **call-forward max-length 0** to disable call forwarding for the first IP Phone. Note that even though call forwarding is disabled, a phone call can still be placed to the phone and from the phone.

```
RouterVoIPX(config-ephone-dn)# call-forward max-length 0
```

List one example of when a company might disable call forwarding for an employee who has an IP Phone.

_____

_____

_____

Step 4.   From the IP Phone that has the lowest phone number (and is associated with the ephone-dn just configured), press the **CFwdAll** softkey button.

What is different from before?

_____

Note: Another option to prevent call forwarding is to modify the ephone template as described at the beginning of this chapter and as demonstrated in Lab 8-2.

Step 5.   Try the **CFwdAll** softkey on the other IP Phone. The softkey on the other phone should work. (Do not forward the calls on this IP Phone.)

Step 6.   View the router configuration and determine which username is associated with the IP Phone that has call forwarding disabled. It will be either **CSchmidt** or **EFriend**.

Step 7.   Use the GUI web interface as the appropriate Phone user for the phone that has the call forwarding softkey disabled. The username will be either **CSchmidt** or **EFriend** with a password of **cisco**.

Step 8.   From the **Configure** menu, select **Phone**.

Step 9.   In the Line Information section, click the hyperlink for **Line 1**.

Step 10.   In the Call Forward: busy and Call Forward: no-answer textboxes, enter the four-digit extension of the other Cisco IP Phone. In the timeout in textbox, enter **8**. (18 seconds is the default.) Figure 8-18 shows these changes.

Figure 8-18   Phone User Account: Call Forward Parameters

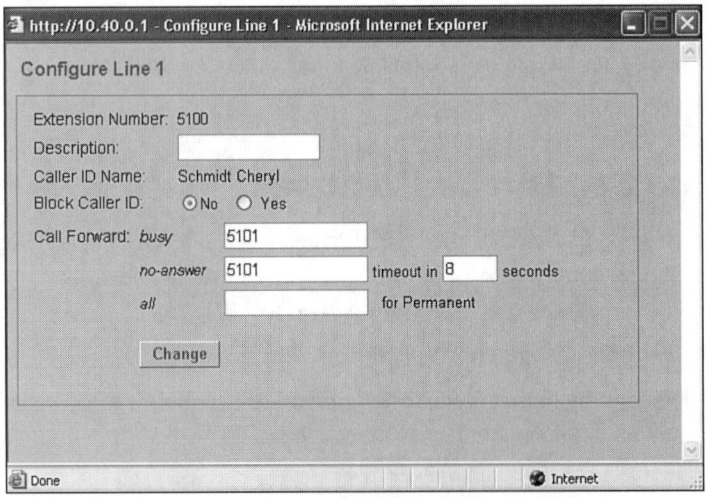

Step 11. Click the **Change** button.

Step 12. Scroll to the bottom of the page and click the **Save Change** button. Click the **OK** button to save the changes. Click **OK** again to acknowledge the changes.

Notice that the user can still configure call forward settings from the GUI even though the **call-forward max-length 0** is set from the router prompt. However, the **CFwdAll** softkey still does not work on the phone.

Step 13. Place a call from the analog phone to the Cisco IP Phone that has just been configured.

What happens to incoming calls when call forward busy and call forward no answer options are active and set to the other IP Phone? Use the analog phone to call the Cisco IP Phone that has just been configured to answer this question.

_____

_____

Step 14. From the web-based interface, put the other Cisco IP Phone number into the Call Forward: all textbox and apply the change.

If a forwarding number was also entered into the Call Forward: all textbox through the web-based interface, what would then happen to calls to that number?

_____

_____

_____

From the analog phone, call the Cisco IP Phones to verify the functionality of the call forwards.

Step 15. Remove the call forwarding from the IP Phone using any method (CLI or GUI).

Step 16. Log out of the GUI and save the router configuration:

```
RouterVoIPX# copy running-config startup-config
```

Lab 8-5: Configure and Use Call Park

In this lab, OCSIC.org can page an employee using speakers in the ceiling. The switchboard operator can page someone who does not answer a transferred consultative call. The ability to *park* the call is needed so that the person being paged can retrieve the call from any phone available using Cisco CallManager Express.

Note: This lab relies on the two IP Phones being able to connect to one another *before* you start this lab. An analog phone connects to the FXS port on the router. This phone should be able to successfully call one of the IP Phones that connects to the same router. Table 8-3 lists the phone numbers used on the analog phone connected to the FXS port. Troubleshoot as necessary.

Table 8-3   FXS Analog Phone Numbers

Pod	Extension Numbers	Router FXS 0 Port
Pod 1	5000 to 5029	5555028
Pod 2	5030 to 5059	5555058
Pod 3	5060 to 5089	5555088
Pod 4	5100 to 5129	5555128

The objective of this lab is to configure and use the call park option.

To perform this lab, you need the following equipment:

- CME-capable router
- Switch/switch module
- Workstation with an Ethernet 10/100 NIC installed
- Two Cisco IP Phones (powered using any method)
- One analog phone connected to the FXS port

Figure 8-19 shows the topology used for this lab. Keep in mind that an integrated switch module in the router could be used instead of the external switch.

Figure 8-19   Lab Topology: Call Park

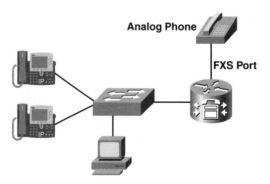

The procedure for this lab consists of the following tasks, described in detail in the following sections:

- **Task 1**—Configure the CME router for call park.
- **Task 2**—Test the call park feature.

Task 1: Configure the CME Router for Call Park

Step 1.   Check connectivity between the analog phone and one of the IP Phones. From the Cisco IP Phone, use seven digits to call the analog phone that connects to the FXS port. From the analog phone, dial one of the IP Phones using four-digit dialing. Do not proceed unless the calls are successful. Refer to Table 8-3, which lists the phone number to use when calling the analog phone.

Step 2.   From the router CLI, verify the current configuration. Remove any call forward commands from ephone-dns:

```
RouterVoIPX# show running-config

RouterVoIPX(config)# ephone-dn X

RouterVoIPX(config-ephone-dn)# no call-forward all XXXX

RouterVoIPX(config-ephone-dn)# no call-forward max-length 0

RouterVoIPX(config-ephone-dn)# no call-forward busy XXXX

RouterVoIPX(config-ephone-dn)# no call-forward noan XXXX timeout 8
```

Step 3.   From the router CLI global configuration mode, create an ephone-dn that will be used as the extension to park a call. This directory number is fake—it is not associated with a real Cisco IP Phone. The ephone-dn is simply a holding spot for a phone call until the desired party picks up the call.

```
RouterVoIPX(config)# ephone-dn 11
```

Step 4.   If a message appears that dn 11 exceeds the max-dn limit, move to telephony-service configuration mode and enter the command **max-dn 15**. Return to global configuration mode and reenter the **ephone-dn 11** command:

```
RouterVoIPX(config)# telephony-service

RouterVoIPX(config-telephony)# max-dn 15

RouterVoIPX(config-telephony)# exit

RouterVoIPX(config)# ephone-dn 11
```

Step 5.   Use the **number** command to assign an extension number of $X800$ (where X is the pod number being used):

```
RouterVoIPX(config-ephone-dn)# number X800
```

Step 6.   Use the command **park-slot timeout 10 limit 3** to set a reminder after 10 seconds and to terminate the call after three reminders:

```
RouterVoIPX(config-ephone-dn)# park-slot timeout 10 limit 3
```

What is the maximum amount of time in hours that can be programmed for the call park feature?

_____

Step 7.   Verify that the **transfer-system full-consult** command is visible in the telephony-service section. This command or **transfer-system full-blind** is required to use the call park feature. If the command is missing, add it.

```
RouterVoIPX# show running-config

RouterVoIPX(config)# telephony-service

RouterVoIPX(config-telephony)# transfer-system full-consult
```

Step 8.   Reset both Cisco IP Phones by using the keys on the IP Phones and pressing the following buttons: * * # * *. This will work on most Cisco 7940 IP Phones, but it may not work on 7960 phones. If this method does not work, reset the IP Phone using the method you learned in Lab 2-2.

Task 2: Test the Call Park Feature

Step 1.   From the analog phone, call one of the IP Phones and answer the call.

Step 2.   Use the **more** softkey button to find and press the **Park** softkey. You may need to press the **more** softkey several times before you see the **Park** softkey.

Wait 10 seconds.

What is heard on the analog phone and on the IP Phone?

_____

_____

Wait another 20 seconds.

What happens to the call?

_____

_____

Step 3.   From the analog phone, call one of the IP Phones and answer the call.

Step 4.   On the IP Phone, use the **more** softkey to locate and then press the **Park** softkey.

Step 5.   From the second IP Phone, use the **more** softkey to find and then press the **PickUp** softkey. When you hear a dial tone, dial *X*800 (where *X* is the pod number) to retrieve the parked call. Notice how the number dialed is the same number you programmed into the virtual ephone-dn earlier in this lab.

The second IP Phone and the analog phone are now connected and can communicate. The first IP Phone has been disconnected. If this does not work, troubleshoot as necessary.

Step 6.   Disconnect the call. The call park feature can also allow the original IP Phone that placed the call in park to pick up the call.

From the analog phone, dial one of the IP Phones and answer the call.

Step 7.   On the same Cisco IP Phone, use the **more** softkey to locate and then press the **Park** softkey. The call is parked to extension *X*800 (where *X* is the pod number).

Use the **more** softkey to find and then press the **PickUp** softkey button. When you hear a dial tone, press * to retrieve the call. The call should connect.

Step 8.   Save the router configuration:

```
RouterVoIPX# copy running-config startup-config
```

Lab 8-6: Customize the IP Phone

In this lab, OCSIC.org wants to customize the IP Phones with the phone's full phone number (area code and seven digits), the company name on the display, and a label on the line. This lab demonstrates both the IOS commands and GUI options.

Note: This lab relies on the two IP Phones being able to connect to one another *before* you start this lab. Also, the PC should be able to access the CME GUI Administrator (http://10.X0.0.1/ccme.html) before you start this lab. Troubleshoot as necessary.

The objectives of this lab are as follows:

■ Customize the Cisco IP Phone display.

■ Configure and customize the top phone line.

■ Configure a system message using GUI and CLI.

To perform this lab, you need the following equipment:

■ CME-capable router

■ Switch/switch module

■ Workstation with an Ethernet 10/100 NIC installed

■ Two Cisco IP Phones (powered using any method)

Figure 8-20 shows the topology used for this lab. Keep in mind that an integrated switch module in the router could be used instead of the external switch.

Figure 8-20   Lab Topology: Phone Customization

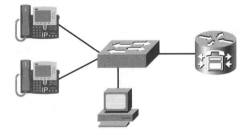

The procedure for this lab consists of the following tasks, described in detail in the following sections:

■ **Task 1**—Customize the IP Phone display.

■ **Task 2**—Reset and verify the phone display.

■ **Task 3**—Perform more GUI customization.

Task 1: Customize the IP Phone Display

Step 1.   Ensure that the two IP Phones can connect to one another before this lab begins. Also ensure that the workstation can connect or ping to 10.X0.0.1 (where X is the pod number being used). Troubleshoot as necessary.

Step 2.   From the PC, browse to the following URL (where X is the pod number) to access the web-based GUI:

```
http://10.X0.0.1/ccme.html
```

Log in using the System administrator credentials of **webadmin** and **cisco**.

Step 3.   From the **Configure** menu, select the **System Parameters** option.

Step 4.   From the list on the left, select **System Message**.

Step 5.   In the System Message textbox, highlight any existing message and delete it. Enter a message of **Welcome to OCSIC**. Click the **Set** button. When you're asked if you want to save the change, click the **OK** button. When the change is successful and that message appears, click **OK**.

Step 6.   From the router CLI, view the running configuration. Notice how the **system message** is shown in the telephony-service section. Change the message using the CLI. Before pressing **Enter** after entering the **system message** command, be ready to look at the Cisco IP Phones as soon as you press the **Enter** key. The message changes quickly.

```
RouterVoIPX# show running-config

RouterVoIPX(config)# telephony-service

RouterVoIPX(config-telephony)# system message Welcome to OCSIC.org!
```

Step 7.   From the router CLI global configuration mode, enter the ephone directory number configuration mode for the first IP Phone:

```
RouterVoIPX(config)# ephone-dn 1
```

Step 8.   Use the **description** command to set the label on the IP Phone header bar:

```
RouterVoIPX(config-ephone-dn)# description Phone1
```

Step 9.   Use the command **label my line** *xxxx* (where *xxxx* is the phone number assigned to the phone) to set a label on ephone-dn 1. Note that nothing will occur until the IP Phone has been reset.

```
RouterVoIPX(config-ephone-dn)# label my line xxxx
```

Step 10.   Enter the ephone directory number configuration mode for the second phone by using the **ephone-dn 2** command:

```
RouterVoIPX(config)# ephone-dn 2
```

Step 11.   Use the **description** *phonenumber* command (where *phonenumber* is the full phone number, including area code). An example for Pod 1 would be **description 5105555001**. An example for Pod 2 would be **description 5105555031**. (The 510555 part of the number is the same for every pod. Simply add the four-digit extension.)

```
RouterVoIPX(config-ephone-dn)# description phonenumber
```

Step 12.   Return to the ephone directory number configuration mode for the first IP Phone.

```
RouterVoIPX(config)# e1phone-dn 1
```

Task 2: Reset and Verify the Phone Display

Step 1.   Reset both IP Phones by pressing ****#**** on the keypad or by using the method shown in Lab 2-2. Some IP Phone firmware versions might require you to select the **Settings** button before pressing ****#****.

Step 2.   After the phones boot and load, notice the changes on the phone. The **description** command used on ephone-dn 2 changed the first line at the top of the phone display. The **label** command is used to uniquely identify a particular button.

Task 3: Perform More GUI Customization

Step 1.   From the GUI, point to **Configure** and click **extensions**.

Step 2.   Click the link for the lowest-numbered Cisco IP Phone (not the call park extension number).

Step 3.   In the Label textbox, enter **Line 1** *xxxx* (where *xxxx* is the phone extension assigned to this phone).

Step 4.   In the Description textbox, enter **Ernie's phone** or an appropriate description for the phone.

Step 5.   Click the **Change** button. Click **OK** to save the change. Click **OK** again when the change is completed.

Step 6.   Point to the **Configure** menu and select **Phones**.

Step 7.   Select the checkbox beside the MAC address of the lowest-numbered IP Phone. Click the **Reset** link to reset the particular phone on which changes have been made. Click **OK** to reset the phone. Click **OK** again to acknowledge the reset.

When the phone reboots and loads, notice the changes made to the description and the label.

Step 8.   Log out of the web interface by clicking the **Logout** link.

Step 9.   From the router, CLI, view the changes made:

```
RouterVoIPX# show running-config | begin tele
```

Step 10.   Save the router changes:

```
RouterVoIPX# copy running-config startup-config
```

Lab 8-7: Configure the Intercom Feature

In this lab, OCSIC.org wants to configure an intercom between the CEO and the administrative assistant. No one else in the company should be able to dial this intercom.

Note: This lab relies on the two IP Phones being able to connect to one another *before* you start this lab. Also, the PC should be able to access the CME GUI Administrator (http://10.X0.0.1/ccme.html) before the start of this lab. Troubleshoot as necessary.

The objectives of this lab are as follows:

- Configure an intercom between two phones.

- Test the intercom feature.

To perform this lab, you need the following equipment:

- CME-capable router

- Switch/switch module

- Workstation with an Ethernet 10/100 NIC installed

- Two Cisco IP Phones (powered using any method)

Figure 8-21 shows the topology used for this lab. Keep in mind that an integrated switch module in the router could be used instead of the external switch.

Figure 8-21   Lab Topology: Intercom

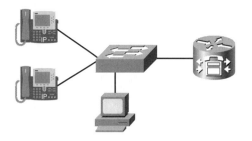

The procedure for this lab consists of the following tasks, described in detail in the following sections:

- **Task 1**—Configure the intercom.

- **Task 2**—Test the intercom configuration.

Task 1: Configure the Intercom

Step 1.   Ensure that the two IP Phones can connect to one another before this lab begins. Also ensure that the workstation can connect or ping to 10.X0.0.1 (where X is the pod number being used). Troubleshoot as necessary.

Step 2.   Access the CME router using the web-based GUI configuration method (**http://10.X0.0.1/ccme.html**). Log in with a username of **webadmin** and a password of **cisco**.

Step 3.   Go to the **Configure** menu and select the **Extensions** option.

Step 4.   Click the **Add** link. In the Extension Number textbox, enter **D3333**, as shown in Figure 8-22. Select a Sequence Number from the drop-down box. This number will be the ephone-dn (directory number) shown in the router configuration. The sequence number must be unique.

Figure 8-22   CME Web Interface: Add Extension for Intercom

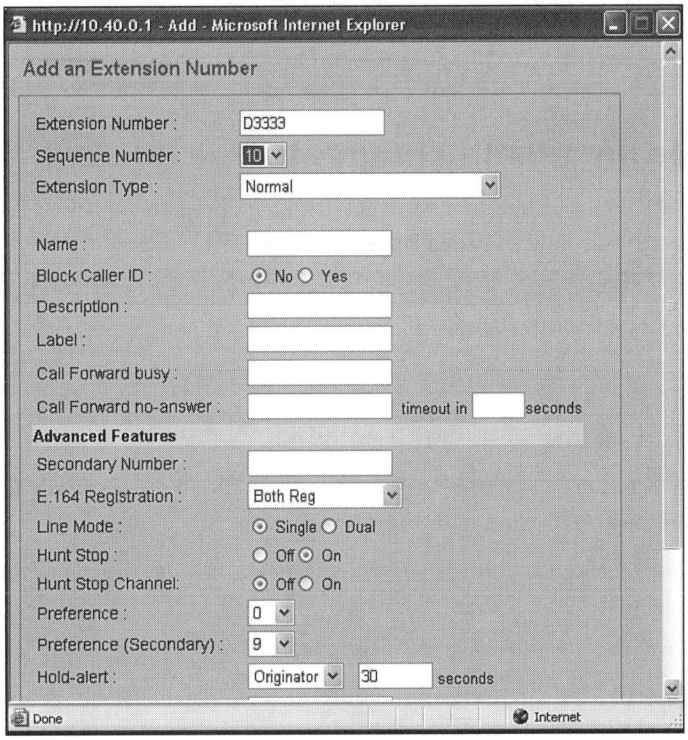

Step 5.   In the Extension Type drop-down menu, select **Intercom**. In the Name textbox, enter **Intercom**. In the first Label textbox, enter **Intercom**. In the Intercom Number textbox, enter **D4444**.

Step 6.   Click the **Add** button to add this extension. When prompted to save the changes, click the **OK** button. A message appears that the extension was added; click **OK**. When prompted to add the new extension to the new phone, click the **OK** button. When a message appears that there is no new phone to add or that there is no free sequence number, click **OK**.

Step 7.   Add a second new extension using the same method. Set the extension number to **D4444** with a unique sequence number, an extension type of **Intercom**, a name of **Intercom**, a label of **Intercom**, an intercom number of **D3333**, and all other settings left at the defaults. Save these changes.

Step 8.   From the **Configure** menu, select the **Phones** option.

Step 9.   Click the MAC address link of the phone that has the lowest phone number.

Step 10.   Go to the Speed Dial Information section and delete any speed dials located there. This is done in case the phone has only two buttons. Even if the phone has multiple buttons, future labs are not affected.

Step 11.   In the Phone Line Buttons section, select an unused button by clicking the button number link located in the Button column.

Step 12.   Locate the D3333 Intercom option and click the checkbox beside the sequence number.

Step 13.   Click the **Save** link at the top of the window. Than click the **Change** button at the bottom of the window. Respond to the next two messages by clicking **OK**. The IP Phone should reboot.

Step 14.   Select the MAC address link of the other IP Phone. Delete any speed dials, and select a free phone line button number link. Locate the D4444 Intercom option and click the checkbox beside the sequence number. Then click the **Save** link at the top of the window. Click the **Change** button. Respond to the next two messages by clicking **OK**. The IP Phone should reboot.

Task 2: Test the Intercom Configuration

Step 1.   After both IP Phones have rebooted and the Intercom option appears beside one of the phone buttons, press the button labeled **Intercom**. Say a few words.

On the other IP Phone, what indication is given that the intercom works? If there is no indication, there is a problem with the intercom. Troubleshoot as necessary.

_____

_____

Step 2.   Press the **Speaker** button (the last button on the right on the bottom right of the phone) on either IP Phone to disconnect the intercom.

Step 3.   Access the router CLI. From privileged exec mode, use the command **show running-config |
begin tele** to view the changes:

```
RouterVoIPX# show running-config | begin tele
```

Step 4.   Notice how the settings changed under the ephone-dn and ephone sections.

Step 5.   Save the router configuration:

```
RouterVoIPX# copy running-config startup-config
```

Lab 8-8: Configure a Dialable Intercom

In this lab, OCSIC.org wants to configure an intercom to the receptionist at the front desk that anyone in the enterprise can dial.

Note: This lab relies on the two IP Phones being able to connect to one another *before* you start this lab. An analog phone connects to the FXS port on the router, and both Cisco IP Phones should be able to successfully call this analog phone. Table 8-4 shows the phone numbers used for the FXS port phones. Also, the PC should be able to access the CME GUI Administrator (http://10.*X*0.0.1/ccme.html) before the start of this lab. Troubleshoot as necessary.

Table 8-4   FXS Analog Phone Numbers

Pod	Extension Numbers	Router FXS 0 Port
Pod 1	5000 to 5029	5555028
Pod 2	5030 to 5059	5555058
Pod 3	5060 to 5089	5555088
Pod 4	5100 to 5129	5555128

The objectives of this lab are as follows:

- Configure a dialable intercom.
- Test the dialable intercom.

To perform this lab, you need the following equipment:

- CME-capable router
- Switch/switch module
- Workstation with an Ethernet 10/100 NIC installed
- Two Cisco IP Phones (powered using any method)
- One analog phone connected to the FXS port

Figure 8-23 shows the topology used for this lab. Keep in mind that an integrated switch module in the router could be used instead of the external switch.

Figure 8-23   Lab Topology: Dialable Intercom

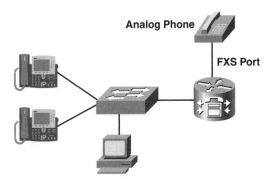

The procedure for this lab consists of the following tasks, described in detail in the following sections:

- **Task 1**—Configure the dialable intercom.

- **Task 2**—Test the dialable intercom.

Task 1: Configure the Dialable Intercom

Step 1.   Check connectivity between the analog phone and one of the IP Phones. From the Cisco IP Phone, use seven digits to call the analog phone that connects to the FXS port. From the analog phone, dial one of the IP Phones. Do not proceed unless the calls are successful. Also ensure that the workstation can connect or ping to 10.X0.0.1 (where X is the pod number being used).

Step 2.   From the PC, access the CME router using a web interface by entering the following URL (where X is the pod number):

`http://10.X0.0.1/ccme.html`

Step 3.   When prompted for a username and password, use **webadmin** and **cisco**.

Step 4.   From the **Configure** menu, select **Extensions**.

Step 5.   Click the **Add** link, and set the Extension Number to *xxxx* (where each *x* is the pod number). An example of the extension number for pod 1 is 1111.

Step 6.   Select an unused Sequence Number. Select an Extension Type of **Intercom**. In both the Name and Label textboxes, enter **Dialable Intercom**. Set the Intercom Number to *xxx***0** (where each *x* is the pod number). An example of an intercom number for pod 1 is 1110. All other settings are left at the defaults.

Make a note of the sequence number. It will be used in a later step.

Step 7.   Click the **Add** button. When you're asked whether you want to save the changes, click **OK**. A confirmation message appears. Click **OK**. When you're asked whether the next extension is to be added to a new phone, click **OK**. When the No new phone to add or No sequence number message appears, click **OK**.

Step 8.   Click the **Add** link and set the Extension Number to *xxx***0** (where *x* is the pod number). An example of an extension number for Pod 1 is 1110. Select an unused Sequence Number. Select an Extension Type of **Intercom** from the drop-down menu. Enter a name of **Dialable Intercom**. Enter a label of **Dialable Intercom** in the Label field. The Intercom Number is set to *xxxx* (where *x* is the pod number). An example of the Intercom Number for pod 1 is 1111. All other settings are left at the defaults.

Make a note of the sequence number. It will be used in a later step.

Step 9.   Click the **Add** button. When you're asked whether you want to save the changes, click **OK**. A confirmation message appears. Click **OK**. When you're asked whether the next extension is to be added to a new phone, click **OK**. When the No new phone to add or no sequence number message appears, click **OK**.

Step 10.   From a command prompt, look at the router configuration and see how there are two new ephone-dn entries. Each new entry has a number using the sequence number.

`RouterVoIPX# `**`show running-config | begin tele`**

Step 11.   From the web interface, click the **Configuration** menu option and select **Phones**. Select the first IP Phone MAC address links. Click a button number. If a checkmark is beside one of the sequence numbers, click the checkbox to remove the checkmark. Click in the checkbox beside one of the new sequence numbers created and noted in this lab.

Step 12. Click the **Save** link located at the top of the page. Then click the **Change** button located at the bottom of the page. When you're asked whether you want to save the changes, click the **OK** button. A confirmation message appears; click **OK**.

Step 13. Select the other IP Phone MAC address link. Click a button number. If a checkmark is beside one of the sequence numbers, click the checkbox to remove the checkmark. Click in the checkbox beside one of the other new sequence numbers (the one *not* used in the preceding step).

Step 14. Click the **Save** link located at the top of the page. Click the **Change** button located at the bottom of the page. When you're asked whether you want to save the changes, click the **OK** button. A confirmation message appears; click **OK**.

Task 2: Test the Dialable Intercom

Step 1. Verify that the intercom connects in both directions on the IP Phones. To test the intercom, press the **Dialable Intercom** button on either IP Phone and speak an audible message. If the dialable intercom does not work in both directions, troubleshoot as necessary.

Step 2. Using the analog phone, dial both **555***xxx***0** and **555***xxxx* (where *x* is the pod number). Note that the intercom works even through an analog phone connection.

Step 3. From privileged exec mode, use the command **show running-config | begin tele** to view the changes:

```
RouterVoIPX# show running-config | begin tele
```

Step 4. Save the router configuration:

```
RouterVoIPX# copy running-config startup-config
```

Lab 8-9: Configure Paging Groups

In this lab, OCSIC.org wants to configure two paging groups that will use the speaker feature of the IP Phones. One paging group is for the sales staff, and a second paging group is for the technical support staff. In addition, when an emergency page is needed, all phones in both groups should receive the page.

Note: This lab relies on the two IP Phones being able to connect to one another *before* you start this lab. An analog phone connects to the FXS port on the router, and both Cisco IP Phones should be able to successfully call this analog phone. Table 8-5 shows the phone number used for the FXS port phones. Also, the PC should be able to access the CME GUI Administrator (http://10.x0.0.1/ccme.html) before you start this lab. Troubleshoot as necessary.

Table 8-5   FXS Analog Phone Numbers

Pod	Extension Numbers	Router FXS 0 Port
Pod 1	5000 to 5029	5555028
Pod 2	5030 to 5059	5555058
Pod 3	5060 to 5089	5555088
Pod 4	5100 to 5129	5555128

The objectives of this lab are as follows:

- Configure two paging groups.

- Configure a phone in each paging group.

- Configure a combined paging group.

- Test the paging feature.

- Configure the paging feature to use multicast.

To perform this lab, you need the following equipment:

- CME-capable router

- Switch/switch module

- Workstation with an Ethernet 10/100 NIC installed

- Two Cisco IP Phones (powered using any method)

- One analog phone connected to the FXS port

Figure 8-24 shows the topology used for this lab. Keep in mind that an integrated switch module in the router could be used instead of the external switch.

Figure 8-24   Lab Topology: Paging Group

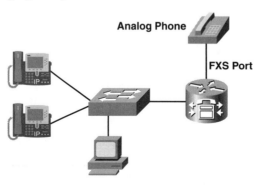

The procedure for this lab consists of the following tasks, described in detail in the following sections:

- **Task 1**—Configure the paging groups.
- **Task 2**—Test the paging groups.
- **Task 3**—Configure a combined paging group.
- **Task 4**—Test the combined paging group.

Task 1: Configure the Paging Groups

Step 1. Check connectivity between the analog phone and one of the IP Phones. From the Cisco IP Phone, use seven digits to call the analog phone that connects to the FXS port. From the analog phone, dial one of the IP Phones. Do not proceed unless the calls are successful. Also ensure that the workstation can connect, or ping to 10.X0.0.1 (where X is the pod number being used).

Step 2. From a workstation connected to an IP Phone (that can ping all router IP addresses), access the CME using a web interface by entering the following URL in the browser address line (where X is the pod number):

`http://10.X0.0.1/ccme.html`

Step 3. When prompted for a username and password, use **webadmin** and **cisco**.

Step 4. From the web interface, click the **Configure** menu option and select **Extensions**.

Step 5. Click the **Add** link. In the Extension Number textbox, enter *x***500** (where *x* is the pod number). Select an unused sequence number. In the Extension Type drop-down box, select **Paging**. In the Name and Description textboxes, enter **Sales**. All other settings are left at the defaults.

Make a note of what sequence number was used. This information is used in a later step.

Step 6. Click the **Add** button. When you're asked whether you want to save the changes, click **OK**. A confirmation message appears. Click **OK**.

Step 7. Using the same procedures, add a second paging extension with an extension number of *x***600** (where *x* is the pod number), an Extension Type of **Paging**, an unused Sequence Number, and a Name and Description of **Support**. Save the changes.

Make a note of what sequence number is used. This information will be needed in a later lab step.

Step 8. Click the **Configure** menu option and select **Phones**. Select a MAC address link for one of the IP Phones being used.

Step 9. Locate the Paging Information section. In the Paging Extension drop-down box, select *x***500** (where *x* is the pod number).

Click the **Change** button. When asked if the change is to be saved, click the **OK** button. When the confirmation message box appears, click **OK**.

Note: The unicast option that is shown on this screen is required only if the IP Phones are on a network that is *not* multicast-enabled. Because the Catalyst switch and the Ethernet switch modules are multicast-enabled and that is the type of equipment being used, multicasting will work, and unicasting is not required.

Step 10. Select the other MAC address link for the other IP Phone. Set the Paging Extension to *x***600** (where *x* is the pod number). Save the changes.

Task 2: Test the Paging Groups

Step 1.   The paging function allows you to dial a number and talk to a group of IP Phones. In this scenario, *x*500 (where *x* is the pod number) represents Sales, which could be a group of Sales representatives who have IP Phones. The other paging function was assigned a number of *x*600, which represents IT support staff.

A help desk call comes in that there is a problem with the mail server. Three administrators can manage the mail server. The help desk staff can now dial one number and page one of the three administrators to pick up on a particular phone line.

From the analog phone, test the paging function by dialing *x*500 (where *x* is the pod number). **555*x*500** can also be dialed.

Step 2.   Also, from the analog phone, test the paging function with the number *x*600 (where *x* is the pod number). The paging function should work. Troubleshoot as necessary.

Task 3: Configure a Combined Paging Group

Step 1.   Access the router CLI, and view the current configuration.

```
RouterVoIPX# show running-config | begin ephone-dn
```

Make a note of which ephone-dns (directory numbers) are in use. Also write down the ephone-dns that are used for the two paging groups (*x*500 and *x*600) that were just created.

Step 2.   From global configuration mode, enter the command **ephone-dn ?**:

```
RouterVoIPX(config)# ephone-dn ?
```

How many dialer numbers are possible?

_____

_____

Step 3.   From global configuration mode, enter the command **ephone-dn** *x* (where *x* is an unused directory number) to create a new directory number. This ephone-dn will be used for a combined paging group.

Step 4.   Assign a directory number to the ephone-dn using the **number *x*700** command (where *x* is the pod number):

```
RouterVoIPX(config-ephone-dn)# number x700
```

Step 5.   Assign the ephone-dn a name of AllCall:

```
RouterVoIPX(config-ephone-dn)# name AllCall
```

Step 6.   The **paging** command specifies that this dialer number is used to broadcast audio paging messages to idle IP Phones. The **ip** parameter, when used with the **paging** command, specifies that multicasting is used to do the audio paging. The number that follows is the multicast group number.

Cisco IP Phones do not support multicasting to a multicast address of 224.*x*.*x*.*x*. The **port** parameter followed by a number defines the UDP port number used to communicate the message to the IP Phone. The number 2000 is recommended because it is already used for normal nonmulticast messaging.

Enter the following command:

```
RouterVoIPX(config-ephone-dn)# paging ip 239.1.1.1 port 2000
```

Step 7. The **paging group** command allows multiple groups already created to be combined into one group. The group numbers that follow are separated by one or more commas. The group number is the sequence number (ephone-dn dial numbers) configured through the web interface earlier in this lab. Refer to the sequence numbers used earlier in the lab. These are the x and y values used in the command. For example, if sequence numbers 9 and 10 were used previously, the command entered would be **paging group 9,10**.

```
RouterVoIPX(config-ephone-dn)# paging group x,y
```

Task 4: Test the Combined Paging Group

Step 1. From privileged exec mode, use the command **show running-config | begin tele** to view the changes:

```
RouterVoIPX# show running-config | begin telephony-service
```

Step 2. Use the analog phone to test the paging function by dialing the paging number **555x700** (where x is the pod number). The page should operate correctly, with both IP Phones (one in each page group) receiving the page.

Step 3. Save the router configuration:

```
RouterVoIPX# copy running-config startup-config
```

CHAPTER 9

H.323

H.323 is a commonly used protocol suite used to connect multiple CallManager Express (CME) sites. H.323 is also commonly used for multimedia conferencing. Other options are available, but the concept is the same, and it is good to learn how this type of protocol works as it relates to voice.

Intersite VoIP

When a company needs to send voice traffic between two different sites, it has three main options—H.323, Media Gateway Control Protocol (MGCP), and Session Initiation Protocol (SIP). All three of these protocols can be used when transmitting voice from a LAN through a circuit-switched network such as the phone company; however, MGCP is not an option when using CME.

H.323

H.323 is one of the most widely deployed protocols for voice and video. H.323 allows voice and video to travel from one LAN through a circuit-switched network to another LAN. H.323 and SIP are supported by CallManager Express.

H.323 is actually composed of many H.*XXX* protocols. Two important ones relate to CME:

- **H.225** establishes connectivity between two H.323 endpoints.
- **H.245** provides signaling rules between two H.323 endpoints.

H.225 uses messages defined in H.245 to establish the call over the Registration, Admission, and Status (RAS) channel. H.245 manages and controls call setup and connection. You can debug H.225 and H.245 messages on a voice-enabled router.

MGCP

MGCP (also known as H.248) handles signaling and session management for a multimedia conference between two sites. This protocol is useful when communication needs to occur between a circuit-switched network (such as the public switched telephone network [PSTN]) and a packet-switched network (such as your company's LAN). MGCP uses a media gateway controller as a "master" that can determine the location of any MGCP communication endpoint and the endpoint's capabilities. Then the media gateway controller can select a level of service that all participants (endpoints) in the conference can use.

SIP

SIP is an increasingly popular protocol to use when connecting multiple LANs through a circuit-switched network. SIP is used to start an interactive user session that involves some type of multimedia, such as voice, video, chat, gaming, and virtual reality applications. SIP can initiate, change, or end multimedia sessions or phone call sessions. SIP also supports the ability to invite a participant to unicast or multicast sessions that do not necessarily have to involve the end device that started the session.

SIP has an advantage over H.323. It can separate inter-site VoIP calls from true external VoIP calls because SIP uses the concept of domains and does name mapping.

A More In-Depth Look at H.323

Lab 9-2 configures two routers that have special functions in the H.323 world—the gateway and the gatekeeper. Lab 9-2 shows connectivity between analog phones at two different sites and focuses on the function of the two H.323 routers. Lab 9-3 builds on the concepts of Lab 9-2 and adds Cisco IP Phones to the configuration and routing of calls.

Gatekeeper and Gateway

Two important terms used with H.323 are gatekeeper and gateway. A *gatekeeper* can provide many functions, but an important one to VoIP is call routing. H.323 provides phone number-to-IP address lookup and conversion functions. This means that the dial plan can be centralized in a single location. This might be desirable in a company that has more than one site. The simplest type of gatekeeper provides only this phone number-to-IP address conversion.

Instead of having a separate VoIP dial peer for every CME router in the company, each CME router could have one dial peer. That dial peer points to the H.323 gatekeeper's IP address. If the dial peer is matched, a telephone call causes the CME router to contact the gatekeeper and request the IP address of the phone number being dialed. As soon as the CME router gets this IP address from the gatekeeper, it sends a call setup message directly to the remote CME router that manages that distant phone number.

A CME router can also serve as a gatekeeper. The gatekeeper can provide other functions, such as call admission control. This means that the gatekeeper monitors the amount of bandwidth being used across the circuit-switched network and can keep a phone call from being made because of lack of resources or because a higher-priority call request has been made.

The major function of a *gateway* is to connect two dissimilar networks (H.323 and non-H.323, such as a LAN and a circuit-switched network). The gateway provides protocol translation for call setup and teardown, converts media formats from one network to the other (traditional phone time-division multiplexing [TDM] to IP), and transfers data between networks separated (connected) by the gateway. A CME router can be configured as a gateway.

E.164 Number Registration

When configuring a CME router (that points to the gatekeeper IP address), the dial peer that is created on the router uses the **session target ras** command instead of the **session target ipv4:***ipaddress* that has been used in previous chapters. This is because the endpoint uses RAS to discover and register with the gatekeeper.

Registration is the process that endpoints (called terminals in the H.323 language) or gateways use to join a zone (an H.323 area that is given a name). Registration is also used to let the H.323 gatekeeper know the endpoint or gateway's E.164 address (a full phone number such as 9045555650) and H.323 ID (cme2@ocsic.org). A zone has only one gatekeeper, and a gateway can register with only one gatekeeper.

RAS is also used as the signaling protocol between a gateway and a gatekeeper. The RAS channel is opened before any other channel and is separate from the call setup and media transport channels. RAS uses UDP port 1719 for the RAS messages and UDP port 1718 for unicast messages sent to discover the gatekeeper.

When an analog phone connects to a Foreign Exchange Station (FXS) port on the CME router, the gateway automatically registers a fully qualified E.164 address for that phone. One purpose of the gateway is to register either the H.323 ID or the E.164 phone number with the gatekeeper. Before an E.164 address is automatically or manually registered with a gatekeeper, you must create a dial peer on the CME router. Then, you assign the FXS port to the peer (using the **port** command) followed by using the **destination-pattern** command to assign an E.164 address. The E.164 address *must* be a fully qualified address. (That is what the gatekeeper expects.) Examples of fully qualified E.164 addresses are +5555650, 5555650, and 9045555650. 904555.... is not a fully qualified number.

The dial peer used for a device connected to an FXS port or an ephone-dn can be programmed with a command not to register its E.164 number with the gatekeeper (**no register e164** with a dial peer and **no-reg** with the ephone-dn). Instead of the gatekeeper having direct knowledge of the device because of registration, the gateway has information about this device, and the gateway is registered with the gatekeeper.

RAS is an important part of H.225, which is a part of the H.323 suite of protocols. H.225 is also used for call setup. H.245, which is also part of the H.323 protocol suite, is used for call control. Figure 9-1 illustrates this concept.

Figure 9-1   H.323 Protocols

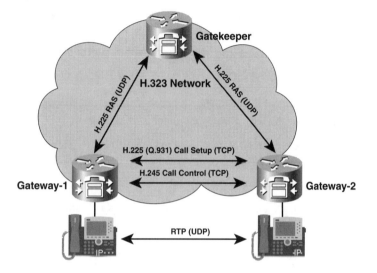

H.323 Gatekeeper Configuration

To configure a router as an H.323 gatekeeper, simply enter the **gatekeeper** command from global configuration mode:

```
Router1(config)#gatekeeper
```

From gatekeeper configuration mode, you can enter two common commands to configure the gatekeeper:

- The **zone local** command allows you to define a zone controlled by the gatekeeper. In this command, you define a name for the gatekeeper and a domain name. Optionally, you can enter an IP address on the router that is used when devices communicate via RAS. The full syntax for this command is

    ```
    Gateway(config-gk)#zone local gatekeeper-name domain-name [ras-IP-address]
    ```

    The *gatekeeper-name* can also be seen or described as the zone name. It is usually the gatekeeper's fully domain-qualified hostname; an example is gk1.ocsic.org. If the gatekeeper is configured to manage multiple zones, the *gatekeeper-name* should be unique for each zone. The gatekeeper cannot operate unless at least one zone is defined. If you decide to configure a RAS IP address (the optional parameter), you can define only one address for all local zones.

- The **no shutdown** command works as it does on any interface: it enables or turns on an interface (in this case, the gatekeeper).

The optional **zone prefix** command, entered in gatekeeper configuration mode, can add an E.164 prefix to dialed numbers. You can also use this command to give a priority number from 0 to 10 (a higher number is a higher priority) for a specific gateway. The default priority for a gateway is 5. The syntax for the command follows:

```
Gateway(config-gk)#zone prefix gatekeeper-name e.164-prefix gw-priority
  priority-number [gw-alias]
```

The optional *gw-alias* parameter is the H.323 ID of a gateway that is registered or will register with the gatekeeper.

Another optional command entered in gatekeeper configuration mode is **bandwidth**, which specifies the maximum aggregate bandwidth for H.323 traffic and verifies the available bandwidth:

```
Gateway(config-gk)# bandwidth {check-destination | interzone | session}
  {default | zone zone-name} bandwidth-size
```

The **check-destination** parameter enables the gatekeeper to verify available bandwidth resources at the destination endpoint. The **interzone** parameter defines the total amount of H.323 traffic bandwidth between zones. The **session** parameter limits the bandwidth for a particular session within the zone. Anything that follows **default** defines the default value for all zones or a particular zone.

H.323 Gateway Configuration

Multiple gateways can exist in a single zone. They register with the gatekeeper. The CME router must be configured so that the router knows the gatekeeper's name and IP address.

To configure a gateway interface as the interface used to connect to non-packet-based networks, enter the following command:

```
Gateway(config-if)#h323-gateway voip interface
```

To configure the appropriate zone, gatekeeper name, and gatekeeper IP address, enter the following command in interface configuration mode:

```
Gateway(config-if)# h323-gateway voip id gatekeeper-id {ipaddr ip-address
  [port-number]¦ multicast} [priority number]
```

It is very important that the gatekeeper ID used here be the fully qualified name (the same one programmed on the gatekeeper).

To give a unique identifier used in H.323 communications between this gateway router and the gatekeeper, enter the following command:

```
GateKeeperX(config-if)# h323-gateway voip h323-id interface-id
```

When the gateway registers with the gatekeeper, use the following command:

```
GateKeeperX(config-if)# h323-gateway voip tech-prefix prefix
```

This feature could be used to inform the gatekeeper that a certain technology is associated with a particular call. An example could be that **4#** is a fax transmission. This feature could also be used like an area code for generic routing. No standard currently exists for its usage, but it is demonstrated in the labs in this chapter. In the Cisco environment, it is common to see the pound sign (#) used as the last character, but this is not required. Because Cisco gatekeepers use an asterisk (*) as a special character, you should never use an asterisk in the tech-prefix.

To designate a local source IP address for the voice gateway, use the following command:

```
GateKeeperX(config-if)# h323-gateway voip bind srcaddr
```

You do not have to issue this command on the interface you define as the voice gateway interface (but it is usually more convenient to do so). The IP address (*srcaddr*) used in this command is the IP address on the same interface being configured.

If your router has redundant WAN connections, the source address typically is bound to a loopback address so that H.323 calls can still be established in the event that the primary WAN connection goes down.

Lab 9-1: Simple H.323 Between Two Pods

In this lab, the company OCSIC.org has decided to deploy H.323 between two CME routers.

Note: This lab requires the CME router to be working. Two Cisco IP Phones are attached to the router, and the phones have connectivity. Refer to the labs in Chapter 2, "Router, Integrated Switch, and IP Phone Basic Configuration," to configure the router and switch. Select a method in Chapter 3, "Managing and Configuring Cisco VoIP Devices," to configure CallManager Express. Also complete Lab 5-1, "Configuring FXS Connectivity," to configure the FXS port.

The two routers should *not* have T1 connectivity.

This lab requires two CME routers, and they have to be configured as two different pod numbers. Pods 1 and 2 must partner, and pods 3 and 4 must partner.

The objectives of this lab are as follows:

- Configure the CME router for serial connectivity to another pod.

- Configure VoIP dial peers for inter-pod connectivity.

To perform this lab, you need the following equipment:

- Two CME-capable routers with a serial interface and the appropriate serial cables

- Two switches/switch modules

- Workstation with an Ethernet 10/100 network interface card (NIC) installed

- Two Cisco IP Phones (powered using any method)

Figure 9-2 shows the topology used with this lab. Keep in mind that an integrated switch module in the router could be used instead of the external switch.

Figure 9-2   Lab Topology: Unity Express Initial Configuration

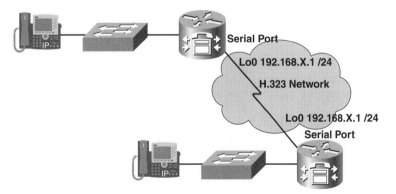

The procedure for this lab consists of the following tasks, described in detail in the following sections:

- **Task 1**—Verify connectivity.

- **Task 2**—Configure and test the routers for serial connectivity.

- **Task 3**—Configure a loopback interface and routing.

- **Task 4**—Configure the H.323 dial peers.

- **Task 5**—Test the dial peers.

Task 1: Verify Connectivity

Step 1.   Power on one of the routers. The router and switch module should be configured with the basic configuration. Both Cisco IP Phones should be operational. From one Cisco IP Phone, call the other IP Phone. The call should succeed. Do not proceed until the IP Phones are configured.

Step 2.   Move both Cisco IP Phones to the other router, and perform the previous procedure on the second router. Do not proceed until the IP Phones connect.

Step 3.   Move one of the Cisco IP Phones back to the other router and ensure that it reregisters with the CME router.

Step 4.   Ensure that no T1 cable attaches to either router.

Task 2: Configure and Test the Routers for Serial Connectivity

Step 1.   Ensure that no configuration commands exist on either router for the lowest-numbered serial interface.

Step 2.   Connect serial cables to the lowest-numbered serial interface between both CME routers.

Step 3.   On both pods, use the **show controllers serial** command on the lowest serial interface, and verify whether the cable is data communications equipment (DCE) or data terminal equipment (DTE):

```
RouterVoIPX# show controllers serial mod/port
```

Examples of this command are **show controllers serial 0/0** and **show controllers serial 0/3/0**.

The output of the **show controllers serial** command looks similar to the following output. The fourth line shows that this router is the DCE and requires the clock rate to be set. The remote router in this case is the DTE.

```
RouterVoIP2#show controllers serial 0/3/0
Interface Serial0/3/0
Hardware is GT96K
DCE V.35, clock rate 2000000
idb at 0x44EEA478, driver data structure at 0x44EF228C
wic_info 0x44EF2880
Physical Port 7, SCC Num 7
```

Step 4.   From interface configuration mode, assign an IP address to the lowest-numbered serial interface on both routers using the following commands. Refer to Table 9-1 for the IP addresses used. On the router that has the DCE cable, provide a clock.

Table 9-1   Router Serial Interface IP Addresses

Pod	Hostname of Router or Switch	Serial Interface IP Address
Pod 1	RouterVoIP1	10.19.0.1/24
Pod 2	RouterVoIP2	10.19.0.2/24
Pod 3	RouterVoIP3	10.39.0.1/24
Pod 4	RouterVoIP4	10.39.0.2/24

```
RouterVoIPX(config)# interface serial x/x/x
RouterVoIPX(config-if)# ip address 10.x9.0.x 255.255.255.0
RouterVoIPX(config-if)# no shutdown
(optional) RouterVoIPX(config-if)# clock rate xxxxx
```

Step 5. From one router, verify that the serial interface is "up and up." Do not proceed until the interface is functional:

```
RouterVoIPX# show ip interface brief
```

Step 6. From one router, ping the serial interface on the other router. Refer to Table 9-1 for the appropriate IP address. Do not proceed until the ping succeeds.

```
RouterVoIPX# ping 10.x9.0.x
```

Task 3: Configure a Loopback Interface and Routing

Step 1. Ensure that no loopback interface currently exists in the router configuration. If it does, remove the interface:

```
RouterVoIPX# show ip interface brief
(optional)RouterVoIPX# config t
(optional)RouterVoIPX(config)# no interface loopbackx
```

Step 2. On both routers, create a loopback address. The x in the IP address is the pod number:

```
RouterVoIPX(config)# interface loopback 0
RouterVoIPX(config-if)# ip address 192.168.x.1 255.255.255.0
```

Step 3. The EIGRP routing protocol (AS number 100) should already be enabled on both routers. If it is not, enable it and advertise all networks.

Advertise the serial network and the network for the loopback address under EIGRP. Look at Table 9-1 to find the appropriate network number for the serial interface.

```
(optional) RouterVoIPX(config)# router eigrp 100
(optional) RouterVoIPX(config-router)# network 10.0.0.0
RouterVoIPX(config)# router eigrp 100
RouterVoIPX(config-router)# network 10.x9.0.0
RouterVoIPX(config-router)# network 192.168.x.0
```

Step 4. On both routers, verify the routing table and ensure that *the other router's networks* appear in the routing table. Do not proceed unless both new networks appear in both routers.

```
RouterVoIPX# show ip route
```

Task 4: Configure the H.323 Dial Peers

Step 1. Before you create a VoIP dial peer, it is important to have the loopback address for the neighbor router.

Neighbor router loopback interface IP address:

Step 2. On both routers, create a dial peer using the following commands. You must know several important pieces of information before configuring.

The x in the dial peer number is the pod number. Refer to Table 9-2 for the appropriate destination pattern. The session target is the loopback address on the neighbor router. This is the IP address recorded in the preceding step.

Table 9-2   Destination Pattern for Inter-pod Connectivity

Pod	Destination Pattern
Pod 1	(to Pod 2) 50[3-5].
Pod 2	(to Pod 1) 50[0-2].
Pod 3	(to Pod 4) 51..
Pod 4	(to Pod 3) 50[6-8]

```
RouterVoIPX(config)# dial-peer voice x00 voip
RouterVoIPX(config-dial-peer)# destination-pattern xxxx
RouterVoIPX(config-dial-peer)# session target ipv4:192.168.x.1
RouterVoIPX(config-dial-peer)# dtmf-relay h245-alphanumeric
RouterVoIPX(config-dial-peer)# codec g729r8
```

Task 5: Test the Dial Peers

Step 1.   From the lowest-numbered Cisco IP Phone, call the other Cisco IP Phone. The call should succeed. Troubleshoot as necessary.

Step 2.   From the Cisco IP Phone connected to the other router, place a call to the other IP Phone. The call should succeed.

Step 3.   The router configuration does not need to be saved for the next lab, but make a copy of the running configuration, and paste it into a text file for your own purposes.

Lab 9-2: H.323 with a Gatekeeper and Analog Phones

In this lab, OCSIC.org has decided to use H.323 in its multisite CME router network. This will reduce the number of dial peers that currently have to be created and will provide more flexibility.

Note: This lab requires an advanced IOS on at least one of the routers so that it can be configured as a gatekeeper. Any IOS image that includes the letters ivs in its filename supports gatekeeper. For example, c2800nm-ipvoice_ivs-mz.123-11.T9.bin is an IOS version that supports both voice and gatekeeper.

To determine if the proper IOS is available, navigate to global configuration mode and enter **gate?**. View the output and see if the **gatekeeper** command is available. If the command is available, the router can be configured as an H.323 gatekeeper.

The objectives of this lab are as follows:

- Configure one CME router as a gatekeeper.

- Configure a second CME router as a gateway.

- Configure two analog phones to communicate using H.323.

To perform this lab, you need the following equipment:

- Two CME-capable routers (with one of the routers having an advanced IOS). See the note at the beginning of this lab.

- Workstation

- Four analog phones

Figure 9-3 shows the topology used with this lab.

Figure 9-3   Lab Topology: Gatekeeper

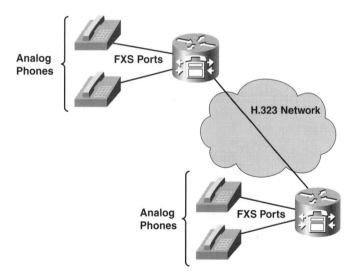

The procedure for this lab consists of the following tasks, described in detail in the following sections:

- **Task 1**—Verify the IOS version.

- **Task 2**—Configure inter-router connectivity.

- **Task 3**—Configure the gatekeeper.

- **Task 4**—Configure the gateway portion of the gatekeeper.

- **Task 5**—Configure the gateway router.

- **Task 6**—Configure the FXS dial peers.
- **Task 7**—Configure the VoIP dial peers.
- **Task 8**—Test H.323 connectivity.

Task 1: Verify the IOS Version

Step 1.   Power on both routers. One of the routers will be configured as an H.323 gatekeeper, and the other router as a gateway.

Step 2.   On both routers, navigate to global configuration mode, and determine if the **gatekeeper** command is available:

```
RouterVoIPX(config)# gate?
```

If the command is missing from both routers, the IOS version on one of the routers must be upgraded to an appropriate IOS. The router IOS must have a software feature set of "INT Voice/Video, IPIP GW, TDMIP, and GW" to perform this lab. The IOS version used in these labs is c2800nm-ipvoice_ivs-mz.124-2.T5.

Make a note of which router will be designated as the gatekeeper.

Step 3.   Erase any currently saved configurations on both routers. Reload both routers:

```
RouterVoIPX# erase startup-config
RouterVoIPX# reload
```

Step 4.   From global configuration mode on the router that will be the gatekeeper, change the hostname. The *x* in the command is the pod number:

```
Router(config)# hostname GateKeeperx
```

Step 5.   From global configuration mode on the router that will be the gateway, change the hostname. The *x* in the command is the pod number:

```
Router (config)# hostname Gatewayx
```

Task 2: Configure Inter-Router Connectivity

Step 1.   Remove any other cables between the two routers. Disconnect the serial or T1 if connected. Connect a crossover cable (or use a switch without VLANs) between the lowest-numbered FastEthernet ports on the routers.

Step 2.   On both routers, determine the interface syntax needed to configure the FastEthernet port. This information will be needed to configure the port:

```
GateKeeperX# show ip interface brief
```

Step 3.   On both routers from FastEthernet interface configuration mode, assign an IP address to the FastEthernet interface. The pod router that will be the gatekeeper will use an IP address that ends in **1**. The gateway router will use an IP address that ends in **2**. Bring up the interface:

```
GateKeeperX(config)#int fastethernet0/0
GateKeeperX(config-if)# ip address 192.168.4.x 255.255.255.0
GateKeeperX(config-if)# no shutdown
GatewayX(config)#int fastethernet0/0
GatewayX(config-if)# ip address 192.168.4.x 255.255.255.0
GatewayX(config-if)# no shutdown
```

Step 4.   From one router, ping the other router. Do not proceed until the ping succeeds.

```
GateKeeperX# ping 192.168.4.x
```

Task 3: Configure the Gatekeeper

Step 1.   In global configuration mode on the router that will be the gatekeeper, enable the gatekeeper function:

```
GateKeeperX(config)# gatekeeper
```

Step 2.   On the gatekeeper router in gatekeeper configuration mode, define the local zone. The gatekeeper H.323 ID is gk, the domain name is zoneA.ocsic.org, and the RAS IP address is 192.168.4.1.

```
GateKeeperX(config-gk)# zone local gk_zoneA.ocsic.org 192.168.4.1
```

Step 3.   In gatekeeper configuration mode, define the zone prefix. In this scenario, the gatekeeper router also serves as a gateway and has phones attached, so two zone prefixes are defined. The phones that connect to the gatekeeper/gateway router FXS ports have phone numbers of 7001 and 7002. The phones that connect to the gateway-only router FXS ports have the phone numbers 8001 and 8002. The gateway function provided on the gatekeeper router has a higher priority than the other router:

```
GateKeeperX(config-gk)# zone prefix gk_7... gw-priority 9 CME1
GateKeeperX(config-gk)# zone prefix gk_8... gw-priority 9 CME2
```

Step 4.   Bring the gatekeeper to an operational mode:

```
GateKeeperX(config-gk)# no shutdown
```

Step 5.   From privileged mode on the gatekeeper, verify the gatekeeper status:

```
GateKeeperX# show gatekeeper zone status
```

The output of the **show gatekeeper zone status** command looks similar to the following:

```
gatekeeper1#show gatekeeper zone stat
                      GATEKEEPER ZONES
                      ================
GK name      Domain Name   RAS Address      PORT  FLAGS
-------      -----------   -----------      ----- -----

gk           zoneA.ocsic.o 192.168.4.1      1719  LS
   BANDWIDTH INFORMATION (kbps) :
      Maximum total bandwidth : unlimited
      Current total bandwidth : 0
      Maximum interzone bandwidth : unlimited
      Current interzone bandwidth : 0
      Maximum session bandwidth : unlimited
   SUBNET ATTRIBUTES :
      All Other Subnets : (Enabled)
   PROXY USAGE CONFIGURATION :
      Inbound Calls from all other zones :
         to terminals in local zone gk : use proxy
         to gateways in local zone gk  : do not use proxy
         to MCUs in local zone gk  : do not use proxy
      Outbound Calls to all other zones :
         from terminals in local zone gk : use proxy
         from gateways in local zone gk  : do not use proxy
         from MCUs in local zone gk  : do not use proxy
```

Verify that the GK name column contains the name **gk**. (That is all it shows.) Ensure that the Domain Name column contains the name **zoneA.ocsic.org**. Ensure that the RAS address is **192.168.4.1** and the Port column number is **1719**. If any of these values is wrong, remove the erroneous command and reenter the appropriate commands.

Step 6. From privileged mode, ensure that the gatekeeper status is up. The zone name can also be seen in the output:

```
GateKeeperX# show gatekeeper status
```

The output of the **show gatekeeper status** command looks similar to the following:

```
gatekeeper1#show gatekeeper status
    Gatekeeper State: UP
    Load Balancing:    DISABLED
    Flow Control:      DISABLED
    Zone Name:         gk
    Accounting:        DISABLED
    Endpoint Throttling:        DISABLED
    Security:          DISABLED
    Maximum Remote Bandwidth:                unlimited
    Current Remote Bandwidth:                0 kbps
    Current Remote Bandwidth (w/ Alt GKs): 0 kbps
```

Task 4: Configure the Gateway Portion of the Gatekeeper

Step 1. The gatekeeper also will be configured as a gateway in this scenario. From global configuration mode, configure the gatekeeper router as a gateway:

```
GateKeeperX(config)# gateway
```

This command turns on the gateway functionality. Enter **exit** to return to configuration mode:

```
GateKeeper1(config-gateway)# exit
```

Step 2. In interface configuration mode for the FastEthernet interface (the interface that connects to the other router), configure the specific H.323 gateway commands.

The second line enables the FastEthernet interface as an H.323 interface. The third line configures the appropriate zone, gatekeeper name, and gatekeeper IP address. The fourth command provides an H.323 ID for this gateway router. The fifth line is a technology prefix used when the gateway registers with the gatekeeper. The last line is the **h323-gateway voip bind srcaddr** command, which designates a local source IP address for the voice gateway. You do not have to issue this command on the interface that you define as the voice gateway interface (but it is usually more convenient to do so):

```
GateKeeperX(config)#interface fastEthernet 0/1
GateKeeperX(config-if)# h323-gateway voip interface
GateKeeperX(config-if)# h323-gateway voip id gk ipaddr 192.168.4.1 1718
GateKeeperX(config-if)# h323-gateway voip h323-id CME1_
GateKeeperX(config-if)# h323-gateway voip tech-prefix 1#
GateKeeperX(config-if)# h323-gateway voip bind srcaddr 192.168.4.1
```

Step 3. Verify the status of the gateway function. Ensure that the H.323 service is up. Also verify that the alias list contains an H323-ID of gw-CME1. If not, check the running configuration for typing errors. Remove any mistyped commands, and reenter the correct command:

```
GateKeeperX# show gateway
```

The output of the **show gateway** command looks similar to the following:

```
gatekeeper1#show gateway
H.323 ITU-T Version: 4.0   H323 Stack Version: 0.1


  H.323 service is up
  Gateway  CME1  is registered to Gatekeeper gk


Alias list (CLI configured)
  H323-ID CME1
Alias list (last RCF)
  H323-ID CME1


  H323 resource thresholding is Disabled
```

Step 4. Look at how the gatekeeper can see the gateway as an H.323 endpoint. Verify that an endpoint exists for the gw-CME1 (gateway on the same router):

```
GateKeeperX# show gatekeeper endpoints
```

The output of the **show gatekeeper endpoints** command looks similar to the following:

```
gatekeeper1#sh gatekeeper endpoints
                     GATEKEEPER ENDPOINT REGISTRATION

                     ==================================

CallSignalAddr   Port  RASSignalAddr   Port  Zone Name          Type       Flags
---------------  ----- --------------- ----- ---------          ----       -----
192.168.4.1      1720  192.168.4.1     58240 gk                 VOIP-GW
     H323-ID: CME1
     Voice Capacity Max.=  Avail.=  Current.= 0
Total number of active registrations = 1
```

Task 5: Configure the Gateway Router

Step 1. In global configuration mode on the router that will be only a gateway, enable the gateway:

```
GatewayX(config)# gateway
```

Step 2. On the FastEthernet interface that connects to the other router, configure the specific H.323 gateway:

```
GatewayX(config)#interface fastEthernet 0/0
GatewayX(config-if)# h323-gateway voip interface
GatewayX(config-if)# h323-gateway voip id gk_ipaddr 192.168.4.1 1718
GatewayX(config-if)# h323-gateway voip h323-id CME2
GatewayX(config-if)# h323-gateway voip tech-prefix 1#
GatewayX(config-if)# h323-gateway voip bind srcaddr 192.168.4.2
```

Step 3. Verify that the gateway registered with the gatekeeper. The H.323 service should be up. The Alias listed in the output should be H323-ID of gw-CME2. If the H.323 service is not up or if the Alias listing is incorrect, remove the improper command and redo it until the output is correct:

```
GatewayX# show gateway
```

The output of the **show gateway** command looks similar to the following:

```
gateway2#sh gateway
```

```
       H.323 ITU-T Version: 4.0    H323 Stack Version: 0.1


       H.323 service is up
       Gateway  CME2  is registered to Gatekeeper gk


    Alias list (CLI configured)
     H323-ID CME2
    Alias list (last RCF)
     H323-ID CME2
```

Step 4.   From the gatekeeper, verify the registration of the new gateway router. The output should show both routers (CallSignalAddr of 192.168.4.1 and 192.168.4.2). Troubleshoot if this information is not correct.

```
GateKeeperX# show gatekeeper endpoints
```

The output of the **show gatekeeper endpoints** command looks similar to the following:

```
gatekeeper1#sh gatekeeper endpoints
                      GATEKEEPER ENDPOINT REGISTRATION
                      ================================

CallSignalAddr  Port  RASSignalAddr   Port  Zone Name       Type      Flags
--------------  ----  -------------   ----  ---------       ----      -----

192.168.4.1     1720  192.168.4.1     51129 gk              VOIP-GW
    H323-ID: CME1
    Voice Capacity Max.=  Avail.=  Current.= 0
192.168.4.2     1720  192.168.4.2     57067 gk              VOIP-GW
    H323-ID: CME2
    Voice Capacity Max.=  Avail.=  Current.= 0
Total number of active registrations = 2
```

Task 6: Configure the FXS Dial Peers

Step 1.   On the gatekeeper router, make a note of the module, port, slot number format of the FXS interfaces:

```
GateKeeperX# show voice port summary
```

The output of the **show voice port summary** command looks similar to the following:

```
gatekeeper1#show voice port summary
                                    IN        OUT
PORT      CH   SIG-TYPE    ADMIN OPER STATUS    STATUS    EC
========= ==   =========== ===== ==== ======== ======== ==
0/2/0     --   fxs-ls      up    dorm on-hook   idle      y
0/2/1     --   fxs-ls      up    dorm on-hook   idle      y
```

Step 2.   On the gatekeeper in global configuration mode, configure a POTS dial peer for the two FXS ports. The number assigned to the analog phone that connects to the lowest-numbered FXS port is 7000; the number assigned to the analog phone that connects to the second FXS port is 7001:

```
GateKeeperX(config)# dial-peer voice 45 pots
GateKeeperX(config-dial-peer)# destination-pattern 7000
GateKeeperX(config-dial-peer)# port x/x/0
```

```
GateKeeperX(config)# dial-peer voice 46 pots
GateKeeperX(config-dial-peer)# destination-pattern 7001
GateKeeperX(config-dial-peer)# port x/x/1
```

Step 3.   On the gateway router, make a note of the syntax for the FXS ports:

```
GatewayX# show voice port summary
```

The output of the **show voice port summary** command looks similar to the following:

```
gateway2#show voice port summary

                                  IN      OUT
PORT      CH   SIG-TYPE   ADMIN OPER STATUS  STATUS   EC
========= == ============ ===== ==== ======== ======== ==
0/2/0     -- fxs-ls       up    dorm on-hook  idle     y
0/2/1     -- fxs-ls       up    dorm on-hook  idle     y
```

Step 4.   On the gateway router, configure the dial peers for the analog phones that connect to the FXS ports. The analog phone that connects to the lowest-numbered FXS port is assigned 8000. The second analog phone that connects to the second FXS port is assigned 8001:

```
GatewayX(config)# dial-peer voice 41 pots
GatewayX(config-dial-peer)# destination-pattern 8000
GatewayX(onfig-dial-peer)# port x/x/0


GatewayX(config)# dial-peer voice 42 pots
GatewayX(config-dial-peer)# destination-pattern 8001
GatewayX(config-dial-peer)# port x/x/1
```

Step 5.   On the gateway router, use the **show gateway** command to see if adding the dial peers has affected the gateway:

```
GatewayX# show gateway
```

Is the output any different from the last time this command was executed?

Step 6.   On the gatekeeper, use the **show gatekeeper endpoints** command to verify that all four analog phones (7000, 7001, 8000, and 8001) have registered with the gatekeeper. Troubleshoot as necessary.

The output of the **show gatekeeper endpoints** command looks similar to the following:

```
GateKeeperx#show gatekeeper endpoints
                GATEKEEPER ENDPOINT REGISTRATION
                ================================
CallSignalAddr  Port  RASSignalAddr   Port  Zone Name        Type     Flags
--------------  ----- --------------- ----- ---------        ----     -----
192.168.4.1     1720  192.168.4.1     51129 gk               VOIP-GW
    E164-ID: 7000
    E164-ID: 7001
    H323-ID: CME1
    Voice Capacity Max.=  Avail.=  Current.= 0
192.168.4.2     1720  192.168.4.2     57067 gk               VOIP-GW
    E164-ID: 8000
```

```
        E164-ID: 8001
        H323-ID: CME2
        Voice Capacity Max.=  Avail.=  Current.= 0
Total number of active registrations = 2
```

What command(s) allowed the analog phones (which are not intelligent devices) to register with the gatekeeper?

Task 7: Configure the VoIP Dial Peers

Step 1.   From global configuration mode on the gatekeeper router, create the VoIP dial peer, and use RAS as the session target. The four periods are part of the command:

```
GateKeeperX(config)# dial-peer voice 50 voip
GateKeeperX(config-dial-peer)# destination pattern ....
GateKeeperX(config-dial-peer)# session target ras
```

Step 2.   From global configuration mode on the gateway router, create the VoIP dial peer, and use RAS as the session target. The four periods are part of the command:

```
GatewayX(config)# dial-peer voice 50 voip
GatewayX(config-dial-peer)# destination-pattern ....
GatewayX(config-dial-peer)# session target ras
```

Step 3.   On the gateway router, determine if the creation of VoIP dial peers affected the H.323 protocol suite:

```
GatewayX# show gateway
```

Is the output any different from the last time this command was executed?

Task 8: Test H.323 Connectivity

Step 1.   From one of the analog phones connected to the gatekeeper, call the phone connected to the gateway at 8000. The call should succeed. Troubleshoot as necessary if the call does not succeed.

Step 2.   From one of the analog phones connected to the gateway, call the phone connected to the gateway at 7000. The call should succeed.

Step 3.   On the gateway, enable H.225 events debugging:

```
GatewayX# debug h225 events
```

Step 4.   From a phone that connects to the gateway, place a call to a phone that connects to the gatekeeper. The **debug h225 events** output shows you how the protocol handles setting up the call.

Step 5.   Turn off all debugging:

```
GatewayX# undebug all
```

Step 6.   Save your configurations on both routers for the next lab:

```
GatewayX# copy running-config startup-config
GatekeeperX# copy startup-config running-config
```

Lab 9-3: H.323 with Analog and IP Phones

In this lab, OCSIC.org has decided to configure the IP Phones to connect sites using H.323.

Note: This lab requires a version of Cisco IOS Software on at least one of the routers that supports gatekeeper and CallManager. Any IOS image that includes the letters ivs in its filename supports gatekeeper. The version of IOS used to create these labs was c2800nm-ipvoice_ivs-mz.124-2.T5.

To determine if the proper IOS is available, navigate to global configuration mode and enter **gate?**. View the output and see if the **gatekeeper** command is available. If the command is available, the router can be configured as an H.323 gatekeeper.

Note: This lab relies on the configuration files from Lab 9-2 being loaded (H.323 used between pods for analog phones). Do not proceed unless H.323 is configured and working between the two analog phones.

The objective of this lab is to configure and verify IP telephony between sites using H.323.

To perform this lab, you need the following equipment:

- Two Cisco CME-capable routers (with one of the routers having an IOS that supports CallManager and Gatekeeper). See the note at the beginning of this lab.

- Switch/switch module

- Workstation

- Two analog phones

- Two Cisco IP Phones (powered using any method)

Figure 9-4 shows the lab topology used with this lab. Keep in mind that an integrated switch module in the router could be used instead of the external switch.

Figure 9-4   Lab Topology: H.323 with IP and Analog Phones

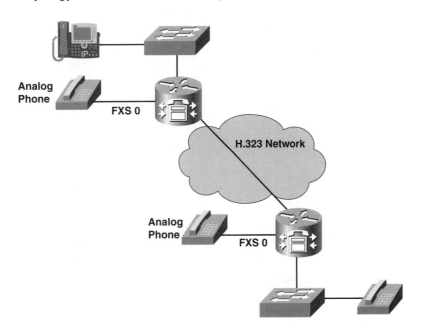

The procedure for this lab consists of the following tasks, described in detail in the following sections:

- **Task 1**—Verify analog phone connectivity.

- **Task 2**—Configure IP Phone connectivity on the gatekeeper.

- **Task 3**—Configure IP Phone connectivity on the gateway.

- **Task 4**—Configure and test the gatekeeper for IP connectivity.

- **Task 5**—Manually register the IP Phone with the gatekeeper.

Task 1: Verify Analog Phone Connectivity

Step 1.   From the analog phone connected to the gatekeeper, call the analog phone connected to the gateway at 8000. The call should succeed. Troubleshoot as necessary if the call does not succeed.

Step 2.   From the analog phone connected to the gateway, call the analog phone (7000) that connects to the gatekeeper router. Do not proceed if the call does not succeed.

Task 2: Configure IP Phone Connectivity on the Gatekeeper

Note: This lab requires that the Cisco IP Phones be configured using CallManager Express. Ensure that the VLANs and routing protocols are configured. Refer to Lab 2-4, "Configuring a Cisco CallManager Express-capable Router and an Integrated Switch," and Lab 2-5, "Configuring a Cisco CallManager Express-capable Router with an External Switch," to configure the router and switch. Disregard the steps in Chapter 2 that require deleting the routers' configuration or changing the routers' hostnames.

Step 1.   On the switch or switch module, program all commands necessary for the phone to connect to the port. If an external switch is being used, create the trunk between the router and the external switch.

Step 2.   Configure the gatekeeper router with the commands necessary to route between VLANs and to exchange routing updates with the gateway router using EIGRP.

Step 3.   On the gatekeeper router, ensure that all routes are up and in the routing table. Troubleshoot as necessary.

Step 4.   On the gatekeeper router, from telephony service configuration mode, use the **telephony-service setup** command to quickly configure the IP Phone. Use the following parameters during this dialog:

DHCP service: **yes**

IP network: **10.X5.0.0**

Subnet mask: **255.255.255.0**

TFTP server: **10.X5.0.1**

Default router: **10.X5.0.1**

IP source address: **10.X5.0.1**

Skinny port: **2000**

Number of phones: **2**

Dual extension: **no**

First phone number: **7010**

Direct-inward-dial: **yes**

Forward calls: **no**

Full E.164: **5105557010**

Voicemail: **no**

Step 5.   The Cisco IP Phone should power up and receive the four-digit number that displays on the phone. The phone may have to be reset. Refer to Lab 2-2 if you need instructions on resetting the phone. Do not proceed unless the phone receives a phone number.

Task 3: Configure IP Phone Connectivity on the Gateway

Step 1.   This configuration is for the router designated as the gateway. On the switch or switch module, program all commands necessary for the phone to connect to the port. If a switch is being used, create the trunk between the router and the switch.

Step 2.   On the gateway router, input the commands necessary to route between VLANs and to exchange routing updates with the gateway router using EIGRP.

Step 3.   On the gateway router, ensure that all routes are up and in the routing table. Troubleshoot as necessary.

Step 4.   On the gateway router, from telephony service configuration mode, use the **telephony-service setup** command to quickly configure the IP Phone. Use the following parameters during this dialog:

DHCP service: **yes**

IP network: **10.***X***5.0.0**

Subnet mask: **255.255.255.0**

TFTP server: **10.***X***5.0.1**

Default router: **10.***X***5.0.1**

IP source address: **10.***X***5.0.1**

Skinny port: **2000**

Number of phones: **2**

Dual extension: **no**

First phone number: **8010**

Direct-inward-dial: **yes**

Forward calls: **no**

Full E.164: **5105558010**

Voicemail: **no**

Step 5.   The Cisco IP Phone should power up and receive the four-digit number that displays on the phone. The phone may have to be reset. Refer to Lab 2-2 if you need instructions on how to reset the phone. Do not proceed unless the phone receives a phone number.

Step 6.   From one Cisco IP Phone, call the IP Phone connected to the other pod. The call should fail.

Task 4: Configure and Test the Gatekeeper for IP Connectivity

Step 1.   From gatekeeper configuration mode, add the following commands so that the IP Phones can register with the gatekeeper:

```
GateKeeper1(config)# gatekeeper
GateKeeperX(config-gk)# shutdown
GateKeeperX(config-gk)# zone prefix gk_zoneA.ocsic.org 7... gw-priority 5 gw_CME1
GateKeeperX(config-gk)# zone prefix gk_zoneA.ocsic.org 8... gw-priority 5 gw_CME2
GateKeeperX(config-gk)# gw-type-prefix 1#* default-technology
GateKeeperX(config-gk)# bandwidth interzone zone gk_ 128
GateKeeperX(config-gk)# no shutdown
```

Step 2.   From one Cisco IP Phone, call the other IP Phone. The call should succeed. If necessary, troubleshoot any problem found. Answer the call and leave the connection active. While the call is being made, use the **show gatekeeper calls** command to determine how the gatekeeper views the call.

The output of the **show gatekeeper calls** command looks similar to the following:

```
gatekeeper1#show gatekeeper calls
Total number of active calls = 1.
                          GATEKEEPER CALL INFO
                          ====================
LocalCallID                         Age(secs)   BW
3-65108                                 4          16(Kbps)
  Endpt(s): Alias                   E.164Addr
    src EP: CME2                       5105558010
            CallSignalAddr  Port  RASSignalAddr   Port
            192.168.4.2     1720  192.168.4.2     53749
  Endpt(s): Alias                   E.164Addr
    dst EP: CME1                       7010
            CallSignalAddr  Port  RASSignalAddr   Port
            192.168.4.1     1720  192.168.4.1     58193
```

What is the source endpoint (src EP)? Why do you think this would be the endpoint shown?

_____

_____

_____

How much bandwidth does the call take?

_____

Task 5: Manually Register the IP Phone with the Gatekeeper

Step 1. On the gateway router from ephone-dn configuration mode for the phone number assigned to the gateway router IP Phone, manually configure the Cisco IP Phone to register with the gatekeeper:

```
GatewayX(config)# ephone-dn x
GatewayX(config-ephone-dn)# number 8010 secondary 5105558010 no-reg primary
```

Step 2. On the ephone that is associated with this number, reset the phone:

```
GatewayX(config)# ephone x
GatewayX(config-ephone)# reset
```

Step 3. From privileged mode on the gateway router, view the effects of the change:

```
GatewayX# show gateway
```

In the output, how is the Cisco IP Phone alias different from the analog phone alias?

Step 4. From privileged mode on the gatekeeper router, view the effects of the change:

```
Gatekeeper# show gatekeeper endpoints
```

Step 5. From the gatekeeper Cisco IP Phone, call the other IP Phone. The call should go through.

Step 6. The configuration can be erased on both routers.

CHAPTER 10

VoIP Quality of Service and Security

Two buzzwords being used in the industry today are *quality of service (QoS)* and *security*. This chapter deals with the basics of these topics. Keep in mind that entire books are dedicated to both QoS and security, so the coverage in this chapter is relegated to what you need to know to complete the labs.

Typically, networks operate on a best-effort delivery basis. This means that all traffic has equal priority and an equal chance of being delivered in a timely manner. Similarly, when congestion occurs, all traffic has an equal chance of being dropped. You can implement QoS on each network device. It can provide an end-to-end solution to ensure that the important traffic gets through but that it does not use so much bandwidth that it prevents other traffic from reaching its destination.

VoIP traffic cannot tolerate large delays or extensive dropped packets. Can you imagine a telephone conversation that had delayed packets? A person would talk, and a second (or more) later, the spoken words would arrive at the other end, or pieces of the conversation could be missing altogether. If the other person repeatedly said something like, "Are you there?", the quality of the conversation would quickly deteriorate. A conversation that has dropped packets means that words (or parts of words) are dropped from the transmitted speech—not a good thing with voice. QoS helps with these issues by prioritizing the speech packets through the IP network and not allowing all the voice traffic to starve the other types of packets from being transmitted or reaching their destination.

Cisco CallManager Express (CME) is vulnerable to attacks on Cisco IOS, similar to any attack to a router. As a result, the same security best practices that are recommended for an IOS router are applicable to a router that is running CME. The labs in this chapter explore a few practices you can implement specifically for VoIP, the Cisco IP Phones, and the overall network design to ensure better security.

Overview of VoIP Quality of Service

When you implement QoS on your network devices, you can implement congestion management and congestion avoidance techniques to give certain frames and packets preferential treatment. This makes your network performance more predictable and bandwidth utilization more effective.

Switch Quality of Service

When implementing QoS on a switch, you can assign a priority value on interfaces that are configured as trunks. 802.1Q frame headers have a 2-byte field called Tag Control Information (TCI). Within this TCI field, the 3 most significant bits are used to classify frames for different priority levels. With 3 bits available, eight priority levels are possible—0 through 7, with 0 being the lowest priority. Figure 10-1 shows the Layer 2 802.1Q frame header and the 3 bits used to prioritize frames.

Figure 10-1   802.1Q Frame Header

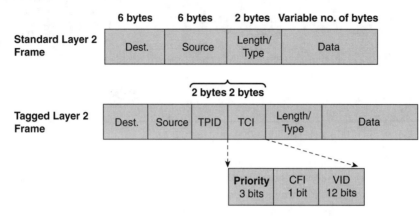

The 3 bits are commonly known as the *class of service (CoS)* value. On interfaces that have been configured as trunks, all traffic in 802.1Q frames (except for traffic coming to/from the native VLAN) can carry CoS values. Frames that are not configured as trunks cannot contain CoS values.

Another type of marking that can be done is within the Layer 3 IP packet; this type of marking is called DiffServ Codepoint (DSCP). The DSCP marking is a 6-bit value contained in the IP header. Figure 10-2 shows the DSCP bits in an IP header.

Figure 10-2   IP Header with DSCP Bits

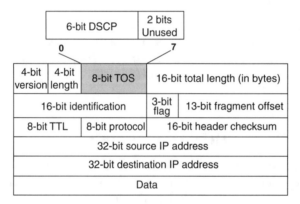

Because the DSCP value is carried within a normal IP header, you do not have to configure the switch port as a trunk to be able to recognize or receive these bits. You can configure the switch to prioritize the traffic using these bits just like you can configure it to prioritize the traffic using the CoS bits.

QoS Queues

Each port on a switch has a single receive buffer queue for incoming frames. When an untagged (no priority value set) frame comes into this port (such as one from the native VLAN), the frame is assigned the priority value that has been configured for that port. This new priority value (if configured) is the frame's new priority value. It follows the frame through the network until it is modified again or until it reaches its destination. You can change this value using the switch CLI.

Switches also have outgoing queues for each port. The number of queues depends on the model of the switch. For example, a 2950 switch has four outgoing queues. You can configure each queue for QoS scheduling. There are two types:

- **Strict priority scheduling** allows packets in the high-priority queue to transmit first. Packets in the low-priority queue have to wait until all the high-priority queues are empty. Strict priority scheduling is the default method.

- **Weighted round robin (WRR) scheduling** allows you to configure a number that indicates how important (or the weight) one queue is over another queue. WRR gives high-priority traffic precedence but still allows lower-priority traffic to be processed. For example, if high-priority traffic is voice (and it should be), a request for a web page might be a lower priority. You would not want your network to ignore the request for a web page just because voice traffic is running on the network. You would, however, want a QoS network design that allows both types of traffic to function properly but at the same time gives the voice traffic a higher priority. With WRR, low-priority traffic is allowed to be sent even though the high-priority queues are not emptied.

If one queue has a weight of 2 assigned to it and another queue has a weight of 3, this means that two packets are sent from the first queue for every three packets that are sent from the second queue.

AutoQoS on the Switch

Cisco switches can enable AutoQoS on a switch interface. AutoQoS enables QoS in an automated fashion for those who might not be too efficient or who don't know their network traffic as well as is required to deploy QoS manually. It is certainly better to use AutoQoS than no QoS. But the manual method allows for a more granular approach to configuring the many advanced features of QoS and can provide a better network design.

You use the **auto qos voip** interface configuration command to enable AutoQoS on a switch interface for VoIP. A network administrator retains complete control over the switch (and therefore the QoS) configuration even when AutoQoS is deployed. As a side note, CiscoWorks has a QoS Policy Manager tool that can help with more extensive VoIP QoS deployments.

Switch Trust State

You can configure switch ports for a particular trust state. The trust state defines how a port reacts to how inbound packets are classified, marked, and scheduled for transfer. Switch ports that have trust enabled assume that inbound packets are marked with some value (CoS, DSCP, or IP precedence [the predecessor to DSCP]) that is assumed to be valid. Untrusted ports are frames that might or might not be marked, but if the frames are marked, the switch doesn't consider them valid.

The different trust states that are supported vary according to switch model. For example, on a 2950 switch, the trust states are untrusted (no trust enabled), trust CoS bits, and trust DSCP bits. On a 3550 switch, the trust states are the same as for a 2950, but they also include trusting the IP precedence bits (the predecessor to DSCP), trusting a Cisco IP Phone, and providing and extending trust on voice and VLANs.

When the command **auto qos voip cisco-phone** is used on a switch interface, it means that the Cisco switch trusts and retains the packets and QoS markings from the Cisco IP Phone. This command is used on ports that have Cisco IP Phones connected.

The default DSCP value for a Cisco IP Phone is 46, otherwise known as *expedited forwarding* (*EF*). This is the highest classification that QoS can put on a device to allow its packets to be sent at a priority level through a network device that has been configured to pay attention to this classification.

The **auto qos voip trust** command is used on some models of switches on ports that connect to more inside parts of the network. This command is used only when the traffic has been classified by another edge device (such as another switch) and the QoS classification that comes into this port is valid and trusted.

When either the **auto qos voip cisco-phone** or **auto qos voip trust** command is used on an interface, the switch automatically generates a QoS configuration. The **auto qos voip cisco-phone** command enables outbound queues:

- Queue 1 is used for CoS values 0 and 1.

- Queue 2 is used for CoS values 2 and 4.

- Queue 3 is used for CoS values 3, 6, and 7.

- Queue 4 is used for CoS value 5.

- Queue 4 is known as the expedite queue. Voice traffic uses this queue. The default CoS value for voice traffic is 5. By default, this queue is used until it has no more frames to transmit.

You must use the **mls qos trust** command when manually configuring a switch interface for a trust state. Inbound traffic can be trusted, and classification can be based on the CoS, DSCP, or IP precedence value.

Another switch command used when configuring QoS is **switchport priority extend**. This switch port interface command is used to set a priority for the incoming untagged frames or to trust the priority received.

By default, the port priority is not set, and the default value for untagged frames received on a switch port is 0. Also by default, the IP Phone that connects to a switch port does not trust traffic that comes in from the PC (or any other device) that connects to the extra port on the bottom of a Cisco IP Phone.

The two options that can be added to this command are **cos** (along with a CoS value that is assigned to a frame) and **trust**. The **cos** command parameter and its associated value override the priority received from the PC. You use the **switchport priority extend cos** command when you do not know what the PC (that connects to the IP Phone) might mark as a CoS value on the frame and you want to use the configured port priority value instead. This method is sometimes called *port-based QoS reclassification*.

The **switchport priority extend trust** command instructs the Cisco IP Phone to trust the tag received across the trunk from the phone or the PC connected to the phone's secondary port. Be careful when using this command. If the user or software application on the PC sets data traffic to a high value, it can negatively affect the quality of voice signals.

The **mls qos trust cos pass-through dscp** or **mls qos trust dscp pass-through cos** commands allow pass-through mode to be enabled. When using the **mls qos trust cos pass-through dscp** command, the inbound packets trust the CoS value and send the packets on through without changing the DSCP value. Comparatively, the other command, **mls qos trust dscp pass-through cos**, trusts the DSCP value and allows the CoS value to be sent without modification.

The default pass-through mode is none. This means that the switch offers best-effort service to each packet regardless of the packet contents or size and sends the packet from a single egress (output) queue.

NBAR

A Cisco-proprietary means of classifying traffic for QoS is *Network-Based Application Recognition (NBAR)*. It is important to note that NBAR classifies, but does not apply, QoS to an interface. NBAR is a handy tool for someone new to QoS because it defines QoS classes for applications based on information that NBAR gathers. NBAR functions only with TCP/IP-type traffic.

NBAR can cause additional CPU processing and memory usage on a router. After traffic is analyzed, NBAR can be removed and then reenabled later if network traffic changes occur. Lab 10-3 demonstrates how NBAR monitors traffic. This lab is more effective and fun if traffic is generated between the two routers. It is best if the two routers are configured as two separate voice pods.

After NBAR is used, a QoS plan and configuration are created. For example, pretend that top three protocols (besides voice, of course, which has to be prioritized) are HTTP, EIGRP, and FTP. QoS could be configured to look for these three protocols and prioritize them over other types of traffic. The actual QoS commands to do this are beyond the scope of this book; however, a good resource to peruse is *Cisco QoS Exam Certification Guide*, Second Edition, from Cisco Press.

Note: NBAR is recommended for testing and planning purposes only. It should be disabled as a live system to prevent excessive CPU utilization on a CME box.

Overview of VoIP Security

Several security functions can be implemented on your Cisco CME router. Some of these security functions are simple things that are done for router security in general. This information is discussed here but is not fully covered in the labs. The details of Lab 10-4 are geared toward commands that should be applied in a VoIP environment with CME installed on a router.

Common Router Security Techniques

You can use the **enable secret** command to encrypt passwords. You can restrict access to various commands using privilege levels using the **privilege** *mode* **level** *level_value* command. You can control who can Telnet to the router by using the **access-class** command. Telnet can be further secured using Secure Shell (SSH) (the **transport input ssh** and **crypto key generate rsa** commands).

The voice VLAN should be separated from the data VLAN, the management VLAN, and the default VLAN. Never should these VLANs be combined in even the smallest of corporate networks (especially those that contain VoIP). These commands are not rehashed in this chapter.

An authentication server can be used to authenticate and track users who log in to the router. All these security functions are CCNA-level material and are beyond the scope of this book. (You are encouraged to research and implement these commands if you are unfamiliar with the concepts.)

VoIP Router Security Techniques

Lab 10-4 demonstrates several security techniques that are applicable to VoIP. This lab details how to control Cisco IP Phone registration so that rogue phones cannot be inserted into the VoIP network. Other security features outlined include how to protect the GUI management environment, how to monitor IP Phone activity, and how to prevent toll fraud when calls are being made outside normal business hours.

By default, the CME GUI management uses HTTP. HTTP over SSL (HTTPS) can be used to provide a more secure environment. Currently, Cisco IP Phones do not serve as HTTPS clients. When HTTPS is enabled on the CME router, IP Phones attempt to connect to port 80. The SSL default port is 443. The workaround for this is to enable both HTTP and HTTPS and use HTTPS for GUI management. Also keep in mind that using a server to authenticate the GUI is one of the most secure methods (but it is beyond the scope of the labs in this chapter).

The Cisco CallManager Express GUI provides call history information so that you can monitor information for unknown callers and then use that information to disallow calling activities based on the call patterns. You can configure the call history log to perform forensics and accounting and allow the administrator to track fraudulent calls and calling patterns. Lab 10-4 provides the commands to do this.

Logging the fraudulent calling pattern information to a Syslog server is a best practice. A free Syslog server that can be used in Lab 10-4 is Kiwi. You should download and install the software before starting the security lab.

Blocking calls after a certain time of day is another way to help with fraudulent calls. The **after-hours day** command can prevent IP Phones from calling a specific dial pattern (defined with the command **after-hours block pattern**) during specific times on specific days. The after-hours blocking technique is demonstrated in Lab 10-4.

Lab 7-2 from Chapter 7, "Configuring Inter-Pod Connectivity," discussed class of restriction (COR). COR helps prevent toll fraud by creating different groups of users who have specific rights concerning where (what types of numbers) they can call. This technique is not covered in this chapter.

Lab 10-1: Configuring AutoQoS on a Router Using an Integrated Switch Module

In this lab, the company OCSIC.org has decided to deploy AutoQoS at a remote site to ensure that the voice traffic has priority but doesn't use all the bandwidth available when traversing the WAN.

Note: This lab relies on the two IP Phones being able to connect to one another *before* you start this lab. The voice-enabled router needs to be connected to another router for QoS to be applied. This connectivity can be through a serial or Ethernet port. From one router, the other router should be reachable using the **ping** command.

The configuration in this lab will not be saved.

The objectives of this lab are as follows:

- Configure AutoQoS on a router.

- Modify AutoQoS.

To perform this lab, you need the following equipment:

- CME-capable router with a switch module

- Cisco router

- Workstation with an Ethernet 10/100 network interface card (NIC) installed

- Two Cisco IP Phones

Figure 10-3 shows the topology used with this lab.

Figure 10-3   Lab Topology: QoS on a Switch Module

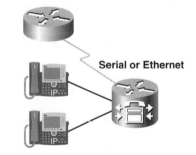

The procedure for this lab consists of the following tasks, described in detail in the following sections:

- **Task 1**—Verify default QoS switch module settings.

- **Task 2**—Enable AutoQoS.

- **Task 3**—Verify AutoQoS settings.

- **Task 4**—Modify and verify AutoQoS parameters.

- **Task 5**—Remove AutoQoS.

Task 1: Verify Default QoS Switch Module Settings

Step 1.   The router and switch module should be configured with the basic configuration. The IP Phones should be plugged into the switch module and should be operational. From one Cisco IP Phone, call the other IP Phone. The call should succeed. Do not proceed until the IP Phones are configured.

Step 2.   Verify connectivity between the routers. Ensure that either a serial or Ethernet connection exists between the two routers. Ping to verify connectivity. Any unused IP addressing scheme can be used for this connection.

Step 3.   Verify the slot/module into which the switch module inserts. Make a note of the format used on the ports to which the IP Phones connect.

For example, on a 2811 router that has a four-port switch module inserted into port 0, port-adapter 1 and the phones connect to the two lowest ports. The format used is FastEthernet 0/1/0 and 0/1/1.

```
RouterVoIPX# show ip interface brief
```

Step 4.   On one of the interfaces to which a Cisco IP Phone connects, verify the default QoS settings:

```
RouterVoIPX# show mls qos interface fastethernet x/x/x
```

In the output, notice that both the trust state and mode are set to not trusted. The CoS override default is disabled (dis). This value can be changed through configuration to override whatever CoS value comes in with one that the switch administrator determines. For example, on a port that has an outside vendor's server attached, the switch administrator may decide to override the QoS markings on the frames from the server and assign them a permanent value such as 0.

The pass-through value in this command output is set to the default of none.

Step 5.   From privileged mode on the router that has IP Phones connected, ensure that AutoQoS is not enabled:

```
RouterVoIPX# show auto qos
```

Task 2: Enable AutoQoS

Step 1.   From global configuration mode on the router that has the IP Phones connected, enter interface configuration mode for the interface used to connect to the other router:

```
RouterVoIPX(config)# interface fastethernet x/x
```

or

```
RouterVoIPX(config)# interface serial x/x/x
```

Step 2.   QoS is to be enabled on the outbound router interface. From interface configuration mode, enable AutoQoS for VoIP:

```
RouterVoIPX(config-if)# auto qos voip
```

Task 3: Verify AutoQoS Settings

From privileged mode on the router that has IP Phones connected, view the effects of enabling AutoQoS:

```
RouterVoIPX# show running-config
```

In the output, notice the three major sections that were added:

- The **class-map** commands
- The policy map
- The extended access list

Pay particular attention to the output shown in the first part of the **policy-map AutoQoS-Policy-UnTrust** section. The first class has the word **priority** in it. The **priority** command designates this class as the priority queue. You can look back to see what class map is associated with this queue. From the class map, you can see what traffic is in the priority queue—it is voice!

On the same line as the **priority** parameter is the **percent 70** parameter. It configures the router so that 70 percent of the bandwidth can be used by voice. The rest is used by the other map classes. This prevents voice from taking over the total amount of bandwidth for a particular link.

The line that follows is also important: **set dscp ef**. Any voice traffic that goes out the interface that connects to the other router is marked with a DSCP value of EF, the highest-priority value. If another type of phone is used or if the switch to which the IP Phone connects does not allow the EF value through or re-marks the packet with the EF value, this router ensures that voice traffic that goes across the link to the other router is marked as the highest priority.

Another way to see the effects of AutoQoS is to use the **show auto qos** command:

```
RouterVoIPX# show auto qos
```

On one of the interfaces to which a Cisco IP Phone connects, verify whether the QoS settings have changed:

```
RouterVoIPX# show mls qos interface fastethernet x/x/x
```

Notice how the QoS settings for the interface have not changed.

Task 4: Modify and Verify AutoQoS Parameters

Step 1.   Even though AutoQoS has been enabled, it can be modified and customized. From global configuration mode on the router with IP Phones connected, enter interface configuration mode on the port connected to an IP Phone:

```
RouterVoIPX(config)# interface fastethernet x/x/x
```

Step 2.   Configure the port to trust the DSCP value automatically marked by the Cisco IP Phone. This command would be used when QoS is implemented on another device that connects to this device through this port, and you want to trust the DSCP markings that come through that port.

```
RouterVoIPX(config-if)# mls qos trust dscp
```

Step 3.   From privileged mode, view the effects of the change:

```
RouterVoIPX# show mls qos interface fastethernet x/x/x
```

Notice how the trust mode is now set to trust the DSCP value.

Step 4.   Suppose a PC connects to a Cisco IP Phone. The router administrator does not want CoS values coming through the switch module port to which the Cisco IP Phone connects. To mark the CoS value, return to interface configuration mode for the port that has a Cisco IP Phone connected. Set the CoS value of 0 to frames sent from the PC that connects to that IP Phone:

```
RouterVoIPX(config-if)# switchport priority extend cos 0
```

Task 5: Remove AutoQoS

Step 1.   Remove AutoQoS from the router port (serial or Ethernet) that has the IP Phones attached. From interface configuration mode, use the following command:

```
RouterVoIPX(config-if)# no auto qos voip
```

Step 2.   Verify that the class maps, the policy map, and the extended access list have been removed from the configuration:

```
RouterVoIPX# show running-config
```

Notice that the QoS parameters that were entered to modify AutoQoS still exist.

Step 3.   Move to interface configuration mode for the port that has a Cisco IP Phone connected. Remove the QoS commands that were previously entered:

```
RouterVoIPX(config-if)# no mls qos trust dscp
RouterVoIPX(config-if)# no switchport priority extend cos 0
```

Step 4.   Save the router configuration:

```
RouterVoIPX# copy running-config startup-config
```

Lab 10-2: Configuring AutoQoS on a Router and External 3550+ Switch

In this lab, OCSIC.org has a remote site with a voice-enabled router and a 3550 switch. The router and switch support Cisco IP Phones. OCSIC.org has decided to deploy AutoQoS at a remote site to ensure that the voice traffic has priority. The company doesn't want the voice traffic to use all the available bandwidth when traversing the WAN.

Note: This lab relies on the two IP Phones being able to connect to one another *before* you start this lab. The voice-enabled router needs to be connected to another router to apply QoS. This connectivity can be through a serial or Ethernet port. From one router, the other router should be reachable using the **ping** command. The voice-enabled router also connects to a 3550 switch that has two IP Phones connected.

The configuration in this lab will not be saved.

The objectives of this lab are as follows:

- Configure AutoQoS on a router.

- Configure AutoQoS on a switch.

- Modify AutoQoS parameters.

To perform this lab, you need the following equipment:

- Cisco CME-capable router

- Second Cisco router

- Cisco external 3550 (or higher) switch

- Workstation with an Ethernet 10/100 NIC installed

- Two Cisco IP Phones

Figure 10-4 shows the topology used with this lab.

Figure 10-4   Lab Topology: QoS on a Switch Module

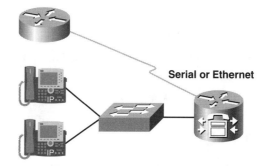

The procedure for this lab consists of the following tasks, described in detail in the following sections:

- **Task 1**—Verify default QoS switch module settings.

- **Task 2**—Enable AutoQoS on the router.

- **Task 3**—Verify AutoQoS settings.

- **Task 4**—Enable AutoQoS on the switch.

- **Task 5**—Modify and verify AutoQoS parameters.

- **Task 6**—Remove AutoQoS.

Task 1: Verify Default QoS Switch Module Settings

Step 1.   Power on the router. The router and switch should be configured with the basic configuration. The IP Phones should be plugged into the switch and should be operational. From one Cisco IP Phone, call the other IP Phone. The call should succeed. Do not proceed until the IP Phones are configured and working properly.

Step 2.   Verify connectivity between the routers. Ensure that either a serial or Ethernet connection exists between the two routers. Ping to verify connectivity. Any IP addresses that are not part of the standard IP addressing scheme can be used for this connection (that is, 192.168.69.0/24).

Step 3.   On one of the switch ports to which a Cisco IP Phone connects, verify the default QoS settings:

```
SwitchVoIPX#show mls qos interface fastethernet x/x
```

In the output, notice that QoS is disabled for this interface. Also notice that if they are enabled, both the trust state and mode are set to not trusted.

By default, the CoS override setting is disabled (dis). This setting can be changed to override whatever CoS value comes into the interface as determined by the switch administrator. For example, on a port that has an outside vendor's server attached, the switch administrator may decide to override the QoS markings on the frames from the server and assign them a permanent value such as 0.

The end of the command output shows that no devices are trusted. These parameters will change as you modify the configuration in this lab.

Step 4.   From privileged mode on the router that connects to a switch, verify that AutoQoS is not enabled:

```
RouterVoIPX# show auto qos
```

Task 2: Enable AutoQoS on the Router

Step 1.   Enter global configuration mode on the router that connects to the switch. Enter interface configuration mode for the port used to connect to the other router:

```
RouterVoIPX(config)# interface fastethernet x/x
```

or

```
RouterVoIPX(config)# interface serial x/x/x
```

Step 2.   The **auto qos voip** command enables QoS on the outbound router interface. From interface configuration mode, enable AutoQoS for VoIP:

```
RouterVoIPX(config-if)# auto qos voip
```

Task 3: Verify AutoQoS Settings

Step 1.   From privileged mode on the router that connects to the switch, view the effects of enabling AutoQoS:

```
RouterVoIPX# show running-config
```

In the output, notice the three major sections that were added: the **class-map** commands, the policy map, and the extended access list.

Pay particular attention to the output shown in the first part of the **policy-map AutoQoS-Policy-UnTrust** section. The first **class** command (AutoQoS-VoIP-RTP-UnTrust) has the word **priority** in it. The **priority** command designates this class as the priority queue. On the same line as the priority parameter is the **percent 70** parameter. It configures the router so that 70 percent of the bandwidth can be used by voice. The rest is used by the other map classes. This is so that voice cannot take over all the bandwidth for a particular link.

To follow the flow of the maps, find the class map with the class name of AutoQoS-VoIP-RTP-UnTrust. Review the **match protocol** statement to identify what protocol has priority and what access group is referenced. In this case, priority is given to RTP audio. RTP audio can be voice traffic. The access group named AutoQoS-VoIP-RTCP is also referenced. The AutoQoS-VoIP-RTCP access group relates to the **ip access-list extended AutoQoS-VoIP-RTCP** command toward the bottom of the router configuration. The AutoQoS-VoIP-RTCP access list permits UDP in port ranges from 16384 to 32767. This port range allows RTP voice media traffic. This entire series of commands gives priority to audio (in this case, voice traffic).

The line that follows is also important: **set dscp ef**. Any voice traffic that goes out the interface that connects to the other router is marked with a DSCP value of EF, the highest-priority value. If another type of phone is used or if the switch to which the IP Phone connects does not allow the EF value through or re-marks the packet with the EF value, this router ensures that voice traffic that goes across the link to the other router is marked as the highest priority.

Step 2. Another way to see the effects of AutoQoS is to use the **show auto qos** command:

```
RouterVoIPX# show auto qos
```

Step 3. Use both of the previous commands on the switch:

```
SwitchVoIPX# show running-config
SwitchVoIPX# show auto qos
```

Notice on the switch how **mls qos** commands are now listed at the beginning of the **show running-config** command output, including the one that enables QoS globally (**mls qos**). Under the interface that has a Cisco IP Phone attached, notice how the **mls** and **wrr** commands were added as a result of enabling AutoQoS.

Step 4. On the switch interface that had QoS enabled, verify that the QoS settings have changed.

```
SwitchVoIPX# show mls qos interface fastethernet x/x
```

Notice how the QoS settings now have a trust state and mode of trust CoS and that the device trusted is a Cisco IP Phone.

Task 4: Enable AutoQoS on the Switch

From global configuration mode on the switch, enter interface configuration mode on one of the ports that connects to the IP Phones. Enable AutoQoS for VoIP:

```
SwitchVoIPX(config)# interface fastethernet x/x
SwitchVoIPX(config-if)# auto qos voip cisco-phone
```

Task 5: Modify and Verify AutoQoS Parameters

Step 1. Even though AutoQoS has been enabled, it can be modified and customized. On the switch, enter interface configuration mode for the port that has an IP Phone attached (that you have configured for AutoQoS).

```
SwitchVoIPX(config)# interface fastethernet x/x
```

Step 2.   Configure the port to trust the DSCP value that comes into this port. The **mls qos trust dscp** command would be used when QoS is implemented on another device that connects to this device through this port, and you want to trust the DSCP markings that come through that port.

A distribution-level switch connects to an access-level switch. The port on the distribution-level switch is a good example of when to use this command. However, just to show its effects, configure the port to trust the DSCP value on the packets that come into this port:

```
SwitchVoIPX(config-if)# mls qos trust dscp
```

Step 3.   Verify the effects of this command:

```
SwitchVoIPX# show mls qos interface fastethernet x/x
```

Notice how the trust state and trust mode have changed.

Step 4.   The default behavior of AutoQoS is to override the priority of the traffic received from a PC attached to the Cisco IP Phone and then reassign it a value of 0, the lowest CoS value. In this way, the PC cannot take advantage of a higher-priority queue based on the CoS markings that the PC (or application on the PC) is putting on the frames.

In some situations (not many), you might want to trust the settings from the PC that connects to the Cisco IP Phone. If AutoQoS is not configured, you can use the **switchport priority extend cos** command to override the priority of the traffic received from the PC and reassign it a value of 0, the lowest value. In this way, you can prevent a PC from taking advantage of a higher-priority queue based on the CoS markings that the PC puts on the frames.

Enter interface configuration mode on a port that connects to an IP Phone (that you have configured for AutoQoS). Modify the AutoQoS configuration to override the PC traffic:

```
SwitchVoIPX(config)# interface fastethernet x/x
SwitchVoIPX(config-if)# switchport priority extend cos 0
```

Step 5.   Another important QoS command that might be used on a switch even when AutoQoS is activated is **mls qos cos override**. This command overrides any CoS value that comes into the interface on which the command is used and replaces the CoS value with the default CoS value (0 unless you change it). This is good on ports that *do not* have Cisco IP Phones attached, but instead have normal workstations. This prevents applications that can set CoS values from using a priority queue, including the one used for voice.

Enter interface configuration mode for an interface that *does not* have a Cisco IP Phone attached. (It does not matter if anything is attached.) Override the CoS value so that it rewrites it to a value of 0, the default:

```
SwitchVoIPX(config)# interface fastethernet x/x
SwitchVoIPX(config-if)# mls qos cos override
```

Step 6.   View the effects of this change. Ensure that you use the interface number that was just configured:

```
SwitchVoIPX# show mls qos interface fastethernet x/x
```

Notice how the CoS override parameter is now enabled.

Task 6: Remove AutoQoS

Step 1.   Enter interface configuration mode on the port that connects to the IP Phone, and remove AutoQoS:

```
RouterVoIPX(config-if)# no auto qos voip
```

Step 2. Verify that the class maps, the policy map, and the extended access list have been removed from the configuration:

```
RouterVoIPX# show running-config
```

Notice that the QoS commands that were entered to modify AutoQoS still exist.

Step 3. From the interface configuration mode of the switch interface that has a Cisco IP Phone attached, remove AutoQoS:

```
SwitchVoIPX(config-if)# no auto qos voip
```

Step 4. From global and interface configuration mode, remove any QoS commands that remain.

Step 5. On both the router and switch, verify that no QoS commands remain. If any remain, remove them:

```
SwitchVoIPX# show running-config
RouterVoIPX# show running-config
```

Step 6. Save the router and switch configuration:

```
RouterVoIPX# copy running-config startup-config
SwitchVoIPX# copy running-config startup-config
```

Lab 10-3: Using NBAR

In this lab, OCSIC.org has decided to deploy AutoQoS at a remote site, but it wants to use NBAR to see the type of traffic that is being generated.

Note: This lab relies on the two IP Phones being able to connect to one another *before* you start this lab. The voice-enabled router needs to be connected to another router to use NBAR and apply QoS. This connectivity can be through a serial or Ethernet port. From one router, the other router should be reachable using the **ping** command.

The configuration in this lab will not be saved.

The objectives of this lab are as follows:

- Configure NBAR.

- View the effects of NBAR.

To perform this lab, you need the following equipment:

- Cisco CME-capable router

- Second Cisco router

- Switch/switch module

- Workstation with an Ethernet 10/100 NIC installed

- Two Cisco IP Phones

Figure 10-5 shows the topology used with this lab. Keep in mind that an integrated switch module in the router could be used instead of the external switch.

Figure 10-5   Lab Topology: NBAR

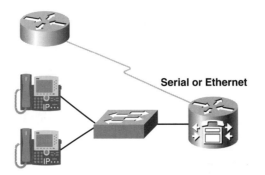

The procedure for this lab consists of the following tasks, described in detail in the following sections:

- **Task 1**—Verify IP Phone connectivity.

- **Task 2**—Enable NBAR.

- **Task 3**—Verify the effects of NBAR.

- **Task 4**—Remove NBAR.

Task 1: Verify IP Phone Connectivity

Step 1. Power on the router. The router and switch or switch module should be configured with the basic configuration. The IP Phones should be plugged into the switch/switch module and should be operational. From one Cisco IP Phone, call the other IP Phone. The call should succeed. Do not proceed until the IP Phones are functional.

Step 2. Verify connectivity between the routers. Ensure that either a serial or Ethernet connection exists between the two routers. Ping to verify connectivity. Any unused IP addressing scheme can be used for this connection.

Task 2: Enable NBAR

On the router interface that connects to the nonvoice router, enable NBAR to discover TCP/IP traffic:

```
RouterVoIPX(config-if)# ip nbar protocol-discovery
```

Task 3: Verify the Effects of NBAR

Step 1. The **show ip nbar protocol-discovery interface** *interface* command (where *interface* is the port being used to connect to the other router) is used to display statistics gathered by NBAR. The output is more interesting if you generate traffic across the WAN. If two voice pods are connected, voice calls can be made:

```
RouterVoIPX# show ip nbar protocol-discovery interface interface
```

Step 2. Quite a few of the NBAR protocol statistics columns are empty. To show you a particular number of protocols based on a value you specify, use the **top-n** *number* option. For example, entering the following command displays the statistics for the top ten protocols:

```
RouterVoIPX# show ip nbar protocol-discovery interface interface top-n 10
```

As soon as you have an idea of the type of traffic that is going through your network, you can create QoS classes that prioritize your most important types of traffic. That process is beyond the scope of this book.

Step 3. If you are connected to another router pod, make a call from one Cisco IP Phone to the remote router pod's IP Phone. Reissue the **show ip nbar protocol-discovery interface** *interface* **top-n 10** command to see the changes on the voice protocols such as RTP and RTCP:

```
RouterVoIPX# show ip nbar protocol-discovery interface interface top-n 10
```

Task 4: Remove NBAR

From interface configuration mode for the interface that connects to the other router, remove NBAR:

```
RouterVoIPX(config-if)# no ip nbar protocol-discovery
```

Lab 10-4: VoIP Security Measures

In this lab, OCSIC.org has decided to deploy some security measures on the CME router that relate to VoIP. These security measures include allowing only specific phones to register, protecting the GUI management, monitoring phone activity, and preventing toll fraud.

Note: This lab relies on the two IP Phones being able to connect to one another *before* you start this lab. Also, the PC should be able to access the CME GUI Administrator (http://10.x0.0.1/ccme.html) before the start of this lab. Troubleshoot as necessary. Do not proceed unless the two phones that connect to the same CME router can call one another and the GUI is accessible from the PC.

Another router is used, but it does not have to be a voice-enabled router. However, the interface between the two routers needs to be in the "up and up" state.

The fraudulent calling information is saved to a Syslog server. Any Syslog server software can be used. If software is not already loaded, download and install it from Kiwi Enterprises at http://www.kiwisyslog.com/downloads.php.

The configuration from this lab will not be needed for any other labs.

The objectives of this lab are as follows:

- Configure IP Phone registration restriction.

- Protect and test GUI management.

- Configure and verify phone activity monitoring.

- Configure the CME router to prevent toll fraud during nonbusiness hours.

To perform this lab, you need the following equipment:

- Cisco CME-capable router

- Cisco router

- Switch/switch module

- Workstation with an Ethernet 10/100 NIC installed

- Two Cisco IP Phones

Figure 10-6 shows the topology used with this lab.

Figure 10-6   Lab Topology: Security

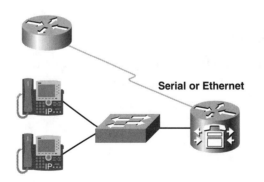

The procedure for this lab consists of the following tasks, described in detail in the following sections:

- **Task 1**—Verify IP Phone and PC connectivity.
- **Task 2**—Restrict phone registration.
- **Task 3**—Protect and test GUI management.
- **Task 4**—Configure IP Phone activity monitoring.
- **Task 5**—Prevent toll fraud.

Task 1: Verify Phone, PC, and Router Connectivity

Step 1.   Check connectivity between the two Cisco IP Phones. Do not proceed unless the calls are successful. Also ensure that the workstation can connect or ping to 10.*x*0.0.1 (where *x* is the pod number being used).

Step 2.   From a workstation connected to an IP Phone (that can ping all router IP addresses), access the CME using a web interface by entering **http://10.x0.0.1/ccme.html** (where *x* is the pod number) in the browser address line.

Step 3.   When prompted for a username and password, use **webadmin** and **cisco**.

Task 2: Restrict Phone Registration

Step 1.   OCSIC.org has 20 Cisco IP Phones that connect to the CME router. Currently, the DHCP pool for the IP Phones is probably configured for 254 addresses. Change the router DHCP pool to allow only 30 IP addresses to be in the DHCP pool. (The last ten addresses will be excluded.)

Verify the name of the DHCP pool. From global configuration mode, modify the subnet mask to be a pool of 30 addresses. The *xxx* in the **ip dhcp pool** command is the name of the DHCP pool used by the Cisco IP Phones. The *x* in the **network** statement is the pod number. Then, from global configuration mode, exclude the last ten IP addresses of the DHCP pool:

```
RouterVoIPX# show running-config

RouterVoIPX(config)# ip dhcp pool xxx

RouterVoIPX(dhcp-config)# network 10.x5.0.0 255.255.255.224

RouterVoIPX(config)# ip dhcp excluded-address 10.x5.0.21 10.x5.0.30
```

Step 2.   Reset the IP Phones using the process described in Lab 2-2. Make a note of what IP addresses the Cisco IP Phones receive by pressing the **Settings** button and using the **3 - Network Configuration** option. Scroll to find the IP address. Ensure that the IP address and subnet mask are correct based on the configuration in Step 1.

Step 3.   Now the **ip source-address** command can be used along with the **strict-match** parameter to restrict which Cisco IP Phones can register with the CME router. The **ip source-address** command is used from telephony-service configuration mode. The *x* in the command is the voice VLAN IP address on the CME router:

```
RouterVoIPX(config-telephony)# ip source-address 10.x0.0.1 port 2000
strict-match
```

Step 4.   Create an access list to block any Cisco IP Phones that might gain access through the WAN. Remember that port 2000 is used by the Skinny (SCCP) protocol to register Cisco IP Phones with the CME router. The second **access-list** command allows any other traffic to be accepted, such as the EIGRP traffic that is sent when two pods connect:

```
RouterVoIPX(config)# access-list 101 deny tcp any any eq 2000

RouterVoIPX(config)# access-list 101 permit ip any any
```

Step 5. On the CME router interface used to connect to the other router, apply the access list. The *xx* in the command is the interface type, slot, and port number used to connect from the CME router to the other router:

```
RouterVoIPX(config)# interface xx
RouterVoIPX(config-if)# ip access-group 101 in
```

Note: CME 4.0 will have a **no auto-reg-ephone** option under telephony-service. It will prevent and log any registration attempts from phones that do not have a MAC address configured under the ephone in the running configuration.

Task 3: Protect and Test GUI Management

Note This lab requires an IOS version that includes security commands. If the **ip http secure-server** command is unavailable, this task cannot be done, so proceed to the next task.

Step 1. By default, the CME GUI management uses HTTP.

Step 2. HTTPS (HTTP over SSL) can be used to provide a more secure environment. Enable HTTPS for GUI management:

```
RouterVoIPX(config)# ip http secure-server
```

Step 3. Create a domain name on the CME router:

```
RouterVoIPX(config)# ip domain-name OCSIC.org
```

Step 4. Use the **crypto key generate** command to manually generate an RSA usage key pair. Even though a key pair is generated automatically the first time HTTPS is used, if the router is rebooted, the keys are lost:

```
RouterVoIPX(config)# crypto key generate rsa usage-keys modulus 1024
```

Step 5. From the PC, access the CME router using HTTPS. The *x* in the command is the pod number. In the browser address line, do not forget to add an "s" to "http":

```
https://10.x0.0.1/ccme.html
```

At the message prompt about accessing the router through a secure connection, click **OK**. If a security alert window appears about the security certificate being issued by a company you have chosen not to trust, click the **Yes** button. When prompted for a username and password, use **webadmin** and **cisco**. The GUI management interface appears. If the management interface does not appear, troubleshoot as necessary.

Task 4: Configure IP Phone Activity Monitoring

Step 1. Ensure that the Syslog server application is active on the PC.

Step 2. Configure the CME router to enable syslogging to a server. The IP address in the command is the IP address that is assigned to the PC:

```
RouterVoIPX(config)# logging ip_address
```

Step 3. The **dial-control-mib** command is used to control attributes (time in minutes and size) of the call history table that is accessible through the GUI. Define the attributes of the CME call history table:

```
RouterVoIPX(config)# dial-control-mib retain-timer 10080
RouterVoIPX(config)# dial-control-mib max-size 500
```

Step 4. The **gw-accounting** command is used to enable VoIP accounting. It allows the accounting information to be output in the form of a Syslog message:

```
RouterVoIPX(config)# gw-accounting syslog
```

Step 5. From one of the Cisco IP Phones, dial some digits that will not make another phone ring. An example of a call is 9999. The call should fail, and it should be logged in the Syslog server. Troubleshoot as necessary.

Step 6. Close the Syslog server when you're finished testing. From global configuration mode, remove the **gw-accounting** command:

```
RouterVoIPX(config)# no gw-accounting syslog
```

Task 5: Prevent Toll Fraud

Step 1. One way to prevent toll fraud in a small business is to prevent calls from being placed after a certain time of day. From telephony-service configuration mode, use the **after-hours day** command to prevent calls from being made after 2 p.m. on Saturday and all day on Sunday:

```
RouterVoIPX(config-telephony)# after-hours day Sat 14:00 23:59
RouterVoIPX(config-telephony)# after-hours day Sun 00:00 23:59
```

Step 2. Use the **after-hours block pattern** command to define the call pattern that cannot be dialed. Because the lab has just two IP Phones connected, we will stop a call between the two phones. In a real business, you might stop a dial pattern that starts with 9, because 9 is used to access an outside line. In the command, the three periods that follow the **5** are part of the command:

```
RouterVoIPX(config-telephony)# after-hours block pattern 1 5...
```

Step 3. Reset both of the Cisco IP Phones. Use the steps in Lab 2-2.

Step 4. Test this configuration by placing a call from one Cisco IP Phone to the other phone. The call should work unless you are doing this particular lab after 2 p.m. on Saturday or on Sunday.

Step 5. Modify the configuration by adding another **after-hours day** command, but have the day and time range include the current day and time. The *day* parameter is the current day, and the *x*'s in the command are the start and ending time:

```
RouterVoIPX(config-telephony)# after-hours day day xx:xx xx:xx
```

Step 6. Test this configuration by placing a call from one Cisco IP Phone to the other phone. The call should *not* go through.

If your phones still work, check the date and time on the router. If the date and time are wrong, use the following privileged mode command to remedy the situation:

```
RouterVoIPX# clock set xx:xx:xx Date Mon Year
```

The call should now be blocked. If it is not, check the commands.

Step 7. Save the configuration to a text file if you want to. Do not save the router configuration to NVRAM. Reload the router:

```
RouterVoIPX# reload
```

CHAPTER 11

Unity Express

Cisco Unity Express (CUE) provides voice mail and automated attendant services in a small-office environment. The automated attendant allows callers to reach any phone extension without the assistance of an operator 24 hours a day, seven days a week. Unity Express can be used in conjunction with CallManager Express. In CUE version 2.3, the following major enhancements have been added:

- Integrated message (IMAP e-mail client access to voice mail)

- Voice View Express (visual voice mail access through phone XML interface and outbound message notification via voice, Short Message Service (SMS), or e-mail)

You can find more information at http://www.cisco.com/univercd/cc/td/doc/product/voice/unityexp/rel2_3/rncue23.htm.

Overview of Unity Express Configuration

Before Unity Express can be activated for the first time, all the basic configurations for CallManager Express must be in place. The Cisco IP Phones should be physically attached and registered. Also, the GUI files should already be loaded in flash memory.

Voice Mail

To have voice mail, a number that is specified in the configuration is used. The labs in this chapter use a configured four-digit extension—6900. When a call goes to voice mail, it references this four-digit extension. A dial peer must also be created to tell the Cisco CallManager Express (CME) router what do with the call when the call gets routed to 6900 or voice mail.

On the Unity Express side, the **ccn trigger sip phonenumber 6900** command is used to define the voice mail number. Further commands are added to customize the voice mail.

SIP

Session Initiation Protocol (SIP) is used for communications between CallManager Express and Unity Express. In the dial peer created on the router, the **session protocol sipv2** command is used. This dial peer defines where to send the call when the system uses the voice mail phone number. On the Unity Express side, the **ccn subsystem sip** command is used, and a gateway address (the address of the CME router) is also configured.

MWI

A common voice mail feature is the *Message-Waiting Indicator (MWI)*. The MWI is a way to let users know they have a phone message waiting by enabling the message-waiting light on the handset when a voice mail message arrives. MWI is configured in a similar manner to call park. To configure MWI, two numbers are placed under two ephone directory numbers. Then **mwi** commands are created on the two ephone directory numbers. Lab 11-2 enables this feature through the Unity Express GUI, but the configuration can also be enabled through the CME router CLI, as demonstrated in the following sample configuration. (The four periods at the end of the **number** command are part of the command.)

```
ephone-dn 80
number 7000....
mwi on
!
ephone-dn 81
number 7001....
mwi off
```

Business Hours Schedule

The Unity Express web interface allows you to create a schedule of normal business operating hours. The default auto attendant scripts use this schedule to determine how to handle an incoming call. You can customize greetings by uploading new prompts and configuring the auto attendant script. (These topics are beyond the scope of this book.) The system allows up to four different business hour schedules.

Night Service Bell

Another useful feature that does not require Unity Express (but that can be configured through the Unity Express GUI) is the night service bell. When this service is active, one or more Cisco IP Phones ring with a unique pattern. Users at the receiving phone can answer the incoming calls by pressing the Call Pickup softkey.

For example, suppose a receptionist is the primary person to answer calls for a company during normal working hours, but the receptionist is unavailable after normal working hours. Several part-time people take turns answering the calls after hours from a different location. The company might not know which person will be working on any given night. The part-time people do not need to answer calls during normal working hours. The night service bell feature can be used in this case to ring all the part-time employee phones only after normal working hours. The part-time people would not receive these calls during the day. All the part-time employees' phones would ring at night, but only the person working that night answers the call.

Another scenario for the night service bell could be applied at a medical supply company. The company could use this feature to enable the security guard to receive all calls from designated phone numbers for staff members who sell critical medical supplies. If a phone rings after hours for someone who sells critical medical supplies, that phone could ring the security guard after hours. The guard could then assess the emergency and contact the salesperson after hours if necessary. During normal working hours, the security desk would not receive calls from the sales staff phones.

The configuration consists of specifying night service hours and optionally a code to disable and reenable night service on the IP Phone. If a configuration code is configured, the code must start with an asterisk (*) and can have a maximum of 22 characters. The code creates a way for the night service bell to be activated without reprogramming Unity Express.

The commands that are issued for the night service bell feature can be a little confusing. To enable a designated phone for night service, use the **night-service bell** command on the ephone-dn that contains the number that people call during off-hours. Use the **night-service bell** on any ephone that you want to be notified of a call during night service hours. This command, used from ephone configuration mode, designates the phone as a night service phone.

If you are configuring the night service bell feature from the router CLI, there are three mandatory steps and one optional one:

Step 1.   The day and time that the night service is to be activated must be configured from telephony-service configuration mode. Multiple days can be configured. Here's a sample entry:

```
telephony-service
night-service day Saturday 00:00 23:59
```

Step 2.   An extension number must be designated as the night service extension (ephone-dn). This is the phone number that people would call during the night service hours. For example:

```
ephone-dn 1
number 5000
night-service bell
```

Step 3.   Any phone that is to ring the special tone when a call comes into the night service extension must be programmed for night service:

```
ephone 2
mac-address AAAA.0000.0001
button 1:2
night-service bell
ephone 8
mac-address BBBB.CCCC.0222
button 1:8
night-service bell
```

Step 4.   Optionally, you can configure a code in telephony-service configuration mode to allow any phone configured for night service to manually turn the night service feature on and off. For example:

```
telephony-service
night-service code *9999
```

Lab 11-1: Accessing Unity Express for the First Time

In this lab, the company OCSIC.org has decided to deploy Unity Express to provide voice mail features. The Unity Express Advanced Integration Module (AIM) has already been installed in the router.

Note: This lab relies on two IP Phones being able to call one another *before* you start this lab. The GUI files should already be installed in flash memory on the router. The workstation should be able to access the CME router using the GUI management system. Lab 8-1, "Configure the GUI for the System Administrator," details how to install the GUI files.

The objectives of this lab are as follows:

- Configure the CME router for Unity Express access.

- Configure basic Unity Express commands so that voice mail can be accessed.

To perform this lab, you need the following equipment:

- Cisco CME-capable router with a Unity Express module installed

- Switch/switch module

- Workstation with an Ethernet 10/100 NIC installed

- Two Cisco IP Phones

Figure 11-1 shows the topology used with this lab. Keep in mind that an integrated switch module in the router could be used instead of the external switch.

Figure 11-1   Lab Topology: Unity Express Initial Configuration

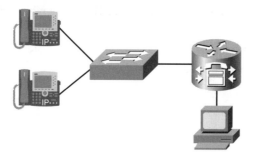

The procedure for this lab consists of the following tasks, described in detail in the following sections:

- **Task 1**—Verify connectivity and installed files.

- **Task 2**—Configure the router for Unity Express.

- **Task 3**—Choose options in the initial configuration dialog.

- **Task 4**—Configure basic Unity Express components.

- **Task 5**—Test voice mail.

Task 1: Verify Connectivity and Installed Files

Step 1.   Power on the router. The router and switch module should be configured with the basic configuration. The IP Phones should be plugged into the switch module and should be operational. From one Cisco IP Phone, call the other IP Phone. The call should succeed. Do not proceed until the IP Phones are configured.

Step 2. Verify that the Unity Express AIM is installed:

```
RouterVoIPX# show inventory
```

The AIM Service Engine should appear if the Unity Express AIM is installed and functioning.

Step 3. Verify that the GUI files are installed on the router. Some of the GUI files include CiscoLogo.gif, admin_user.html, ephone_admin.html, and telephony_service.html.

```
RouterVoIPX# show flash:
```

If the files are missing, install them. Refer to Chapter 8, "GUI and IOS Intermediate Administration," for installation instructions.

Step 4. From the PC, access the CME GUI using a userid of **webadmin** and a password of **cisco**. If the userid and password do not seem to work, check the running configuration file in the telephony-service section. There should be a line that says **web admin system name webadmin password cisco**. If this command is missing or another name is configured, reconfigure it.

Do *not* proceed unless the GUI works. Return to Chapter 8 for instructions.

Step 5. From the command prompt, examine the running configuration, and verify that the Service-Engine interface now appears. Make a note of the interface number shown directly after the words **interface Service-Engine**. This number will be needed for the configuration steps that follow.

```
RouterVoIPX# show running-config
```

Task 2: Configure the Router for Unity Express

Step 1. The Cisco Unity Express module will use IP unnumbered. A VLAN interface or another subinterface will be created as the interface used to apply IP unnumbered. This depends on whether you are using an integrated switch module (VLAN interface) with the router or an external switch (the subinterface on the port that connects to the switch). The *x* in the **interface** and **ip address** commands is the pod number being used:

```
RouterVoIPX(config)# interface fastethernet 0/0.x6
RouterVoIPX(config-if)# encapsulation dot1q x6
RouterVoIPX(config-if)# ip address 10.x6.0.1 255.255.255.0
```

or

```
RouterVoIPX(config)# interface vlan x6
RouterVoIPX(config-if)# ip address 10.x6.0.1 255.255.255.0
RouterVoIPX(config-if)# no shutdown
RouterVoIPX(config-if)# end
RouterVoIPX# vlan database
RouterVoIPX(vlan)# vlan x6 name Unity state active
RouterVoIPX(vlan)# exit
```

Step 2. The *x/x* in the **interface service-engine** command is the Unity Express module interface number (interface Service-Engine) noted in Step 5 of Task 1. If your interface Service-Engine number is 0/*x*, you are using the AIM hardware. If it is 1/*x*, 2/*x*, 3/*x*, or 4/*x*, you are using NM hardware.

Where to apply the **ip unnumbered** command depends on whether you are using an integrated switch module (**ip unnumbered vlan x6**) or an external switch (**ip unnumbered fastethernet0/0.x6**):

```
RouterVoIPX(config)# interface service-engine x/x
RouterVoIPX(config-if)# ip unnumbered fastethernet 0/0.x6
```

or

```
RouterVoIPX(config-if)# ip unnumbered vlan x6
```

Step 3.   The Service-Engine interface must have an IP address and default gateway configured in the same network as the interface identified in the **ip unnumbered** command in the preceding step. For example, if pod 1 were being used with an integrated switch module, the command would be to create interface VLAN 16 and assign the IP address of 10.16.0.1. For this step, the service-module IP address would be 10.16.0.2, and the default gateway would be 10.16.0.1.

The *x/x* in the **interface** command is the interface number documented in Step 5 of Task 1. The *x* in the IP address is the pod number being used:

```
RouterVoIPX(config)# interface service-engine x/x
RouterVoIPX(config-if)# service-module ip address 10.x6.0.2 255.255.255.0
RouterVoIPX(config-if)# service-module ip default-gateway 10.x6.0.1
RouterVoIPX(config-if)# no shutdown
```

Step 4.   Create a static route to the Cisco Unity Express module. The *x* in the network address part of the command (10.*x*6.0.2) is your pod number. The *x/x* at the end of the command is the Unity Express (interface Service-Engine) module interface number noted in Step 5 of Task 1:

```
RouterVoIPX(config)# ip route 10.x6.0.2 255.255.255.255 service-engine x/x
```

Step 5.   Define the base path used to locate files for use by the HTTP server:

```
RouterVoIPX(config)# ip http path flash:
```

Step 6.   A dial peer must be created for Unity Express to work. This lab uses the extension number of 6900 to forward calls to voice mail. The destination pattern in this dial peer matches the number 6900 (69..). This VoIP dial peer uses SIP to connect to the Unity Express service engine. When a match is made with the 6900 extension, the session target forwards it to the IP address 10.*x*6.02 (the IP address of the Unity Express service module, where *x* is the pod number). The IP packet uses the G711ulaw codec type. The two periods that follow the number 69 in the **destination-pattern** command are part of the command. The *x* in the **session target** command is the pod number being used:

```
RouterVoIPX(config)# dial-peer voice 6000 voip
RouterVoIPX(config-dial-peer)# destination-pattern 69..
RouterVoIPX(config-dial-peer)# session protocol sipv2
RouterVoIPX(config-dial-peer)# dtmf-relay sip-notify
RouterVoIPX(config-dial-peer)# session target ipv4:10.x6.0.2
RouterVoIPX(config-dial-peer)# codec g711ulaw
RouterVoIPX(config-dial-peer)# no vad
```

Step 7.   Ensure that the VTY Telnet ports are enabled on the CME router. If they are not, enter these commands:

```
RouterVoIPX(config)# line vty 0 4
RouterVoIPX(config-line)# password cisco
RouterVoIPX(config-line)# login
```

Step 8.   You will use the four-digit number of 6900 for voice mail. This can be any number, but it has to be consistent with the voice mail number that will be used in the ephone-dn and when programming commands in Unity Express. From telephony-service configuration mode, enter the voice mail phone number:

```
RouterVoIPX(config-telephony)# voicemail 6900
```

Step 9. Verify which ephone-dn is the one for the lowest-numbered IP Phone by looking at the running configuration. Make a note of this ephone-dn number. Under this ephone directory number, create a name, and specify that if the phone line is busy, the call will be forwarded to the phone number 6900, the voice mail number. Also, if there is no answer after a certain period (3 seconds), the call is forwarded to voice mail. The *x* in the **ephone-dn** command is the number researched from the running configuration:

```
RouterVoIPX# show running-config

RouterVoIPX# config t

RouterVoIPX(config)# ephone-dn x

RouterVoIPX(config-ephone-dn)# name CSchmidt

RouterVoIPX(config-ephone-dn)# call-forward busy 6900

RouterVoIPX(config-ephone-dn)# call-forward noan 6900 timeout 3
```

Step 10. On the ephone that corresponds to the directory number that was just programmed, a username is created. This username matches the username created on Unity Express.

```
RouterVoIPX(config)# ephone x

RouterVoIPX(config-ephone)# username CSchmidt password null
```

Note: This username can be a different one, but the username on the router and the username on Unity Express must be the same. Also, the username is case-sensitive.

Step 11. From privileged mode, access the Unity Express module. The *x/x* at the end of the command is the Unity Express (interface Service-Engine) module interface number noted in a previous step. After you enter the command, when the prompt states that the session is open, press **Enter**. (This may take a few seconds.)

```
RouterVoIPX# service-module service-engine x/x session

    [Press Enter when a message similar to "Trying 10.X6.0.1, 2258...Open"
    appears]
```

Note: If your session to the Unity Express service module hangs, or if the remote host refuses your connection, try the **service-module service-engine** *x/x* **session clear** command (where *x/x* is the number of your service module). This clears your previous session. After clearing the session, use the **service-module service-engine** *x/x* **session** command again to reestablish the connection.

Task 3: Choose Options in the Initial Configuration Dialog

Step 1. The first time you install and access Unity, you are asked whether you want to start the configuration dialog. This question appears only the first time. If this prompt does not appear, skip to the next task.

Step 2. If the "Do you wish to start configuration now?" prompt appears, press **Y**.

```
Are you sure (y,n)? Y
```

Step 3. When you're prompted for the hostname, press **Enter** to accept the default (which is the IP address of the SE).

Step 4. When prompted for a domain name, press **Enter** to accept the default.

Step 5. When asked if you would like to use DNS for CUE, enter **N**. When asked if you are sure, enter **Y**.

Step 6.   When you're asked to enter the IP address of the primary NTP server, press **Enter** to accept the default of 10.x6.0.1 (even though you do not have the router set up as an NTP server). A message appears that 10.x6.0.1 could not be reached. When you are asked if you want to continue without the primary NTP server, press Y.

Step 7.   When you're asked to enter the IP address of the secondary NTP server, press **Enter** to bypass.

Step 8.   Press the number that corresponds to your location in the world. For example, the U.S. and Canada are number **2**.

Step 9.   Press the number that corresponds to your country. For example, the U.S. is **45**, Brazil is **9**, Canada is **10**, and Mexico is **30**.

Step 10.   You may be prompted for a time zone region. If so, select the number that corresponds to your correct time zone.

Step 11.   When you're asked if the information provided is correct, press **1** for yes even if the time and date are incorrect. You will be able to correct these later.

Step 12.   When you're asked to enter the system time, do so in the correct format. For example, a sample system time is Mon Nov 20 23:21:00 2007.

Step 13.   A message appears that says "Configuring the system. Please wait...". The initial configuration may take 6 to 10 minutes. Next, an important message about the administrator account appears. When you're asked to enter the administrator user ID, enter **cisco**. When you're asked to enter a password, enter **cisco**, and confirm the password by entering **cisco** again. The Unity Express prompt appears (se-10-x6-0-2>), where x is the pod number.

Task 4: Configure Basic Unity Express Components

Step 1.   At the Unity Express enable prompt, enter **enable**. When prompted for a password, press **Enter**.

```
se-10-x6-0-2> enable
```

Step 2.   At the privileged mode prompt, enter **show running-config** to view the basic configuration. Notice how the entire configuration is shown at once. Also make notes about any name shown after any **username** commands.

```
se-10-x6-0-2# show running-config
```

Step 3.   From global configuration mode, create a username that is to match the username programmed on the router ephone. If the username on the router ephone is already programmed in Unity Express, use the **no** *username* [*optional parameters*] command from Unity Express global configuration mode to remove those commands before proceeding.

The four *x*'s in the commands are the four-digit phone number of the lowest-numbered Cisco IP Phone:

```
se-10-x6-0-2(config)# username CSchmidt create
se-10-x6-0-2(config)# username CSchmidt phonenumberE164 510555xxxx
se-10-x6-0-2(config)# username CSchmidt phonenumber xxxx
```

Note: This username can be a different one, but the username on the router and the username on Unity Express must be the same. Also, the username is case-sensitive.

Step 4.   Unity Express must be configured for SIP. From global configuration mode, use the **ccn subsystem sip** command, and configure the default gateway. The *x* in the **gateway address** command is the pod number.

```
se-10-x6-0-2(config)# ccn subsystem sip
se-10-x6-0-2(config-sip)# gateway address 10.x6.0.1
se-10-x6-0-2(config-sip)# end subsystem
```

Step 5. From global configuration mode, Unity Express must be configured for the voice mail four-digit number:

```
se-10-x6-0-2(config)# ccn trigger sip phonenumber 6900
se-10-x6-0-2(config-trigger)# application voicemail
se-10-x6-0-2(config-trigger)# enabled
se-10-x6-0-2(config-trigger)# maxsessions 4
se-10-x6-0-2(config-trigger)# end trigger
```

Step 6. The default language used in the voice mail attendant is defined with the **voicemail default language** command. The language choices are not shown in some versions of the IOS (such as 12.3.11T8). The *xx* is the language code, and the *YY* is the country code. Some common ones are en_US, de_DE, fr_FR, and es_ES.

```
se-10-x6-0-2(config)# voicemail default language xx_YY
```

Step 7. You must configure the voice mail for the user who was created on the router and as a user in Unity Express. The name is case-sensitive.

```
se-10-x6-0-2(config)# voicemail mailbox owner CSchmidt size 2700
se-10-x6-0-2(config-mailbox)# description "CSchmidt mailbox"
se-10-x6-0-2(config-mailbox)# end mailbox
```

Step 8. From privileged mode, copy the configuration:

```
se-10-x6-0-2# copy running-config startup-config
```

Step 9. To return to the router prompt, hold down the **Shift**, **Ctrl**, and **6** keys simultaneously. Let go of the keys and press the **X** key. The router prompt appears.

Step 10. Save the router configuration. Use the **show sessions** command to verify that a session to the Unity Express module is still active:

```
RouterVoIPX# copy running-config startup-config
RouterVoIPX# show sessions
```

Step 11. The session to Unity Express is listed as the number 1 session. Press the **1** key, and then press **Enter**. The prompt changes to the Unity Express prompt.

Task 5: Test Voice Mail

Step 1. From the highest-numbered Cisco IP Phone, call the other Cisco IP Phone. Do not answer the call. After 3 seconds, you should see the number 6900 appear on the phone from which the call was made. Then, the attendant can be heard. Leave a voice message.

Step 2. If these voice mail features do not work, troubleshoot as necessary.

Step 3. On the Cisco IP Phone that has the lowest phone number, press the **Messages** key. This key looks like the back of an envelope.

Step 4. The first time this key is pressed, an attendant states that your settings can be personalized. Follow the directions and create a name, a greeting, and a password of **123**. Then follow the directions to listen to the voice message that was left in Step 1. If no voice mail was left, redo this task from the first step.

Congratulations! You now have voice mail in your company.

Lab 11-2: Configuring Unity Express from a Web Interface

In this lab, OCSIC.org has decided to allow remote access to the Unity Express router so that user configurations can be done more easily. Also, OCSIC.org wants the MWI feature turned on.

Note: The two IP Phones must be able to connect, *and* voice mail must be enabled and working for the lowest-numbered Cisco IP Phone *before* you start this lab. The PC should be able to ping the Unity Express IP address of 10.*X*6.0.2.

The objective of this lab is to configure voice mail and MWI from the web interface.

To perform this lab, you need the following equipment:

- Cisco CME-capable router with a switch module

- Cisco CME-capable router with a Unity Express module installed

- Switch/switch module

- Workstation with an Ethernet 10/100 NIC installed

- Two Cisco IP Phones

Figure 11-2 shows the topology used with this lab. Keep in mind that an integrated switch module in the router could be used instead of the external switch.

Figure 11-2   Lab Topology: Web-Based Unity Express

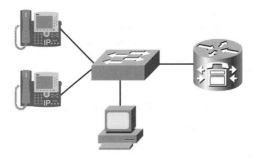

The procedure for this lab consists of the following tasks, described in detail in the following sections:

- **Task 1**—Verify phone and PC connectivity.

- **Task 2**—Prepare the router and Unity Express for web access.

- **Task 3**—Configure voice mail using the web interface.

- **Task 4**—Test voice mail.

- **Task 5**—Configure and test the MWI.

Task 1: Verify Phone and PC Connectivity

Step 1.   The router and switch should be configured with the basic configuration. The IP Phones should be plugged into the switch and should be operational. From the Cisco IP Phone that has the highest phone number, call the other IP Phone, but do not answer the call. The call should succeed, and voice mail should work. Do not proceed until the IP Phones are configured.

Step 2. From a command prompt, verify connectivity between the PC and Unity Express. The PC should be connected to a switch port that is configured for the data VLAN. You can manually assign an IP address in the data VLAN address range. Or you can obtain an IP address from the DHCP pool configured on the router for the data VLAN. The *x* in the command is the pod number. Do not proceed until the ping succeeds and the PC has a properly configured IP address.

```
> ping 10.x6.0.2
```

Task 2: Prepare the Router and Unity Express for Web Access

Step 1. From privileged mode on the router, ensure that an enable secret password is configured:

```
RouterVoIPX(config)# enable secret cisco
```

Step 2. From telephony-service configuration mode, ensure that the web admin is configured with a username and password of **cisco**:

```
RouterVoIPX(config-telephony)# web admin system name cisco password cisco
```

Step 3. Access Unity Express from privileged mode by using the **service-module** command. The *x* in the command is the proper interface number for the service-engine interface. (View the running configuration if you forgot this interface number.) Press **Enter** after a session is opened.

```
RouterVoIPX# service-module service-engine 0/x session
```

Note: You can press **Shift-Ctrl-6** (release) and then press **X** to return to the router prompt. Enter the **show sessions** command. Then press the number (usually 1) of the session that corresponds to Unity Express, and press **Enter** to return to the Unity Express prompt.

Step 4. From privileged mode on Unity Express, disable the Run Initialization Wizard:

```
se-10-X6-0-2# web skipinitwizard
```

Note: A Run Initialization Wizard option is available from the main Unity Express web interface window. This wizard is not used in the lab, because it can be used only once (so the lab would work only once).

Step 5. From privileged mode, create a web admin userid that can be used to access Unity Express through a web page:

```
se-10-X6-0-2# web admin cme hostname 10.x6.0.1 username cisco password cisco
```

Task 3: Configure Voice Mail Using the Web Interface

Step 1. On the PC, open a browser window. Enter the following URL in the address line:

```
http://10.x6.0.2
```

The *x* in the address is the pod number. The Cisco Unity Express Voice Mail/Auto Attendant window appears.

Step 2. In the Authentication window, at the username and password prompt, enter **cisco** and **cisco**. Click the **Login** button. The Cisco Unity Express Voice Mail/Auto Attendant screen appears.

Note: If the userid does not work, verify or redo the steps in Lab 11-1. The following steps can also be used to troubleshoot the web access problem.

After web access is gained from the PC, if the system displays the Lost Contact screen, network connectivity issues might exist between Unity Express and CallManager Express. The Lost Contact screen might also appear if the CME web administrator username and password and the Unity Express web administrator username and password do not match. The lab reconfigures both of these to match, but a typing error could cause this problem. The hostname that is requested on the Lost Contact screen is the hostname or IP address of the CME router.

Step 3.   From the main window, select the **Configure** menu option and select **Users**. Click the **Add** link.

Step 4.   In the Add a New User window, shown in Figure 11-3, enter **EFriend** in the User ID textbox. (This is a case-sensitive userid.) In the First Name textbox, enter **Ernie**; in the Last Name textbox, enter **Friend**. The Nick Name and Display Name fields are automatically populated.

Figure 11-3   Unity Express: New User Window

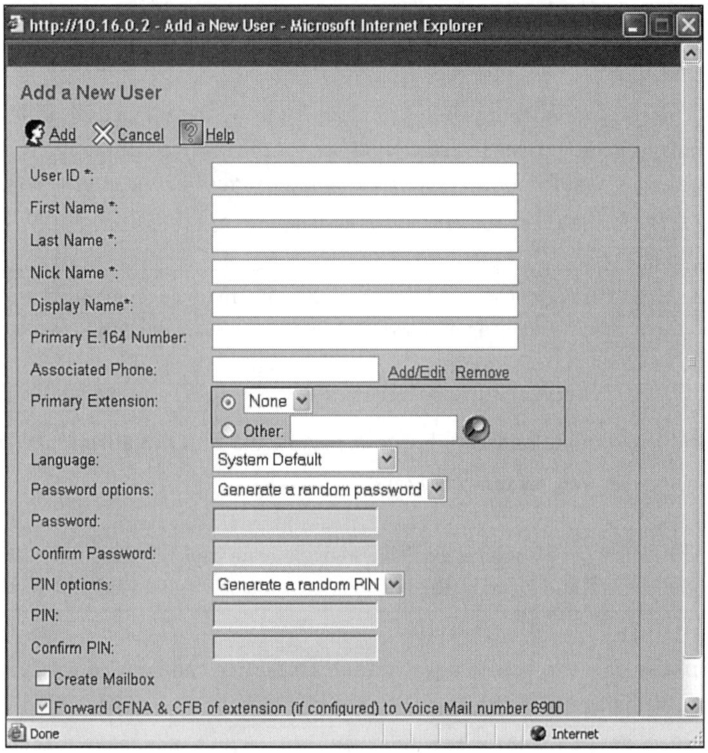

Step 5.   In the Primary E.164 Number textbox, enter the full E.164 number of the highest-numbered Cisco IP Phone. An example for Pod 1 is 5105555001.

Step 6.   In the Associated Phone section, click the **Add/Edit** link. The Select Phone window appears; the second IP Phone number should be listed. Click the radio button beside the extension number of the highest IP Phone number. Click the **Select phone** link.

Step 7.   In the Password options drop-down menu, select the **Password specified below** option. In the Password and Confirm Password textboxes, enter **12345**.

Step 8.   In the PIN options drop-down menu, select the **PIN specified below** option. In the PIN and Confirm PIN textboxes, enter **12345**.

Step 9.   Select the **Create Mailbox** checkbox. Click the **Add** link at the top of the page.

Step 10.   From the Add a New Mailbox window, shown in Figure 11-4, accept all the defaults, and click the **Add** link.

Figure 11-4 Unity Express: Add a New Mailbox Window

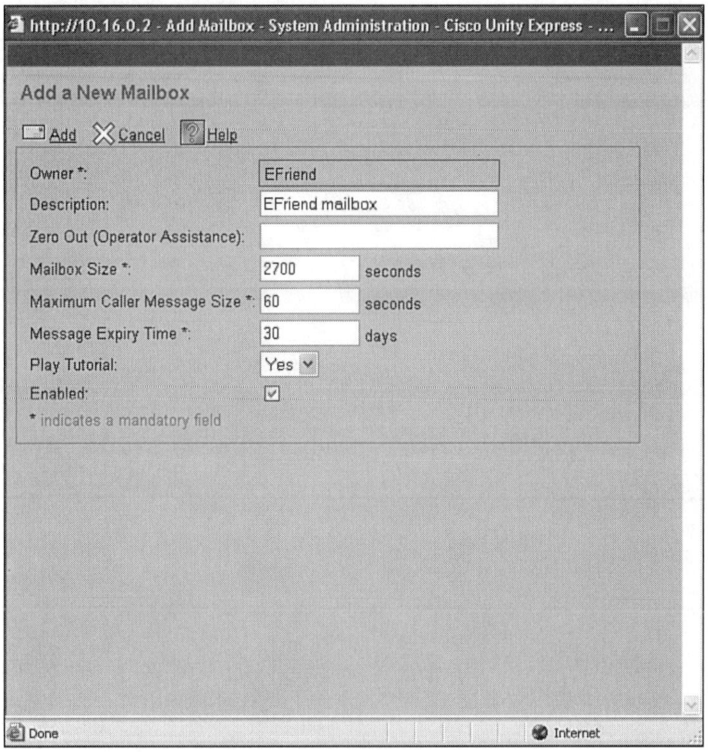

Step 11. From the lowest-numbered Cisco IP Phone, place a call to the other IP Phone. Do not answer the call. Voice mail *does not* work properly. Instead, an error message appears. This is because the directory number associated with this phone was configured for a different voice mail box (not the voice mail box that is used for Unity Express—6900).

Step 12. From the main Unity Express web interface, select the **Configure** menu option and choose **Extensions**. Click the link for the four-digit extension for the highest-numbered IP Phone that is currently being used. The Change Extension window opens, as shown in Figure 11-5.

Step 13. In the Name textbox, enter **EFriend**.

Step 14. Locate the Call Forward busy and Call Forward no-answer textboxes. Change the number inside these textboxes to **6900**. Change the timeout in seconds textbox to **3**.

Step 15. Click the **Change** button at the bottom of the window. When prompted to save the change, click **OK**, and click **OK** again to confirm the change.

Figure 11-5   Unity Express: Change Extension Window

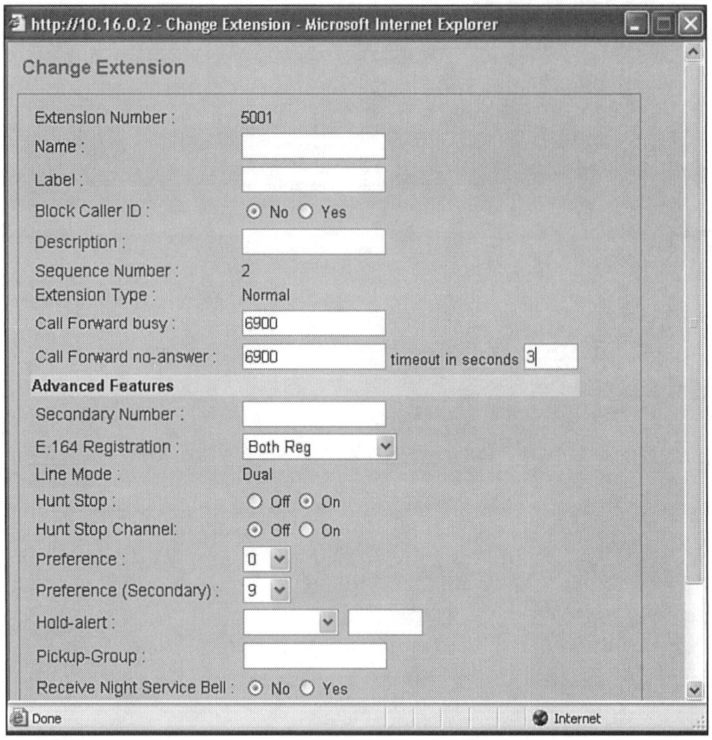

Task 4: Test Voice Mail

Step 1.   From the lowest-numbered Cisco IP Phone, place a call to the other IP Phone. Do not answer the call. The voice mail attendant speaks, and a voice mail can be left. See the following note if a problem occurs.

Note: If the attendant states that a mailbox has not been configured for this extension, go to the main Unity Express web interface. Select the **Configure** option, and then select **Users**. Check whether the EFriend user has a primary extension associated with it. If it does not, click the user ID of **EFriend**. Locate the Primary Extension section, click the **Other** radio button, and select the magnifying glass icon. The Select Extension window appears. Click the appropriate extension number of the highest-numbered IP Phone. Click the **Select Extension** link. Click the **Apply** link from the User Profile window. Click **OK**. Close the User Profile window. Try the call again. Also, resetting the IP Phone sometimes clears up problems.

Step 2.   To access the voice mail on the highest-numbered Cisco IP Phone, perform the same procedure that was performed on the other IP Phone.

Task 5: Configure and Test the MWI

Step 1.   From the Unity Express web interface, select **Configure** and then the **Extensions** option. Click the **Add** link. If an error message appears, see the following note.

Note: If an error message appears, saying that there are no more extensions to add during the first step, access the router CLI. From telephony-service configuration mode, modify the **max-dn** and **max-ephones** commands to a digit that is two numbers higher than the current configuration.

Also, if the router is not configured correctly for GUI access and the correct options to edit things such as extensions, the Add extensions option disabled message appears. See Lab 8-1 for these configuration commands.

Step 2. In the Extension Number textbox, enter **7000....** (the four periods are part of the command). In the Extension Type drop-down menu, select **Message Waiting Indication (MWI)**. Ensure that the MWI Mode option is set to On.

Step 3. Click the **Add** button. Click **OK** to save the change. Click **OK** again to confirm the change. The 7000.... number appears in the extensions.

Step 4. Create a second extension of 7001 by clicking the **Add** link. In the Extension Number textbox, enter **7001....** (the four periods are part of the command). In the Extension Type drop-down menu, select **Message Waiting Indication (MWI)**. Change the MWI Mode option to **Off**.

Step 5. Click the **Add** button. Click **OK** to save the change. Click **OK** again to confirm the change. The 7001.... number appears in the extensions.

Step 6. From the Unity Express main menu, select **Voice Mail**, point to **Message Waiting Indicators**, and click the **Numbers** option. The 7000.... and 7001.... numbers should appear in the MWI on and MWI off boxes.

Note: If the two numbers do not appear, select **Voice Mail**, point to **Message Waiting Indicators**, and click the **Refresh** option.

Step 7. From the Unity Express main menu, select **Administration**, point to **Synchronize Information**, and click the **Synchronize** link.

Step 8. From one of the Cisco IP Phones, make a call to the other IP Phone, but do not answer it. Instead, leave a voice message. The light on the IP Phone handset should illuminate after the message is left. This is MWI in action.

Step 9. From the Unity Express web interface, save both the CME router and Unity Express configurations. Click the **Save CallManager Express Configuration** button. Click **OK** in any message window that appears. Click the **Save Unity Express Configuration** button. Click the **OK** button in any message window that appears.

Lab 11-3: Configuring Business Hours and Night Service Bell Features

In this lab, OCSIC.org has decided to deploy the night service bell feature from 8 a.m. to 1 p.m. on Saturdays. Also, the company wants the phones to automatically go to voice mail before and after normal operating hours. This requires configuring the business hours feature.

Note: The three IP Phones must be able to connect to one another, and the voice mail system must be working before you start this lab. The PC should be able to access the web interface for Unity Express.

The objectives of this lab are as follows:

- Configure and verify the business hours settings.

- Configure and verify the night service bell feature.

To perform this lab, you need the following equipment:

- Cisco CME-capable router with a switch module

- Cisco CME-capable router with a Unity Express module installed

- Switch/switch module

- Workstation with an Ethernet 10/100 NIC installed

- Three Cisco IP Phones

Figure 11-6 shows the topology used with this lab. Keep in mind that an integrated switch module in the router could be used instead of the external switch.

Figure 11-6   Lab Topology: Night Service Bell Configuration

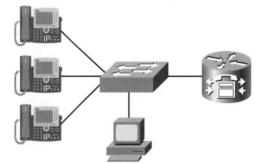

The procedure for this lab consists of the following tasks, described in detail in the following sections:

- **Task 1**—Verify IP Phone and PC connectivity.

- **Task 2**—Configure the business hours settings.

- **Task 3**—Verify the business hours settings.

- **Task 4**—Configure the night service bell.

- **Task 5**—Test the night service bell.

Task 1: Verify IP Phone and PC Connectivity

Step 1.   The router and switch/switch module should be configured with the basic configuration. The IP Phones should be plugged into the switch and should be operational. From the highest Cisco IP Phone, call the other IP Phones, but do not answer the call. The call should succeed, and voice mail should be working. Do not proceed until the IP Phones are configured.

Step 2.   From a command prompt, verify connectivity between the PC and Unity Express. The PC should be connected to a switch port that is configured for the data VLAN. You can manually assign an IP address in the data VLAN address range. Or you can obtain an IP address from the DHCP pool configured on the router for the data VLAN. The x in the command is the pod number. Do not proceed until the ping succeeds and the PC has a properly configured IP address:

```
> ping 10.x6.0.2
```

The PC should be able to access Unity Express from a web interface. Enter the following URL in the PC browser address line. Both the username and password are **cisco**. Do not proceed unless the Unity Express web interface is accessed.

```
http://10.x6.0.2
```

Task 2: Configure the Business Hours Settings

Step 1.   From the Unity Express web interface main menu, select **Voice Mail**, and click the **Business Hours Settings** option. Figure 11-7 shows the Business Hours Settings window.

Figure 11-7   Unity Express: Business Hours Settings Window

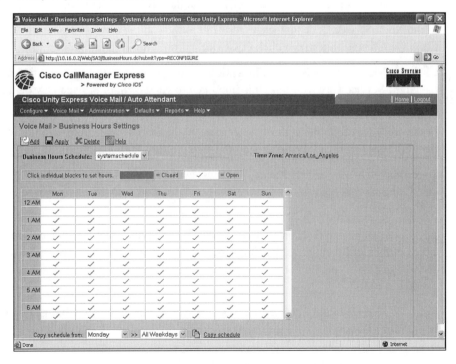

Step 2.   The normal business hours for OCSIC.org are Monday through Friday, 8 a.m. to 5 p.m. Locate the Monday column, and click inside all the boxes *except* those for normal business hours. This causes the "closed" times to appear grayed out. When you are finished, ensure that the Copy schedule from drop-down menu has **Monday** selected. Ensure that the drop-down box to the right of the >> symbol is set to the **All Weekdays** option. Click the **Copy schedule** link. The other weekdays now look like the Monday column.

Step 3.   Locate the Saturday column, and click in every cell to gray them out (indicating closed). In the Copy schedule from drop-down menu, select **Saturday**. In the drop-down box to the right of the >> symbol, select **Sunday**. Click the **Copy schedule** link. Sunday now appears the same as Saturday.

Step 4.   Click the **Apply** link at the top of the page. Click **OK**.

Task 3: Verify the Business Hours Settings

Step 1.   From one IP Phone, call the other IP Phone, but do not answer the call. Leave a voice message. This should work (unless you are performing this lab outside normal business hours).

Step 2.   From the Unity Express GUI main menu, click **Configure**, select **System Parameters**, and click **System Time**.

Step 3.   Change the day to a day that is a Saturday or Sunday. Click the **Set** button. Click **OK** twice.

Step 4.   From one of the Cisco IP Phones, call the other IP Phone, but do not answer the call. The auto attendant should automatically say that the specific person (if configured) is unavailable. This is because it is outside normal business hours.

Step 5.   Using the **System Time** option, set the day back to the correct date.

Task 4: Configure the Night Service Bell

Step 1.   From the Unity Express web interface, point to **Configure**, select **System Parameters**, click **Night Service Bell Configuration**, and click the **Night Service Code** link. This code is the number that users press to manually activate and deactivate the night service bell.

Step 2.   In the Night Service Code textbox, enter ***789** as the code to activate/deactivate the service. Click the **Change** button, and click **OK** twice.

Step 3.   Click the **Night Service Bell Configuration** option to return to the configuration menu. Select the **Night Service Day Add** link. It is important to get the Night Service Day (and not the Night Service Date) link.

Step 4.   In the Week Day drop-down menu, select **Sat**. In the Start Time textboxes, enter **08** and **00**. In the End Time text boxes, enter **13** and **00**. Click the **Add** button and both of the **OK** buttons.

Step 5.   To test the night service bell feature, you must configure a "Night Service Day" for the current day. Using the process described in the two previous steps, add the night service feature for the current day.

Step 6.   The lowest-numbered IP Phone will be designated as a phone that is the extension number called during off-hours. From the Unity Express GUI, point to **Configure**, and select **Extensions**. Click the link for the lowest-numbered Cisco IP Phone. The Change Extension window appears.

Step 7.   Click the **Receive Night Service Bell Yes** radio button, and click the **Change** button. Click both of the **OK** buttons that appear.

Note: The process of configuring the option under **Extensions** affects the ephone-dn that can be seen from the router CLI. The next step, which configures an option under **Phones**, affects the ephone.

Step 8. The highest-numbered IP Phone will be able to receive a ring when anyone calls the night service extension during night service hours. From the Unity Express GUI, point to **Configure**, and select **Phones**. Click the MAC address link that relates to the highest-numbered Cisco IP Phone. The Change Phone window appears. If the Change Phone window does not appear, see the following note.

Note: The authors have noticed that on certain versions of IOS (such as 12.3(11)T8), the GUI files must be upgraded to the next-higher version. Refer to Lab 8-1 for how to upload and extract the files to the router.

Step 9. In the Change Phone window, select the **Receive Night Service Bell Yes** radio button. Scroll to the bottom of the window, and select the **Change** button. Click **OK** twice.

Task 5: Test the Night Service Bell

Step 1. From the Cisco IP Phone that has not been configured for the night service bell (the IP Phone that has the second-highest phone number), call the phone number of the IP Phone that has the words "Night Service Active" displayed. Notice how the other IP Phone rings in addition to the extension that was dialed. If the night service bell does not work properly, troubleshoot the commands entered in the previous task.

Step 2. From telephony-service configuration mode, or using the GUI, remove the night service "day" for the current day. The phone with the lowest extension number no longer displays the words "Night Service Active."

```
RouterVoIPX(config-telephony)# no night-service day xxx xx:xx xx:xx
```

Step 3. On the phone that has the extension that has been designated the night service extension (the lowest-numbered phone extension), press the speaker button, and press the keys ***789** (the night service code). The words "Night Service Active" appear, because the night service feature has been manually enabled. If this does not work, there was a problem with how you configured the **night-service code** configuration in Task 4, Steps 1 and 2.

Step 4. On the same phone, press the speaker button, and press the keys ***789** again. After a few seconds, the words "Night Service Disabled" appear on the phone.

Step 5. From the router CLI, manually remove the configurations that relate to the night service bell feature:

```
RouterVoIPX(config)# ephone-dn X
RouterVoIPX(config-ephone-dn)# no night-service bell
RouterVoIPX(config-ephone-dn)# ephone X
RouterVoIPX(config-ephone)# no night-service bell
RouterVoIPX(config-ephone)# telephony-service
RouterVoIPX(config-telephony)# no night-service code *789
RouterVoIPX(config-telephony)# no night-service day Sat
```

Step 6. From the Unity Express GUI, select the **Configure** main menu option, and click **Users**. Figure 11-8 shows this window. Select all the users you have created for the exercises in this chapter.

Figure 11-8   Unity Express: Configure Users Window

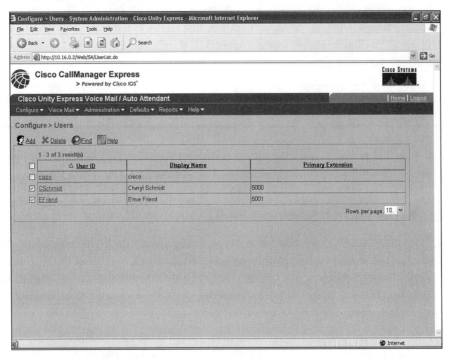

Step 7.   Select the **Delete** link. Click the **OK** button when a confirmation window appears. The users and associated mailbox are deleted.

Step 8.   Save the Unity Express configuration:

```
se-10-X6-0-2# copy running-config startup-config
```

Step 9.   Save the router configuration:

```
RouterVoIPX# copy running-config startup-config
```

CHAPTER 12

Case Studies

This chapter provides three case studies designed to help you practice configuration concepts from Chapters 1 through 11. You can work through these case studies individually or in a group setting. Keep in mind that the case studies were written with the smallest amount of equipment needed, but they still let you practice VoIP commands. The case studies are progressively harder—the first case study is easier than Case Study 12-2 or 12-3.

Case Study 12-1: Configuring Cisco CallManager Express Connectivity Between Two Pods

The company OCSIC.org has decided to design and build a new two-site voice network using two CallManager Express (CME) routers, IP Phones, and analog phones. These sites need to be able to dial from one Cisco IP Phone to an IP Phone at the other site.

The objectives of this lab are as follows:

- Create a new IP addressing scheme.

- Create a new five-digit dial plan.

- Build and configure a two-router voice network with CME.

- Configure an analog phone on each router.

- Verify IP Phone and analog phone connectivity.

To perform this lab, you need the following equipment:

- Two Cisco CME-capable routers

- Two switches/switch module

- Workstation with a FastEthernet 10/100 network interface card (NIC) installed

- Two Cisco IP Phones (powered using any method)

- Two analog phones

Figure 12-1 illustrates the topology used for this case study. Keep in mind that you can use an integrated switch module in the router instead of the external switch.

Figure 12-1   Lab Topology: CCME Cisco, Switch/Switch Module, and IP Phone Connectivity

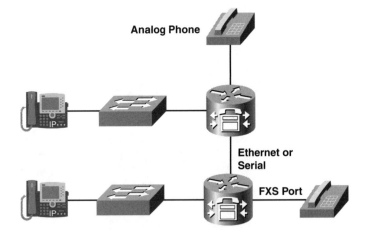

The procedure for this case study consists of the following tasks. The following sections describe each task in detail.

- **Task 1**—Create a new IP addressing scheme.
- **Task 2**—Create a new five-digit dial plan.
- **Task 3**—Build and configure a two-router voice network with CME.
- **Task 4**—Configure an analog phone on each router.
- **Task 5**—Verify IP Phone and analog phone connectivity.

Task 1: Create a New IP Addressing Scheme

Step 1. Create a new IP addressing scheme that accommodates the IP addresses necessary to configure a two-router CME voice network with either an external switch or an internal switch module. The IP address ranges must be different from the ones used in previous labs.

Step 2. Complete Table 12-1 using the new IP addressing scheme.

Table 12-1   IP Telephony Addressing Scheme

Pod	Hostname of Cisco CME Router or Switch	IP Address on Ethernet Interface	Type	DHCP Pool Exclusion	IP Network for DHCP Pool	Default Router	Option 150
Pod 1	VoiceRouter1	_____	Data	_____ _____	_____	_____	___
		_____	Voice	_____ _____	_____	_____	_____
		_____	Mgmt	—	—	—	—
	VoiceSwitch1	_____	Mgmt	—	—	_____	—
Pod 2	VoiceRouter2	_____	Data	_____ _____	_____	_____	___
		_____	Voice	_____ _____	_____	_____	_____
		_____	Mgmt	—	—	—	—
	VoiceSwitch2	_____	Mgmt	—	—	_____	—

Task 2: Create a New Five-Digit Dial Plan

Step 1. Create a new five-digit dial plan that accommodates the CME IP Phones and two analog phones. The dial plan phone numbers must be different from the ones used in previous labs.

Step 2. Complete Table 12-2 using the new dial plan.

Table 12-2   IP Telephony Dial Plan

Pod	Extension Numbers	First E.164 DID Number	Voice Mail Extension Number (Analog Numbers)
1	_____	_____	_____
2	_____	_____	_____

Task 3: Build and Configure a Two-Router Voice Network with CME

Step 1.   Cable two routers, external switches, or switch modules. Install the necessary IOS and CME files, and cable IP and analog phones.

Step 2.   Configure two routers, external switches, or switch modules using the IP addressing scheme and dial plan created in Tasks 1 and 2.

Task 4: Configure an Analog Phone on Each Router

Configure one analog phone on each router using the dial plan created in Task 2.

Task 5: Verify IP Phone and Analog Phone Connectivity

Step 1.   Verify that each IP Phone can call every other IP Phone or analog phone.

Step 2.   Verify that each analog phone can call every other IP Phone or analog phone.

Case Study 12-2: Elementary School (Multiple CMEs)

In this lab, you configure a two-router CME network to interoperate in an elementary school environment.

The objectives of this lab are as follows:

- Configure two CME routers that allow connectivity to a phone connected to the Adtran (or a similar unit).

- Configure the routers so that call routing is somewhat controlled.

To perform this lab, you need the following equipment:

- Two Cisco CME-capable routers with a serial interface and the appropriate serial cables

- Two switches/switch modules

- Two workstations with an Ethernet 10/100 NIC installed

- Four Cisco IP Phones

- One analog phone

- Adtran (or a similar WAN emulation unit)

Figure 12-2 shows the lab topology used with this lab. Keep in mind that an integrated switch module in the router could be used instead of the external switch.

Figure 12-2   Lab Topology: Case Study 12-2

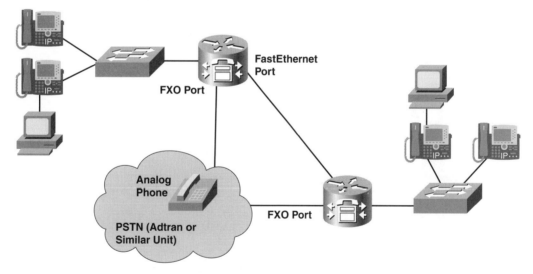

The procedure for this case study consists of the following tasks. Complete each task to build an operational VoIP network.

- **Task 1**—Create an IP addressing scheme using 192.168.*x.x*, and place it in a spreadsheet or table.

- **Task 2**—Develop a four-digit dial plan that is different from the labs or any other case study, and place it in a spreadsheet or table.

- **Task 3**—Provide a dial peer summary that lists every dial peer and dial peer number and configuration commands in an organized manner.

- **Task 4**—Configure all Cisco IP Phones so that they communicate with each other using a four-digit extension.

- **Task 5**—Configure each CME router so that it can communicate with the analog phone located outside the school. The CME router reaches this phone using a Foreign Exchange Office (FXO) port. The analog phone does not call the Cisco IP Phones. (Pretend that the analog phone is an external fax machine at another company.)

- **Task 6**—Configure at least one PC that connects to a Cisco IP Phone on each pod. Configure the PC for DHCP, and provide the IP address from the CME router. The PC must be on a different network than the IP Phones.

- **Task 7**—Create a call routing policy with the following requirements:

   — Allow only administrators with Cisco IP Phones (one phone on one pod) to access the external fax (analog phone).

   — Do not allow any of the Cisco IP Phones on one pod to access a particular Cisco IP Phone number on the other pod.

Case Study 12-3: IT Company

In this lab, you configure two CME routers to interoperate in a small multisite IT company environment.

The objectives of this lab are as follows:

- Configure two CME routers that allow connectivity between Cisco IP Phones to an analog phone connected to the Adtran (or a similar unit) and to an analog phone connected to the Foreign Exchange Station (FXS) port.

- Configure GUI administration access.

- Configure translation rules.

- Configure an intercom between two IP Phones.

- Configure phone monitoring.

- Configure speed dialing.

To perform this lab, you need the following equipment:

- Two Cisco CME-capable routers with a serial interface and the appropriate serial cables

- Two switches/switch modules

- At least one workstation with an Ethernet 10/100 NIC installed

- Four Cisco IP Phones

- Three analog phones

- Adtran (or a similar WAN emulation unit)

Figure 12-3 shows the lab topology used with this lab. Keep in mind that you could use an integrated switch module in the router instead of the external switch.

Figure 12-3   Lab Topology: Case Study 12-3

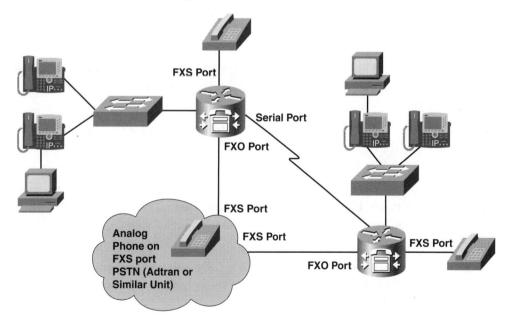

The procedure for this case study consists of the following tasks. Complete each task to build an operational VoIP network.

- **Task 1**—Create an IP addressing scheme using 172.30.*x.x*, and place it in a spreadsheet or table.

- **Task 2**—Use the same dial plan (and phone numbers) that was used for labs such as Lab 3-1, "Configuring VoIP Using the **telephony-service setup** Program."

- **Task 3**—Provide a dial peer summary that lists every dial peer and dial peer number and configuration command in an organized manner. You cannot use the same dial peer numbers that were used in the labs.

- **Task 4**—Configure all Cisco IP Phones so that they communicate with each other using a four-digit extension. The codec used between sites is G729.

- **Task 5**—Configure an analog phone that connects to the first FXS port so that the IP Phones can reach it using four-digit dialing. The analog phone should be able to reach the Cisco IP Phones using four-digit dialing as well. Do this on both CME routers.

- **Task 6**—Configure each CME router so that the Cisco IP Phones and the analog phone connected to the FXS port can communicate with the analog phone located outside the company (connected to an FXS port on the Adtran or a similar unit). The CME router reaches this phone using an FXO port.

  The analog phone that connects to the Adtran unit (FXS port) cannot communicate with the Cisco IP Phones or the analog phone connected to the CME router FXS ports.

- **Task 7**—Configure at least one PC to connect to the data VLAN, and connect the PC directly to a switch port (not the back of the IP Phone). Statically configure the appropriate IP address and default gateway on the PC.

- **Task 8**—On the lowest-numbered CME router, enable GUI phone administration, and protect it by enabling HTTPS if the IOS supports it. For example, if one CME router is named RouterVoIP1 and the other router is named RouterVoIP2, enable GUI phone administration and add the security component on RouterVoIP1.

- **Task 9**—On the highest-numbered CME router, configure phone activity monitoring, and send the results to a syslog server. Save the log results of at least two phone calls, and put them in a presentable format.

- **Task 10**—Using the CLI on the highest-numbered CME router, configure an intercom system between two IP Phones. Assign a button on each Cisco IP Phone, and label it with the word Intercom. Test the intercom.

- **Task 11**—Using the CLI on the lowest-numbered CME router, configure one speed dial on one of the Cisco IP Phones to reach the other IP Phone. Place a label on the speed dial button, and test the speed dial.

- **Task 12**—On the lowest-numbered CME router, the CEO has a Cisco IP Phone that has four digits, like every other IP Phone. However, the CEO wants everyone to dial BOSS-MAN (267-7626) when they call him. Create a translation rule that makes this happen on the phone that simulates the CEO's phone.

- **Task 13**—On the highest-numbered CME router is a LAN with top-secret projects. This LAN has one phone. No one should ever know the phone number assigned to this phone. Employees should dial SECRET (732738) to reach this phone.

Reference Tables

This appendix provides three tables—IP addressing, dial plan, and dial peers. These are a combination of addresses and numbers given throughout the labs in Chapters 1 through 11. Many people find it helpful to have the numbers in one place rather than having to search through the chapters to find the exact syntax and/or parameters.

IP Addressing

Table A-1 shows the IP addressing scheme used for the majority of the labs in this book.

Table A-1   IP Addressing

Pod	Hostname	Ethernet IP Address	VLAN Type	DHCP Pool Network	Default Router	DHCP Option 150	Serial Interface IP Address
1	RouterVoIP1	10.10.0.1/24	Data	10.10.0.0/24	10.10.0.1	N/A	10.19.0.1/24
		10.15.0.1/24	Voice	10.15.0.0/24	10.15.0.1	10.10.0.1	N/A
		10.1.0.1/24	Mgmt	N/A	N/A	N/A	N/A
	SwitchVoIP1	10.1.0.4/24	Mgmt	N/A	10.1.0.1	N/A	N/A
2	RouterVoIP2	10.20.0.1/24	Data	10.20.0.0/24	10.20.0.1	N/A	10.19.0.2/24
		10.25.0.1/24	Voice	10.25.0.0/24	10.25.0.1	10.20.0.1	N/A
		10.2.0.1/24	Mgmt	N/A	N/A	N/A	N/A
	SwitchVoIP2	10.2.0.4	Mgmt	N/A	10.2.0.1	N/A	N/A
3	RouterVoIP3	10.30.0.1/24	Data	10.30.0.0/24	10.30.0.1	N/A	10.39.0.1/24
		10.35.0.1/24	Voice	10.35.0.0 24	10.35.0.1	10.30.0.1	N/A
		10.3.0.1/24	Mgmt	N/A	N/A	N/A	N/A
	SwitchVoIP3	10.3.0.4	Mgmt	N/A	10.3.0.1	N/A	N/A
4	RouterVoIP4	10.40.0.1/24	Data	10.40.0.0/24	10.40.0.1	N/A	10.39.0.2/24
		10.45.0.1/24	Voice	10.45.0.0/24	10.45.0.1	10.40.0.1	N/A
		10.4.0.1/24	Mgmt	N/A	N/A	N/A	N/A
	SwitchVoIP4	10.4.0.4/24	Mgmt	N/A	10.4.0.1	N/A	N/A

Dial Plan

Table A-2 shows the dial plan scheme used for the majority of the labs in this book.

Table A-2   Dial Plan

Pod	Extension Numbers	Voice Mail Extension Number	First E.164 DID Number	Router FXS 0 Port	Router FXS 1 Port
1	5000 to 5029	5555028	5105555000	5555028	5555029
2	5030 to 5059	5555058	5105555030	5555058	5555059
3	5060 to 5089	5555088	5105555060	5555088	5555089
4	5100 to 5129	5555128	5105555100	5555128	5555129

Dial Peers

Table A-3 shows the dial peers used for the majority of the labs in this book.

Table A-3   Dial Peers

Purpose	Dial Peer Tag	Dial Peer Type	Destination Pattern	Target IP Address or Port	Optional Manipulation
Communicate with analog phone connected to first FXS port	1	POTS	5555XXX Pod1—028 Pod2—058 Pod3—088 Pod4—128	FXS port 0 (example 0/2/0)	—
Use the PRI to access PSTN	2	POTS	555[4-6]... (3 dots)	T1 port 0 (example 1/0/0:23)	**forward-digits all**
Outside analog phone to analog phone connected to FXS 0 (through T1)	3	POTS	—	T1 port 0 (example 1/0/0:23)	**incoming called-number 5555...** (3 dots) **direct-inward-dial**
Use first FXO port to connect to outside analog phone (on Adtran or similar unit)	5	POTS	5556... (3 dots)	FXO port 0 (example 0/0/0)	**forward-digits all**
Pod 1 to Pod 2 serial interface connectivity	6	VoIP	50[3-5]. (1 dot)	**session target ipv4:** *partner_ip_address*	**codec g729br8** (config-telephony-service)# **dialplan-pattern 1 555.... extension-length 4**
Pod 2 to Pod 1 serial interface connectivity	6	VoIP	50[0-2]. (1 dot)	**session target ipv4:** *partner_ip_address*	**codec g729br8** (config-telephony-service)# **dialplan-pattern 1 555.... extension-length 4**
Pod 3 to Pod 4 serial interface connectivity	6	VoIP	51[0-1]. (1 dot)	**session target ipv4:** *partner_ip_address*	**codec g729br8** (config-telephony-service)# **dialplan-pattern 1 555.... extension-length 4**

continues

Table A-3   Dial Peers   *continued*

Purpose	Dial Peer Tag	Dial Peer Type	Destination Pattern	Target IP Address or Port	Optional Manipulation
Pod 4 to Pod 3 serial interface connectivity	6	VoIP	50[6-8]. (1 dot)	**session target ipv4:** *partner_ip_address*	**codec g729br8** (config-telephony-service)# **dialplan-pattern 1 555.... extension-length 4**
Communicate with analog phone connected to second FXS port	12	POTS	5555059	FXS port 1 (example port 0/2/1)	—
Gateway: analog phone connected to first FXS port	41	POTS	8000	FXS port 0 (example port 0/2/0)	—
Gateway: analog phone connected to second FXS port	42	POTS	8001	FXS port 1 (example port 0/2/1)	—
Gatekeeper: analog phone connected to first FXS port	45	POTS	7000	FXS port 0 (example port 0/2/0)	—
Gatekeeper: analog phone connected to second FXS port	46	POTS	7001	FXS port 1 (example port 0/2/1)	—
Gatekeeper and gateway: communication with another pod	50	VoIP	.... (4 dots)	—	**session target ras**
Pod 1 to Pod 2 for basic H.323	100	VoIP	50[3-5]. (1 dot)	**session target ipv4:** *partner_loopback_ address*	**dtmf-relay h245-alphanumeric** **codec g729r8**
Pod 2 to Pod 1 for basic H.323	100	VoIP	50[0-2]. (1 dot)	**session target ipv4:** *partner_loopback_ address*	**dtmf-relay h245-alphanumeric** **codec g729r8**
Pod 3 to Pod 4 for basic H.323	100	VoIP	51.. (2 dots)	**session target ipv4:** *partner_loopback_ address*	**dtmf-relay h245-alphanumeric** **codec g729r8**

Purpose	Dial Peer Tag	Dial Peer Type	Destination Pattern	Target IP Address or Port	Optional Manipulation
Pod 4 to Pod 3 for basic H.323	100	VoIP	50[6-8]. (1 dot)	**session target ipv4:** *partner_loopback_ address*	**dtmf-relay h245-alphanumeric** **codec g729r8**
Communicate with voice mailbox of 6900 on Unity module	6000	VoIP	69.. (2 dots)	**session target ipv4:10.***x***6.0.2**	**dtmf-relay sip-notify** **session protocol sipv2** **codec g711ulaw** **no vad**

Command Reference

The commands provided in this appendix (in alphabetical order) are those used in the labs throughout this book.

Table B-1   CallManager Express/Unity Express Commands Used in the Labs

Command Example	Description
access-list *number* [**permit** | **deny**] *protocol source source_wildcard_mask destination destination_wildcard_mask* [**eq** *parameter*]	Creates an extended access list.
after-hours block pattern *number*	Specifies a pattern that cannot be dialed, such as 9 for local calls or 9 1 for long-distance calls.
after-hours day *day start* **end**	Blocks specific days and times for non-business-hours calls.
application voicemail	From within Unity Express, configures the voice mail with the name of the application to start when a trigger is entered.
archive tar /xtract *source destination*	Extracts the contents of a .tar file to the destination specified.
auto assign *X* **to** *X*	Turns on auto registration and configuration of new ephone-dns.
auto qos voip	Enables AutoQoS for VoIP on the outbound router interface.
auto qos voip cisco-phone	Enables AutoQoS for VoIP on a port that has a Cisco IP Phone attached.
bandwidth interzone zone *zone_name kbps*	Defines the maximum aggregate bandwidth for H.323 traffic.
button *button_number:ephone-dn_number*	Assigns an ephone-dn to a line on the ephone.
call-forward busy *number*	The voice mail number to send a call if the phone line is busy.
call-forward max-length 0	Disables call forwarding for a specific ephone-dn.
call-forward noan *number* **timeout** *seconds*	Defines the voice mail number to send a call if there is no answer for a particular phone line.
card type t1 *slot_number* **1**	Enables a T1 interface. (The 1 indicates the use of onboard controllers and may not be needed.)
ccn subsystem sip	Enters SIP configuration mode.
ccn trigger sip phonenumber *number*	Configures Unity Express for a voice mail number.
clock rate *rate*	Defines the clock rate on a specific interface.

continues

Table B-1   CallManager Express/Unity Express Commands Used in the Labs   *continued*

Command Example	Description
clock set *hour:minute:seconds date month year*	Sets the date and time.
clock source line	Specifies that the T1 link uses the recovered clock from the line.
codec g711ulaw	Defines a dial peer to use the G711ulaw codec.
codec g729br8	Defines a dial peer to use the G729BR8 codec, which is a higher compression than G711.
codec g729r8	Defines a dial peer to use the G729R8 codec, which is a higher compression method than G711.
configure terminal	Enters global configuration mode.
controller t1 *slot/port*	Enters T1 port configuration mode.
copy running-config startup-config	Saves the changes made in RAM to NVRAM on a router or switch.
cor incoming *name*	Applies a COR in the incoming direction to an ephone-dn.
corlist outgoing *name*	Associates a COR list with a dial peer.
create cnf-files	Creates XML files for configuring the IP Phones.
crypto key generate rsa usage-keys modulus 1024	Manually generates an RSA usage key pair.
debug ephone pak	Displays packets used in communication between the ephone and the CME router.
debug ephone register	Used to troubleshoot IP phone registration with CME problems.
debug h225 events	Enables H.225 (part of the H.323 suite) events debugging.
debug translation detail	Used to troubleshoot translation rules.
debug voice dialpeer all	Used to troubleshoot dial peers (incomplete calls).
default-router *IP_address*	Sets the default gateway that will be assigned to the DHCP clients.
delete flash:vlan.dat	Deletes the VLAN database from a switch or router that has a switch module installed.
description *words*	Sets the label on the IP phone header bar.
destination-pattern *phone_number*	Defines a number dialed for a specific dial peer.
dial-control-mib max-size *bytes*	Controls the maximum size of call history table entries.
dial-control-mib retain-timer *minutes*	Controls how long call history entries are retained.
dial-peer cor custom	Specifies that named class of restrictions apply to dial peers.
dial-peer cor list *name*	Defines a dial peer class of restriction list.
dial-peer cor list *name*	Defines a class of restriction list name.

Command Example	Description
dial-peer voice *number* **pots**	Creates a POTS dial peer.
dial-peer voice *number* **voip**	Creates a VoIP dial peer.
dialplan-pattern *pattern* **extension-length** *length* [**extension-pattern** *pattern*] [**no-reg**]	Creates a global prefix that can be used to expand the abbreviated extension numbers into fully qualified E.164 numbers.
direct-inward-dial	Enables DID call treatment for an incoming called number for a specific dial peer. The incoming call is treated as if the digits were received from the DID trunk.
dn-webedit	Allows directory number changes to be made via the web interface.
dtmf-relay h245-alphanumeric	Specifies the way an H.323 or SIP gateway relays DTMF tones between telephony interfaces and an IP network.
dtmf-relay sip-notify	Forwards DTMF tones using SIP NOTIFY messages.
enable	Accesses privileged mode.
enable password *cisco*	Assigns a password to enter privileged exec mode.
enabled	In Unity Express, starts a trigger for SIP.
encapsulation dot1q *vlan_number*	Configures an interface or subinterface for IEEE 802.1Q trunking for the specified VLAN.
encapsulation dot1q *vlan_number* **native**	Defines the native VLAN.
encapsulation hdlc	Configures the serial link to use the HDLC encapsulation.
end mailbox	Returns from voice mail mailbox configuration mode.
end subsystem	Returns from a configuration mode (such as **ccn subsystem sip**).
end trigger	Returns from a configuration mode (such as **ccn trigger sip**).
ephone *number*	Enters and creates an ephone.
ephone-dn *number* **dual-line**	Enters and creates an ephone-dn.
erase startup-config	Erases the configuration stored in NVRAM from a router or switch.
exit	Goes back one configuration level.
forward-digits all	Forwards the full length of the destination dial pattern.
framing esf	Defines the type of framing used to be ESF (Extended Superframe).
gatekeeper	Enables the gatekeeper function.
gateway	Enables the gateway function.
gateway address *IP_address*	Defines the Unity Express default gateway for SIP.

continues

Table B-1   CallManager Express/Unity Express Commands Used in the Labs   *continued*

Command Example	Description
gw-accounting syslog	Enables VoIP accounting and outputs in Syslog message format.
gw-type-prefix *prefix_type* **default-technology**	Configures the gatekeeper for the specified technology prefix.
h323-gateway voip h323-id *gateway_name*	Defines the H.323 name for a gateway.
h323-gateway voip id *gatekeeper_id* {**ipaddr** *IP_address* [*port_number*]}	Defines the name and location of the gatekeeper for a router functioning as a gateway.
H323-gateway voip interface	Enables the specific interface being configured as an H.323 interface.
H323-gateway voip tech-prefix *prefix*	Defines the technology prefix used when the gateway registers with the gatekeeper.
H323-gateway voip vind scraddr *local_IP_address*	Designates a local source IP address for the voice gateway.
hostname *name*	Assigns a hostname to the router.
interface *fastethernet x/x*	Enters FastEthernet 0/0 configuration mode.
interface fastethernet *x/x.x*	Creates a subinterface for the FastEthernet interface.
interface loopback 0	Creates a loopback interface.
interface service-engine *x/x*	Configures parameters for the Unity Express module.
interface vlan *x*	Enters VLAN configuration mode.
ip access-group *number* [**in** | **out**]	Applies an access list to an interface.
ip address *address mask*	Sets the IP address on an interface.
ip default-gateway *IP_address*	Assigns a default gateway address to be used by a switch.
ip dhcp excluded-address *starting_address ending_address*	Sets a range of addresses to be excluded from the DHCP pool.
ip dhcp pool *pool_name*	Defines a DHCP pool and enters a DHCP pool mode.
ip domain-name *name*	Creates a domain name.
ip http authentication local	Specifies a local userid and password.
ip http path flash:	Defines the location of the HTML files.
ip http secure-server	Enables HTTPS.
ip http server	Enables the HTTP service on a router or switch.
ip nbar protocol-discovery	Enables NBAR on an interface.
ip route *network mask* **service-engine** *x/x*	Creates a static route to the Cisco Unity Express module.
ip source-address *IP_address* **port** *port_number*	Sets the interface where Cisco CallManager Express listens for skinny messages.

Command Example	Description
ip source-address *IP_address* **port** *port_number* **strict-match**	Restricts from telephony-service configuration mode which Cisco IP Phones can register with the CME router.
ip unnumbered fastethernet *x/x*	Uses the IP address from the specified FastEthernet port.
ip unnumbered vlan *x*	Uses the IP address from the specified VLAN interface.
isdn switch-type primary-ni	Defines the type of ISDN switch used in T1 communications between the router and the ISDN switch (or simulated ISDN switch).
keepalive 10	Sets the keepalive to 10 seconds.
label *words*	Applies a label to a specific ephone-dn.
line vty 0 4	Enters line configuration mode.
linecode b8zs	Defines the type of line code to be used as B8ZS.
load *model filename*	Loads the firmware file for the specified model of IP phone.
logging *ip_address*	Enables Syslogging to the specified IP address (logging server).
login	Enables logins on vty connections.
mac-address *H.H.H*	Associates a physical device with an ephone.
max-dn *number*	Sets the maximum ephone-dn that can be present.
max-ephones *number*	Sets the maximum ephones that can be present.
maxsessions *number*	In Unity Express, specifies the maximum number of users who can access a SIP trigger simultaneously.
member *name*	Associates a member with a COR list.
mls qos cos override	Overrides the CoS value so that it is rewritten to a value of 0, the default.
mls qos trust dscp	Configures a port to trust the DSCP value. (If a Cisco IP Phone is attached, the DSCP value is automatically marked.)
name *John Smith*	Assigns a name (such as John Smith) to the ephone-dn.
name *name*	Associates a specific name with a COR.
network *10.0.0.0*	Allows EIGRP to advertise networks for all interfaces with a 10.0.0.0 network number.
network *network_number mask*	Enters a network range and subnet mask to use to assign addresses and masks to the DHCP clients.
network-clock-participate slot *T1_slot*	Allows a port on a specific module or voice WAN interface card (VWIC) to use the network clock for timing. Whether you use the WIC or the slot option is based on output shown in the **show diag** command.

continues

Table B-1   CallManager Express/Unity Express Commands Used in the Labs   *continued*

Command Example	Description
network-clock-participate wic *T1_slot*	Allows a port on a specific module or VWIC to use the network clock for timing. Whether you use the WIC or the slot option is based on output shown in the **show diag** command.
no vad	Disables voice activity detection (VAD).
number *extension_number*	Assigns a directory (extension) number to the ephone-dn.
number *number* **secondary** *e.164_number* **no-reg primary**	Manually configures the Cisco IP Phone to register with the gatekeeper.
option 150 ip *IP_address*	Sets the TFTP server that will be assigned to the DHCP clients.
paging group *x,y*	Allows multiple paging groups already created to be combined into one group.
paging ip *multicast_ip_address* **port** *port_number*	Defines the multicast address and port number used to broadcast audio paging messages to idle IP phones.
park-slot timeout *seconds* **limit** *number_of_reminders*	Sets a call reminder (ringback) after the specified number of seconds and defines a maximum number of reminders.
password *cisco*	Sets a password of cisco on the vty lines.
ping	Checks Layer 3 connectivity between two IP devices.
port *port_number*	Defines the port to be used by a specific dial peer.
pri-group timeslots *beginning_channel-ending_channel*	Defines the channels to be assigned to the Primary Rate Interface (PRI).
reload	Reloads the router or switch.
ring number *number*	Configures a Foreign Exchange Office (FXO) port to answer after the specified number of rings.
router eigrp *100*	Enters EIGRP configuration mode for autonomous system (AS) 100.
rule *priority_number match_pattern replace_pattern*	Creates a specific translation rule.
rule *priority_number /match_pattern/ /replace_pattern/*	Creates a specific voice translation rule.
service-module ip address *ip_address mask*	Defines the IP address of the Cisco Unity Express module.
service-module ip default-gateway *ip_address*	Defines the default gateway for the Cisco Unity Express module.
service-module service-engine *x/x* **session**	Accesses the Unity Express module.
session target ipv4:*ip_address*	Used for a specific dial peer to route a call toward the specified IP address.
session target ras	Allows an analog phone to register to a gateway using RAS (a part of the H.323 protocol suite).

Command Example	Description
show auto qos	Displays AutoQoS information.
show controllers serial *mod/port*	Displays information that is specific to the interface hardware.
show diag	Displays hardware information.
show dial-plan number *dialed_number*	Displays which outgoing dial peer is reached when a particular phone number is dialed.
show ephone	Verifies IP phone registration.
show flash:	Displays the contents of the flash.
show gatekeeper calls	Displays the status of each ongoing call of which a gatekeeper is aware.
show gatekeeper endpoints	Verifies the devices that register with the gatekeeper, including the gateway(s).
show gatekeeper status	Displays the gatekeeper's status.
show gatekeeper zone status	Displays the status of zones related to a gatekeeper.
show gateway	Verifies the gateway function.
show hardware	Displays the hardware installed in a router.
show interfaces fastethernet *slot/port-adapter/port* **switchport**	Displays trunking information for a particular interface.
show interfaces serial *slot/port-adapter/port***:23**	Verifies the status of the T1 connection (up and up and spoofing).
show interfaces trunk	Displays trunking information for all interfaces.
show inventory	Verifies the installation of hardware such as an AIM.
show ip interface brief	Displays a summary of interfaces on the devices.
show ip nbar protocol-discovery interface *interface*	Displays NBAR statistics for the specified interface.
show ip nbar protocol-discovery interface *interface* **top-n** *number*	Displays NBAR statistics for the specified interface for the most widely used protocols (the number of protocols defined in the command).
show isdn status	Displays the status of the ISDN port. Used in verifying and troubleshooting T1 connectivity.
show mls qos interface fastethernet *slot/port-adapter/port*	Displays QoS information for a specific interface.
show num-exp *dialed_number*	Displays the number expansions created.
show running-configuration	Displays the current configuration that is loaded and running in RAM on the router or switch.
show sessions	Displays open Telnet or rlogin connections.
show translation-rule	Displays translation rules, match pattern, replacement pattern, and whether the rule is being used.

continues

Table B-1   CallManager Express/Unity Express Commands Used in the Labs   *continued*

Command Example	Description
show voice port	Displays detailed information about all voice ports.
show voice port *port_number*	Displays information about a specific voice port.
show voice port summary	Displays a short list of voice ports.
switchport mode trunk	Sets a physical interface or subinterface to trunking mode (in contrast to access mode).
switchport priority extend cos 0	Sets the CoS value of 0 for frames originating from a PC that attaches to a Cisco IP Phone.
switchport trunk encapsulation dot1q	Sets a physical interface or subinterface to the IEEE 802.1Q trunking encapsulation standard.
switchport trunk native vlan *vlan_number*	Defines the native VLAN. (In VoIP, this should be the data VLAN so that a PC connected to the IP phone can receive an IP address.)
switchport voice vlan *vlan_number*	Defines the voice VLAN.
system message *message*	Displays a message on all the IP phones.
telephony-service	Enters telephony-service configuration mode.
telephony-service setup	Enters the VoIP setup utility.
test translation-rule *rule_number* *number_to_be_tested*	Tests a translation rule offline.
test voice translation-rule *rule_number* *number_to_be_tested*	Tests a voice translation rule offline.
time-webedit	Allows Cisco CME time to be configured through the web interface.
transfer-system full-consult	Enables consultative phone transfers.
translate called *number*	Associates a translation rule with an ephone-dn.
translation-rule *number*	Creates a translation rule.
type *7960*	Assigns a model of IP phone to the ephone.
undebug all	Turns off all debugging.
username *name* **create**	Creates a username on the Unity Express module.
username *name* **password** *password*	Defines a username and password for an ephone.
username *name* **phonenumber** *number*	Defines an extension number for a specific username.
username *name* **phonenumberE164** *number*	Defines an E.164 number for a specific username.
username *name* **privilege** *level* **secret** *password*	Creates a username and encrypted password.
vlan database	Enters VLAN database configuration mode from privileged mode on a switch or router that has a switch module installed.
vlan X name *name* **state active**	Manually creates a VLAN in the VLAN database and places the VLAN in an active condition.

Command Example	Description
voice translation-rule *number*	Creates a voice translation rule.
voice-port *slot/subunit/port*	Enters port configuration mode for a specific voice port.
voicemail default language *xx_yy*	Specifies the default language used in the Unity Express voice mail attendant.
voicemail mailbox owner *name* **size** *seconds*	Creates a Unity Express mailbox and defines the mailbox size.
voicemail *number*	Defines the phone number used for voice mail.
web admin system name *name* **password** *password*	Defines a userid and password to be used when performing web-based voice configurations.
web customize load *filename*	Specifies the XML file to be used with the Customer administrator account via the web interface.
web skipinitwizard	Skips the Unity Express GUI initialization wizard.
zone local *gatekeeper_name domain-name* [*ras_Ipaddress*]	Specifies a zone controlled by the gatekeeper.
zone prefix *gatekeeper_name pattern* [**gw-priority** *priority_number gateway_name*]	Adds a specific dialed prefix to the gatekeeper zone list. This is like the call routing table definitions for the gatekeeper.

Installing a Unity Express AIM in a 2811 Router

This lab works with other routers, but the placement of the Advanced Integration Module (AIM) is specific for a 2811 series router. If you have another type of router, you can use this lab, but it is recommended that you go to Cisco.com and locate the AIM installation procedure for your specific router model.

Cover Removal

The hardest part of this lab is removing the router cover. Four screws hold the cover in place. Ensure that the router is powered off and unplugged. The rear of the router contains the slots for the different modules. At the rear of the router, notice the two metal clips on the outermost part of the router. These clips are attached to the top cover and get inserted into the router frame. The clips prevent the cover from sliding forward toward the front of the chassis.

After you remove the screws, the cover slides toward the rear of the chassis. Only when the clasps are completely away from the router frame can you remove the cover. On new routers, it might help to hold the palm of your hand firmly on the cover and push the cover toward the rear of the chassis. As you do this, you will see the two clips move away from the chassis. Use this same technique (but in the reverse direction) to reinstall the router cover.

Lab C-1: Installing a Unity Express AIM in a 2811 Router

In this lab, the company OCSIC.org has decided to provide voice mail with its Cisco IP Phones. Before you can deploy voice mail, you must install a Unity Express AIM module in the CME router.

The objective of this lab is to install a Unity Express AIM.

To perform this lab, you need the following equipment:

- Cisco 2811 CallManager Express (CME)-capable router

- Unity Express AIM

- Number 1 and Number 2 Phillips screwdrivers

Figure C-1 shows a 2811 router with the cover removed for reference in this lab.

Figure C-1   Lab Topology: 2811 Router

The procedure for this lab consists of the following tasks, which are described in detail in the following sections:

- **Task 1**—Remove the router cover.

- **Task 2**—Install a Unity Express AIM.

- **Task 3**—Reinstall the router cover.

- **Task 4**—Verify the AIM installation.

Task 1: Remove the Router Cover

Step 1.   Power off the router. Cisco recommends removing the power cord. Remove any cables that attach to the router ports.

Step 2.   Remove the screws that are used to hold the router top cover in place.

Step 3.   Slide the top cover toward the rear of the router (the part that contains the modules) to remove the top cover.

Step 4.   Remove any jewelry you are wearing. Remove the disposable antistatic wrist strap from the Unity Express AIM box, and read the instructions. Insert your hand through the strap so that it rides on your wrist, and attach the strap to the router as shown in the directions.

Task 2: Install a Unity Express AIM

Step 1. Before you can install the AIM, you must remove three screws. Figure C-2 shows how to remove them from AIM slot 1. The three screws from AIM slot 0 are also shown. Remove the screws from AIM slot 1 as shown.

Figure C-2   AIM Slot 1 Screws

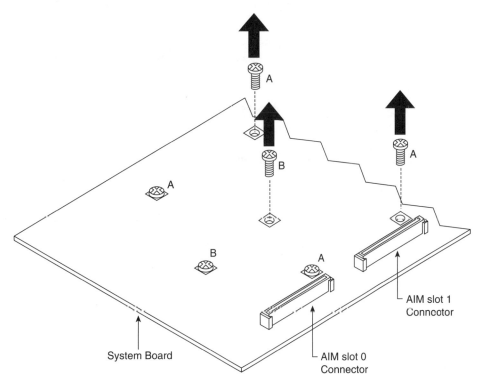

Step 2. Metal standoffs and a plastic standoff are provided with the AIM. Locate the two machine-thread standoffs, as shown in Figure C-3.

Figure C-3   Machine-Thread Standoffs

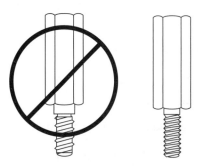

Step 3.   Install the two machine-thread metal standoffs and the plastic standoff, as shown in Figure C-4.

Figure C-4   Unity Express AIM Installation

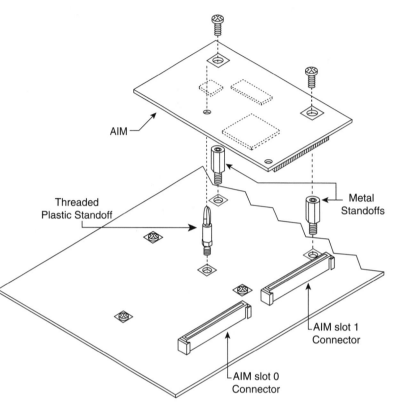

Step 4.   Install the Unity Express AIM. Refer to Figure C-4 for its placement. Press down firmly on the side that fits over the plastic standoff.

Step 5.   Locate the two screws that came in the same plastic bag as the standoffs.

Step 6.   Install the two screws that attach through the AIM to the metal standoffs. The original screws will not fit properly. Again, press down firmly on the side that fits over the plastic standoff to ensure that the board is seated properly in the connector.

Task 3: Reinstall the Router Cover

Step 1.   Reattach the router cover.

Step 2.   Reinstall the router cover screws.

Step 3.   Reattach the power cords and any cabling you removed.

Step 4.   Locate the stickers that came with the Unity Express AIM. (They say AIM-CUE.) Place one of them on the router. Do not place it on a module cover (such as slot 1) that might be removed. It is important that you be able to easily identify which router has this module inserted without removing the cover.

Task 4: Verify the AIM Installation

Step 1. Connect to the router via a HyperTerminal session, and power on the router.

Step 2. As the router boots, watch the HyperTerminal screen. The boot process provides a couple of indications that the AIM has been installed properly and that the router recognizes it. Scroll up toward the top of the boot process and notice the line under the **smart init is sizing iomem** statement. The words **Service Engine AIM** appear. Also, scroll to the part of the boot process that displays the different interfaces installed. You might see a line for FastEthernet, Serial, FXS, and so on. Just below that section you might see a line that states **SETUP: new interface Service-Engine0/1 placed in "shutdown" state**.

Step 3. On the rear of the router (the bottom-right corner), under the FE 0/0 port for a 2811 router, are LEDs for AIM slot 0 and AIM slot 1. The LED for AIM slot 1 should be illuminated.

Step 4. Use the **show inventory** command and verify that the AIM Service Engine was detected. If it was not, reinstall the AIM. You are now ready to use the Unity Express module. Refer to the Chapter 11 labs on configuring Unity Express.

Configuring the Adtran Dial Plan

The lab in this appendix provides the basic instructions to verify and configure the dial plans using the Adtran 550. The correct dial plan is critical to ensuring that the labs work as written. If no dial plan or the wrong dial plan is configured on the Adtran, the calls will not reach their destination, and the labs will not function.

An Adtran configuration file will be available to match the labs. For the supplied Adtran configuration file to work properly, the Adtran must be physically configured to match the configuration file. For example, if the software configuration is set to look for the Octal FXS card in port 3 of the Adtran, but you installed it in port 2, the configuration file will not load. Physically configure the Adtran as per Table D-1.

Table D-1   Adtran Physical Configuration

Slot	Service Card
1	V35Nx
2	V35Nx
3	FXS-8
4	T1/PRI-4
N1	Central (single T1)
N2	Central (single T1)

The Quad T1/PRI card in slot 4 is optional. The single T1 Network Module goes into Network Slot 1 (the slot in the lower-left corner of the Adtran). The other Adtran ports are not used in this lab, but you can install the V35 cards in slots 1 and 2. This lab provides the basic steps to verify and configure the Adtran voice port dial plan.

Lab D-1: Configuring the Adtran Dial Plan

The company OCSIC.org has decided to use an Adtran Atlas 550 for its voice network. You must configure the Adtran to match the OCSIC.org dial plan.

The objectives of this lab are as follows:

- Connect to the Adtran.

- Verify and configure the Adtran octal FXS ports.

- Verify and configure the Adtran T1/PRI ports.

To perform this lab, you need the following equipment:

- Adtran Atlas 550 with an octal FXS, a single T1 module, and/or a Quad T1/PRI module configured as per Table D-1

- Workstation

- Adtran nine-pin-to-RJ-45 connector

Figure D-1 illustrates the topology that is used for this lab.

Figure D-1   Lab Topology: Workstation to Adtran Connectivity

**Workstation with Straight
Through
Cable and Adtran 9-Pin
Connector**

The procedure for this lab consists of the following tasks. The following sections describe each task in detail.

- **Task 1**—Connect a workstation to the Adtran.

- **Task 2**—Verify and configure the Adtran octal FXS ports.

- **Task 3**—Verify and configure the Adtran T1/PRI ports.

Task 1: Connect a Workstation to the Adtran

Step 1. Connect a straight-through cable from the Craft port on the Adtran to the RJ-45 side of the special nine-pin Adtran connector. Connect the nine-pin side of the Adtran connector to the computer. The Adtran nine-pin-to-RJ-45 connector is a specially wired connector. A standard RJ-45-to-nine-pin connector used to console into a router will not work. If you do not have the Adtran connector, you can find more information on the pinouts for the connector at www.adtran.com.

Step 2. Configure HyperTerminal or some other terminal emulator to interface with the Adtran. The HyperTerminal settings are 9600 data rate, no parity, 8 data bits, 1 stop bit, and no flow control.

Step 3. Power on the Adtran. The Adtran boot sequence should show in HyperTerminal.

Step 4. After the Adtran boots completely, a login window appears in the center of the screen. By default, the password for the Adtran is "password." The default password is case-sensitive and is all lowercase.

Step 5. The Adtran System Info screen, shown in Figure D-2, appears after you enter the password. The System Info screen provides basic information, including firmware, uptime, and memory.

Figure D-2   Adtran System Info Screen

```
ATLAS 550/System Info
System Info      System Name              ATLAS 550
System Status    System Location          Adtran ATLAS 550
System Config    System Contact           Adtran ATLAS 550
System Utility   Firmware Revision        ATLAS 550  Rev. C.09.04 08/24/04 11:06:
Modules          System Uptime            0 days  0 hours  19 min  8 secs
Packet Manager   Startup Mode             Power cycle
Router           Current Time/Date (24h)  Saturday October 14  10:24:49  2006
Dedicated Maps   Installed Memory         Flash:2097152 bytes   DRAM:16777216 byte
Circuit Status   Serial Number            B30B1576
Dial Plan        Boot ROM Rev             B.02 07/13/00




                                         |




SYS: OK    NETWK1: OK    NETWK2: --          1:ONLN   2:ONLN   3: OK    4:ALRM
System Information menu                                      ^Z=help 10:24_
```

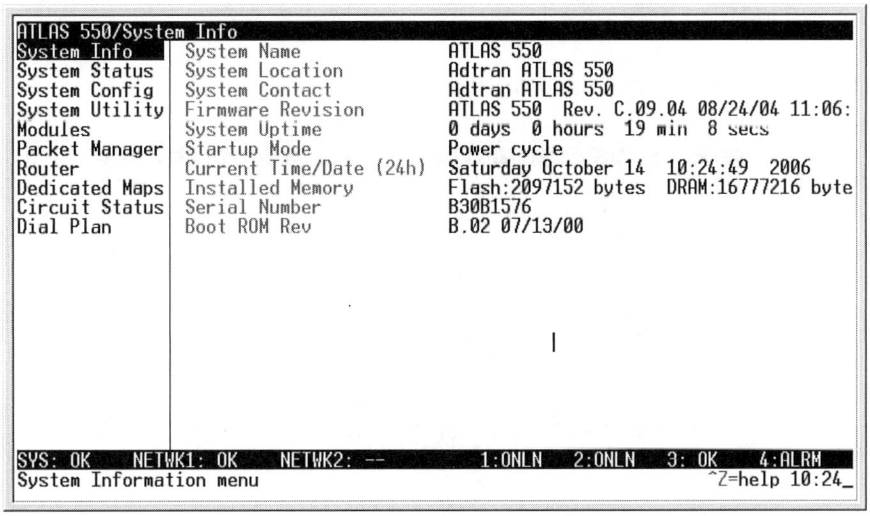

Task 2: Verify and Configure the Adtran Octal FXS Ports

Step 1. From the System Info screen, use the arrow keys to move down to the **Dial Plan** option.

Step 2. From the **Dial Plan** option, shown in Figure D-3, move right and down to the **User Term** option and press the **Enter** key.

Figure D-3   Dial Plan Screen

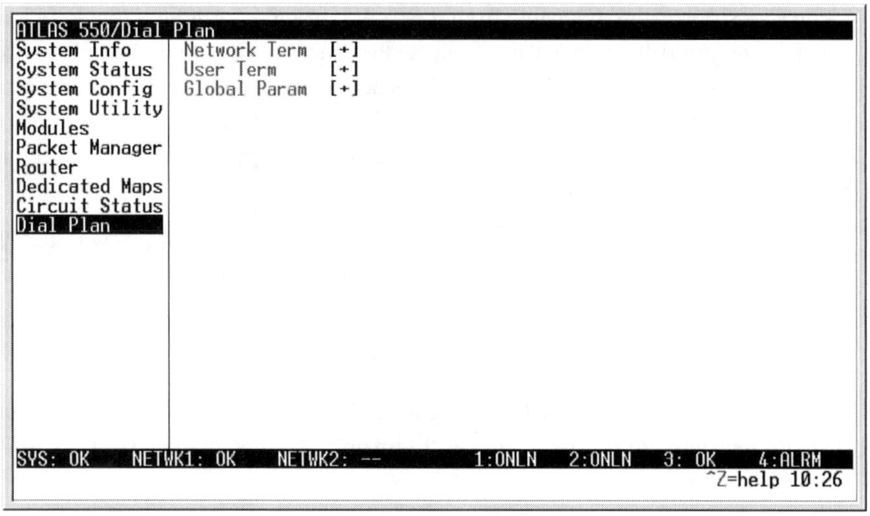

```
ATLAS 550/Dial Plan
System Info      Network Term  [+]
System Status    User Term     [+]
System Config    Global Param  [+]
System Utility
Modules
Packet Manager
Router
Dedicated Maps
Circuit Status
Dial Plan




















SYS: OK    NETWK1: OK    NETWK2: --        1:ONLN    2:ONLN    3: OK    4:ALRM
                                                              ^Z=help 10:26
```

Step 3.   From the **User Term** screen, shown in Figure D-4, you can see the cards that are configured in each slot. If the FXS-8 card is installed in slot 3 and the single PRI card is installed in slot N1, the screen should be similar to Figure D-4. If the four-port T1/PRI card is installed, it shows up in slot 4.

Figure D-4   User Term Screen: Card/Slot Configuration

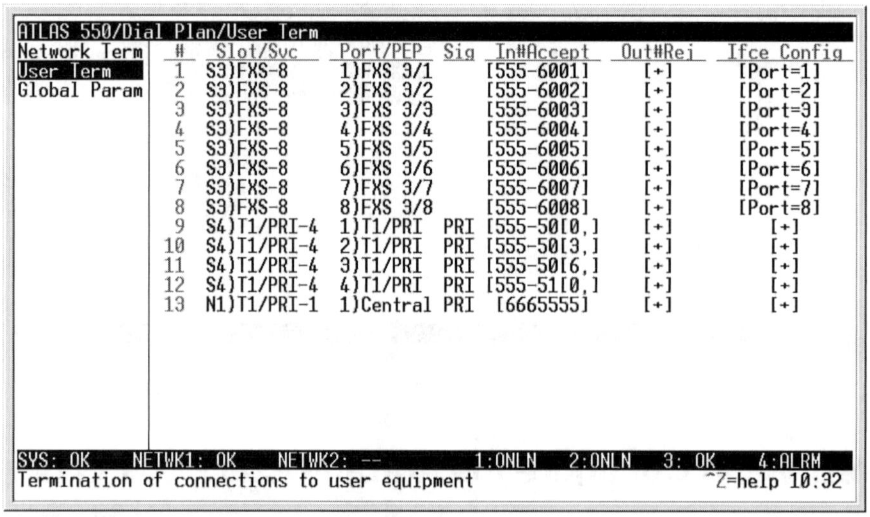

```
ATLAS 550/Dial Plan/User Term
Network Term  #   Slot/Svc     Port/PEP   Sig  In#Accept   Out#Rej  Ifce Config
User Term      1  S3)FXS-8     1)FXS 3/1       [555-6001]    [+]    [Port=1]
Global Param   2  S3)FXS-8     2)FXS 3/2       [555-6002]    [+]    [Port=2]
               3  S3)FXS-8     3)FXS 3/3       [555-6003]    [+]    [Port=3]
               4  S3)FXS-8     4)FXS 3/4       [555-6004]    [+]    [Port=4]
               5  S3)FXS-8     5)FXS 3/5       [555-6005]    [+]    [Port=5]
               6  S3)FXS-8     6)FXS 3/6       [555-6006]    [+]    [Port=6]
               7  S3)FXS-8     7)FXS 3/7       [555-6007]    [+]    [Port=7]
               8  S3)FXS-8     8)FXS 3/8       [555-6008]    [+]    [Port=8]
               9  S4)T1/PRI-4  1)T1/PRI   PRI  [555-50[0,]   [+]    [+]
              10  S4)T1/PRI-4  2)T1/PRI   PRI  [555-50[3,]   [+]    [+]
              11  S4)T1/PRI-4  3)T1/PRI   PRI  [555-50[6,]   [+]    [+]
              12  S4)T1/PRI-4  4)T1/PRI   PRI  [555-51[0,]   [+]    [+]
              13  N1)T1/PRI-1  1)Central  PRI  [6665555]     [+]    [+]







SYS: OK    NETWK1: OK    NETWK2: --        1:ONLN    2:ONLN    3: OK    4:ALRM
Termination of connections to user equipment                  ^Z=help 10:32
```

Step 4.   The dial plan for the labs requires FXS port 3/1 to use the analog number 555-6001. Use the arrow keys to move to the **In#Accept** option for port 3/1, and press the **Enter** key. Use the **In#Accept** option to change or verify the analog number (see Figure D-5). Use the arrows to select the **Accept Number** option for the **Incoming Number Accept List**. The Accept Number window opens, as shown in Figure D-6. Verify the Accept Number or change it to 555-6001, and then press the **Enter** key. The Adtran saves the configuration. No other action is required to save the configuration.

Figure D-5   User Term Screen

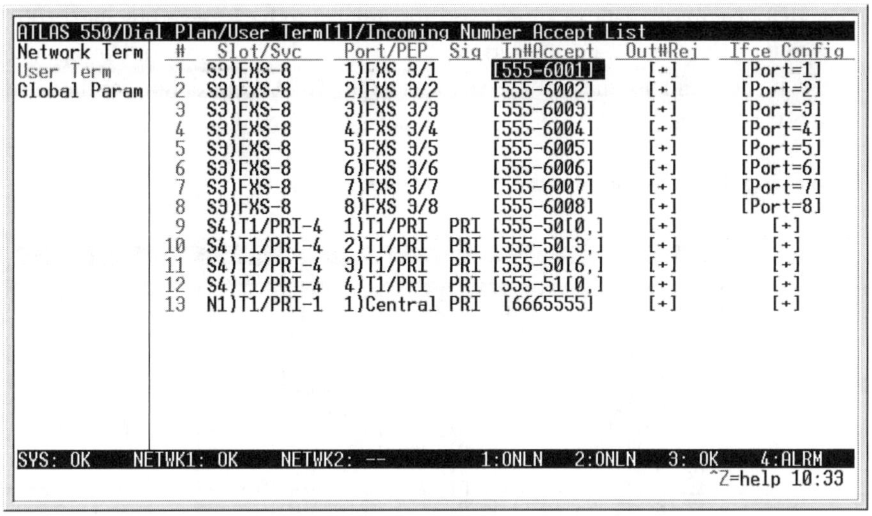

```
ATLAS 550/Dial Plan/User Term[1]/Incoming Number Accept List
Network Term   #   Slot/Svc     Port/PEP   Sig  In#Accept    Out#Rej   Ifce Config
User Term       1  S3)FXS-8     1)FXS 3/1       [555-6001]    [+]      [Port=1]
Global Param    2  S3)FXS-8     2)FXS 3/2       [555-6002]    [+]      [Port=2]
                3  S3)FXS-8     3)FXS 3/3       [555-6003]    [+]      [Port=3]
                4  S3)FXS-8     4)FXS 3/4       [555-6004]    [+]      [Port=4]
                5  S3)FXS-8     5)FXS 3/5       [555-6005]    [+]      [Port=5]
                6  S3)FXS-8     6)FXS 3/6       [555-6006]    [+]      [Port=6]
                7  S3)FXS-8     7)FXS 3/7       [555-6007]    [+]      [Port=7]
                8  S3)FXS-8     8)FXS 3/8       [555-6008]    [+]      [Port=8]
                9  S4)T1/PRI-4  1)T1/PRI   PRI  [555-50[0,]   [+]       [+]
               10  S4)T1/PRI-4  2)T1/PRI   PRI  [555-50[3,]   [+]       [+]
               11  S4)T1/PRI-4  3)T1/PRI   PRI  [555-50[6,]   [+]       [+]
               12  S4)T1/PRI-4  4)T1/PRI   PRI  [555-51[0,]   [+]       [+]
               13  N1)T1/PRI-1  1)Central  PRI  [6665555]     [+]       [+]




SYS: OK    NETWK1: OK    NETWK2: --         1:ONLN    2:ONLN   3: OK    4:ALRM
                                                              ^Z=help 10:33
```

Figure D-6   Incoming Number Accept List

```
ATLAS 550/Dial Plan/User Term[1]/Incoming Number Accept List[1]/Accept Number
Incoming Number Accept List  #   Src ID   Accept Number   Search   Data 64K   Data 56
Outgoing Number Reject List  1     0         555-6001     Primary  Enabled    Enable
Interface Configuration
Substitution Template




                          ┌Accept Number───────────┐
                          │555-6001                 │
                          └─────────────────────────┘








SYS: OK    NETWK1: OK    NETWK2: --         1:ONLN    2:ONLN   3: OK    4:ALRM
Match pattern - Digits 0-9, [], N, X, and $              ^A=more ^Z=help 12:12
```

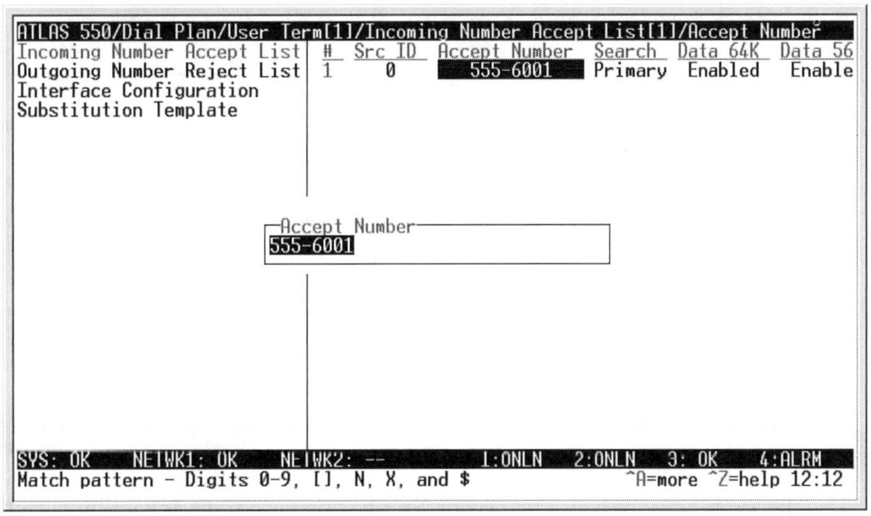

Step 5.   Change or verify the remaining FXS ports. Configure FXS port 3/2 for the analog number **555-6002**, FXS 3/3 for the number **555-6003**, FXS 3/4 for **555-6004**, port 3/5 for **555-6005**, port 3/6 for **555-6006**, port 3/7 for **555-6007**, and port 3/8 for **555-6008**. Use the arrow keys to back out to the **User Term** option.

Task 3: Verify and Configure the Adtran T1/ PRI Ports

Step 1.   The dial plan for the labs requires a specific number to be accepted by the T1/PRI ports. You assign the accepted dial numbers to the T1/PRI ports by using the **In#Accept** option. From the **User Term** menu, use the arrow keys to select the **In#Accept** option for the T1/PRI card in slot N1, as shown in Figure D-7, and then press the **Enter** key.

Figure D-7   Displaying the Accepted Incoming Numbers

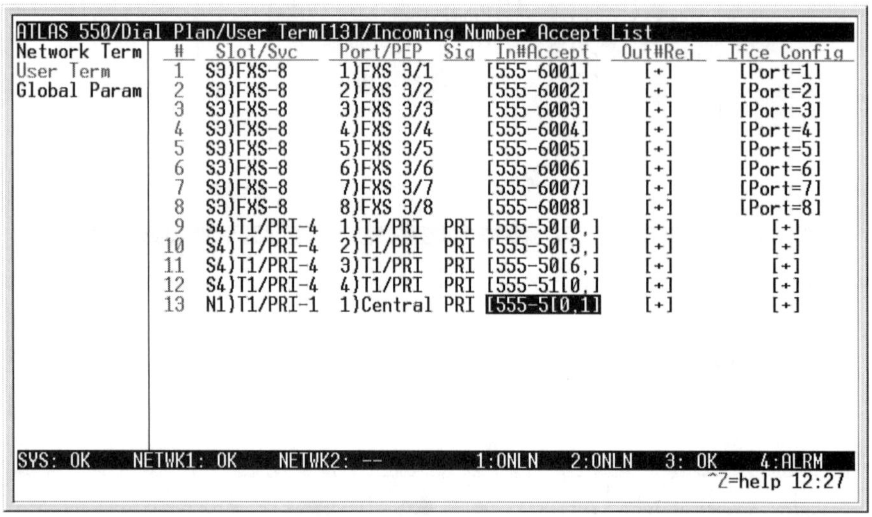

```
ATLAS 550/Dial Plan/User Term[13]/Incoming Number Accept List
Network Term    #    Slot/Svc    Port/PEP   Sig   In#Accept    Out#Rej   Ifce Config
User Term        1   S3)FXS-8    1)FXS 3/1         [555-6001]    [+]      [Port=1]
Global Param     2   S3)FXS-8    2)FXS 3/2         [555-6002]    [+]      [Port=2]
                 3   S3)FXS-8    3)FXS 3/3         [555-6003]    [+]      [Port=3]
                 4   S3)FXS-8    4)FXS 3/4         [555-6004]    [+]      [Port=4]
                 5   S3)FXS-8    5)FXS 3/5         [555-6005]    [+]      [Port=5]
                 6   S3)FXS-8    6)FXS 3/6         [555-6006]    [+]      [Port=6]
                 7   S3)FXS-8    7)FXS 3/7         [555-6007]    [+]      [Port=7]
                 8   S3)FXS-8    8)FXS 3/8         [555-6008]    [+]      [Port=8]
                 9   S4)T1/PRI-4 1)T1/PRI    PRI   [555-50[0,]   [+]         [+]
                10   S4)T1/PRI-4 2)T1/PRI    PRI   [555-50[3,]   [+]         [+]
                11   S4)T1/PRI-4 3)T1/PRI    PRI   [555-50[6,]   [+]         [+]
                12   S4)T1/PRI-4 4)T1/PRI    PRI   [555-51[0,]   [+]         [+]
                13   N1)T1/PRI-1 1)Central   PRI   [555-5[0,1]   [+]         [+]

SYS: OK    NETWK1: OK    NETWK2: --        1:ONLN   2:ONLN   3: OK   4:ALRM
                                                              ^Z=help 12:27
```

Step 2.   Use the arrow keys to select the **Accept Number** option for the **Incoming Number Accept List**. The Accept Number window opens. Verify the Accept Number or change it to **555-5[0,1][0-5]X** (the **X** is part of the configuration), and then press the **Enter** key. The Adtran saves the configuration. No other action is required to save the configuration.

Step 3.   If you are using the four-port T1/PRI module, go to Step 5. Otherwise, the Adtran is ready to work properly with the labs. Close the HyperTerminal application, and disconnect the cable from the Adtran and computer.

Step 4.   From the **User Term** menu, use the arrow keys to select the **In#Accept** option for the T1/PRI card in slot 4 port 1, and then press the **Enter** key.

Step 5.   Use the arrow keys to select the **Accept Number** option for the **Incoming Number Accept List**. After you select the Accept Number option for the T1/PRI card in slot 4 port 1, the Accept Number window opens, as shown in Figure D-8. Verify the number or change it to **555-50[0,1,2]X** (the **X** is part of the configuration), and then press **Enter** (refer to Figure D-6). The Adtran saves the configuration automatically after you press **Enter**. No other action is required to save the configuration.

Figure D-8   User Term Screen for T1/PRI Slot 4 Port 1

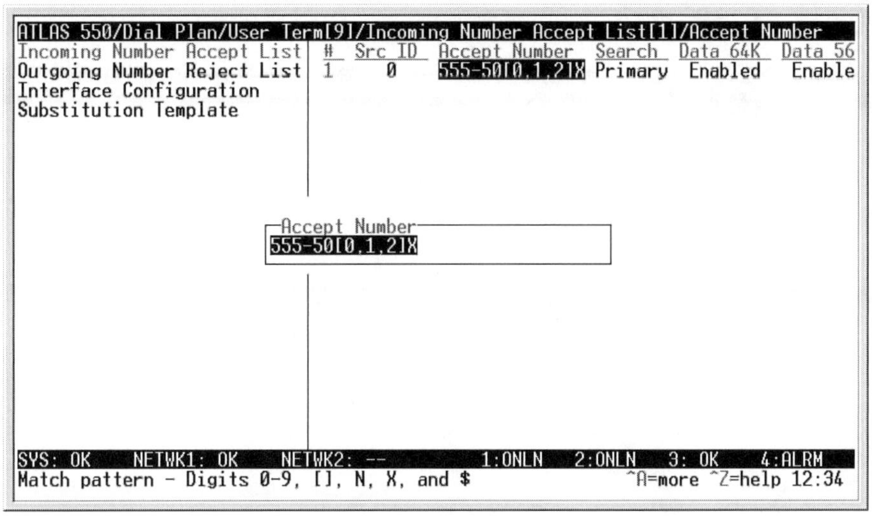

```
ATLAS 550/Dial Plan/User Term[9]/Incoming Number Accept List[1]/Accept Number
Incoming Number Accept List| #  Src ID  Accept Number  Search  Data 64K  Data 56
Outgoing Number Reject List| 1    0     555-50[0,1,2]X Primary  Enabled   Enable
Interface Configuration
Substitution Template

                          ┌Accept Number────────────────┐
                          │555-50[0,1,2]X               │
                          └─────────────────────────────┘




SYS: OK    NETWK1: OK    NETWK2: --        1:ONLN   2:ONLN   3: OK    4:ALRM
Match pattern - Digits 0-9, [], N, X, and $            ^A=more ^Z=help 12:34
```

Step 6.   Configure the three remaining T1/PRI ports with the following dial peers: Port 2 for the number **555-50[3,4,5]X** (the **X** is part of the configuration), Port 3 for **555-50[6,7,8]X**, and Port 4 for **555-51[0,1,2]X**.

Step 7.   The Adtran is ready to work properly with the labs. Close the HyperTerminal application, and disconnect the cable from the Adtran and computer.

Resetting 7970 Cisco IP Phones

You cannot reset the 7970 Cisco IP Phone with the same procedures used with the 7940 or 7960 IP Phone. Instead, you use a similar process. This appendix is provided in case you use 7970 Cisco IP Phones as part of your lab equipment.

Lab E-1: Resetting a 7970 Cisco IP Phone to the Defaults

In this lab, the company OCSIC.org has decided to deploy CallManager Express (CME) in the enterprise. You must reset the 7970 Cisco IP Phones if they have been used before. In this company, the network support staff used them in a test lab, and they currently have various configurations. You should use this process when configuring any IP Phone that might have been previously configured.

The objective of this lab is to erase the current configuration from an IP Phone.

To perform this lab, you need the following equipment:

- Cisco IP Phone 7970 series (powered using any method)

- Switch/switch module

Figure E-1 shows a typical Cisco IP Phone.

Figure E-1   Lab Topology: 7970 Cisco IP Phone

The procedure for this lab consists of the following steps:

Step 1.   On the 7970 Cisco IP Phone, press the **Settings** button. If the phone buttons are unlabeled, this button has a check mark. A menu appears.

Step 2.   Press the number **2** on the keypad to select the **Network Configuration** option.

Step 3.   Notice how a closed lock symbol appears in the upper-right display. Press the ****#** keys on the keypad.

Step 4.   Press the **Erase** softkey. The phone restarts.

Configuring Cisco IP Communicator

Cisco IP Communicator is a software application that provides the same functionality as a physical Cisco IP Phone. Many people also refer to this technology as a *SoftPhone*. The Cisco IP Communicator software is configured and managed using a CallManager server or CallManager Express router. The Cisco IP Communicator phone is configured on the CallManager Express router in the same manner as a physical IP Phone.

After the Cisco IP Communicator software is installed and configured on a computer or laptop, users can initiate and receive calls on the computer, check voice mail, and have all the features of a physical Cisco IP Phone. This application is useful for people who travel and for small remote offices with just a few phones. Cisco IP Communicator can be configured as part of a user's desk phone, or it can have a separate number. For example, a manager could have an extension number of 6578 on the phone in her office. That same extension could be associated with her laptop running Cisco IP Communicator. When someone inside or outside the company dials the desktop phone extension, the office phone rings, as does the laptop with Cisco IP Communicator configured. This offers the manager complete mobility, and her location is transparent to anyone who calls.

It should be noted that, like any other application that runs over the Internet, Cisco IP Communicator software phones are susceptible to congestion. During times of extreme congestion on the Internet, the audio quality of a Cisco IP Communicator phone might be diminished. In addition to assigning the MAC address of the Ethernet card on the computer or laptop, you also can assign the MAC address of the wireless card. This would allow someone to use the Cisco IP Communicator phone via a wireless connection. For the best audio quality, a headset with a microphone should be used with Cisco IP Communicator SoftPhones. Many companies make a headset with built-in digital signal processors (DSPs) that provide near-perfect audio quality.

Lab F-1: Configuring Cisco IP Communicator

In this lab, the company OCSIC.org has decided to deploy Cisco IP Communicator in the CallManager Express (CME) network. The company wants to test the Cisco IP Communicator application to allow small remote offices to expand their number of IP Phones.

Note: This lab relies on the two IP Phones being able to connect to one another *before* you start this lab. You should configure the router and switch with the basic configuration. Plug the IP Phones into the switch or switch module and configure them with a basic configuration using any of the methods previously demonstrated.

The objectives of this lab are as follows:

- Install the Cisco IP Communicator application.
- Configure and test Cisco IP Communicator.

To perform this lab, you need the following equipment:

- Cisco CallManager Express-capable router

- Appropriate licensed copy of the Cisco IP Communicator application

- Switch/switch module

- Workstation with an Ethernet 10/100 NIC installed

- Two Cisco IP Phones (powered using any method)

Figure F-1 shows the topology used for this lab. Keep in mind that you could use an integrated switch module in the router instead of the external switch.

Figure F-1   Lab Topology: Cisco IP Communicator

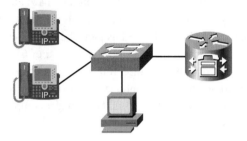

The procedure for this lab consists of the following tasks, both of which are described in detail in the following sections:

- **Task 1**—Install the Cisco IP Communicator application.

- **Task 2**—Configure and test Cisco IP Communicator.

Task 1: Install the Cisco IP Communicator Application

Step 1.   Configure the router and switch with the basic configuration. Plug the IP Phones into the switch or switch module and configure them with a basic configuration using any of the methods previously demonstrated.

Step 2.   Download a licensed copy of Cisco IP Communicator to the computer that will be used in this lab. To download the file, a registered user must log into Cisco.com. After logging in, select the **Technical Support & Documentation** option and then the **Software Downloads** option. From the Downloads page, select **Voice Software** under the Software Products & Downloads section. On the Voice Software page, scroll down to the Cisco IP Phone section and select the **Cisco IP Communicator** option. Select the latest version of the Cisco IP Communicator software. Follow the instructions to download the file to the computer. After you have downloaded the file, unzip it, but do not start the application.

Step 3.   From one of the phones, dial the other phone.

Does the call go through properly? If not, troubleshoot as necessary.

Step 4. If required, configure an additional port on the switch or switch module to allow the computer to receive a DHCP IP address from the router.

Step 5. Connect the computer to the switch or switch module, and configure the PC for DHCP.

Step 6. Test the computer's connectivity to the router by pinging the IP address of the voice VLAN.

Is the ping successful? If not, troubleshoot as necessary.

Task 2: Configure and Test Cisco IP Communicator

Step 1. In the directory where Cisco IP Communicator was downloaded and unzipped, double-click the file **CiscoIPCommunicatorSetup (Windows Installer Package)**.

Step 2. Click **Run** if the File Download-Security Warning screen appears.

Step 3. Click **Next** on the Cisco IP Communicator welcome screen. Read the User License agreement. Click **Next** if you agree with the terms.

Step 4. Click **Next** to install the application in the default directory.

Step 5. Click **Install**. After the installation, click **Finish**.

Step 6. Click the **Restart** option when you are asked to restart the computer.

Step 7. Launch the Cisco IP Communicator application.

Step 8. On the Audio Tuning Wizard screen, click **Next**.

Step 9. Select the appropriate audio devices on the Select Audio Devices screen, and click **Next**.

Step 10. Click **Play** on the Adjust Listening Volume screen, and then click **Next**.

Step 11. Click **Test** on the Adjust Microphone Volume screen, and then click **Next**.

Step 12. Click **Finish**.

Step 13. Click **OK** if you see the Unable to reach TFTP server screen.

Step 14. On the Network tab, select the **Use these TFTP servers** radio button.

Step 15. Enter the IP address of the Cisco CallManager Express in the TFTP Server 1 field. The Cisco CallManager Express IP address for the labs in this book is the IP address used for the voice VLAN. You can verify the IP address by viewing the router configuration in the telephony-service section. The TFTP server IP address is the one used as the **ip source-address** *xxx.xxx.xxx.xxx* **port 2000** command in the telephony-service section of the router configuration. After you enter the address, click **OK**.

Step 16. After you enter the correct address, a window appears that is similar to a Cisco 7960 IP Phone.

Step 17. The Cisco IP Communicator functions in the same manner as the 7960 phone. Test the Cisco IP Communicator by calling one of the 7960 IP Phones.

Step 18. Call from the other 7960 IP Phone to the phone number of the IP Communicator.

Are the calls successful? If not, troubleshoot as necessary.

Common problems and solutions include the following:

- **You see the error message "Registering" or "Defaulting to TFTP server," and the phone is never configured**—These error messages indicate that Cisco IP Communicator is unable to contact the TFTP server. Check network connectivity to the TFTP server. Try to ping the TFTP server on the CallManager Express routers. If the ping isn't successful, the Cisco IP Communicator application will not register. Troubleshoot basic network connectivity issues.

- **Cisco IP Communicator fails to register and shows the error "Error DBConfig"**—The solution to this problem is to enable Auto-Registration. If Auto-Registration is disabled on the CallManager Express router and no MAC address is assigned on the router for the device using Cisco IP Communicator, the phone will not configure. If Auto-Registration is disabled on the CallManager Express router, you must manually configure the ephone and ephone-dn for the Cisco IP Communicator device. If a wireless card has not been configured on the CallManager Express router, ensure that the wireless card with the configured MAC address is installed in the computer, laptop, PDA, and so on. Finally, ensure that the correct TFTP server IP address is configured in the Cisco IP Communicator software.

The following link provides detailed information on Cisco IP Communicator: www.cisco.com/univercd/cc/td/doc/product/voice/c_ipphon/english/ipc/